ACTING FUNNY

ACTING FUNNY

Comic Theory and Practice
in Shakespeare's Plays

Edited by
Frances Teague

Rutherford ● Madison ● Teaneck
Fairleigh Dickinson University Press
London and Toronto: Associated University Presses

© 1994 by Associated University Presses, Inc.

Associated University Presses
440 Forsgate Drive
Cranbury, NJ 08512

Associated University Presses
25 Sicilian Avenue
London WC1A 2QH, England

Associated University Presses
P.O. Box 338, Port Credit
Mississauga, Ontario
Canada L5G 4L8

The paper used in this publication meets the requirements
of the American National Standard for Permanence of Paper
for Printed Library Materials Z39.48-1984.

Library of Congress Cataloging-in-Publication Data

Acting funny : comic theory and practice in Shakespeare's plays /
edited by Frances Teague.
    p. cm.
Includes bibliographical references.
ISBN 0-8386-3524-5 (alk. paper)
1. Shakespeare, William, 1564–1616—Comedies.   2. Comic, The, in
literature.   3. Comedy.   I. Teague, Frances N.
PR2981.A28   1994
822.3'3—dc20   92-55090
                                                     CIP

PRINTED IN THE UNITED STATES OF AMERICA

To the Teagues,
who've always put up
with those who act funny.

Contents

Introduction

FRANCES TEAGUE

> The great actor lay dying. . . . By his bedside a grieving
> friend watched. "Ah," said the friend mournfully, "Dying
> must be hard."
> "Dying's easy," said the actor. "It's comedy that's hard."

When I teach *Othello*, I like to compare it to *Much Ado about
Nothing* and *The Winter's Tale*.[1] All three have the same plot, of
course: a man suspects the woman he loves of sexual infidelity.
In each case, he accuses her and she seemingly dies; Hero, Desdemona, and Hermione all return from death and forgive their un-
just lover. Yet the plays conclude differently: in the comedy,
Claudio and Hero marry (as do Beatrice and Benedick); in the
tragedy, Desdemona dies again and Othello soon follows her by
killing himself; while in the romance, Hermione awaits not her
husband, but her daughter Perdita, whose restoration prompts
the queen's return. The plot similarities always engage my students' attention as the class tries to account for the way different
genres use the same materials.

That pedagogical exercise led me to this collection. A few years
ago, I realized that of the three plays, the one that had the stock
characters familiar from Roman New Comedy was *Othello*; recognizing the braggart soldier, blustering father, and clever servant,
I wrote an essay about what happens to our understanding of
the play if the tragedy is rooted in the comic tradition. I have
continued to think about the implications of that insight, so when
the Shakespeare Association of America asked me to direct one
of its seminars in 1990, I choose as the topic "Acting Funny:
Comic Theory and Practice in Shakespeare's Plays," hoping that
what other Shakespeareans had to say about the topic would
enlighten me.[2]

The seminar exceeded my hopes. The participants who joined

me that spring afternoon in Philadelphia were lively and enliv-
ening. Some participants remarked on the way that recent critical
theory has neglected or misunderstood comic elements in Shakespeare's plays, focusing instead on the multivocality of his work,
examining central dramatic moments, often in the tragedies, for
alternative readings. Those critics interested in the genre of comedy have concentrated on either the problem plays and the romances or on the features that the comedies may share.
Meanwhile, other Shakespeareans have reconsidered the plays
as cultural artifacts: such studies examine the histories and the
tragedies more often than the comedies or even comic elements.
The work that the seminar participants contributed was original
both in making use of new critical approaches to old problems
and in reassessing certain critical givens about the nature of comedy and the comic. The most prominent of these assumptions is
that tragedy is more important than comedy, an assumption that
has impeded the study of Shakespearean comedy.

Before discussing new approaches or critical givens, however,
I should explain how comedy and the comic differ. In the broadest
sense, comedy refers to a form, and comic to tone. The anecdote
about the dying actor, which serves as epigraph for this chapter,
illustrates the distinction between comedy and the comic: what
the actor says is comic and makes us laugh because we forget
that comedy is serious business to a performer. We have to reas-
sess our assumptions about comedy in light of the actor's precept—that "comedy's hard"—and may even recognize that not all
comic moments occur in comedies (they might even occur on
deathbeds) nor do all comedies seek to make us laugh. Those
points have confused virtually all discussions of the subject and
provide a convenient place for me to try either to achieve a happy
ending for this essay, suitable to comedy, or to make a fool of
myself by my comic inadequacy.

If a comedy may be serious and need not be comic, how then
does it differ from tragedy, the form that is usually regarded as its
opposite and superior? The relation between comedy and tragedy
might be defined in terms of a psychological model that articulates a dialectic between dependence and autonomy in human
development. The recognition not only that others exist, but also
that the individual needs another person for nurturance is crucial
in human development.[3] Recognizing dependence can elicit a
range of responses, but two responses are particularly significant,
since they mark the ends of the range and provide models for
tragedy and comedy.[4] One may respond by denying that the indi-

vidual must depend on others. Such a response insists that to be dependent is to be in danger, for the other person may not be good enough as a source of nurture or may fail altogether. The individual strives for autonomy; although others exist, the individual deals with them by using strategies of competition and aggression. This response provides the impetus for tragedy with its essential message that when the hero—necessarily an individual—becomes involved with others, he meets disaster. The polar response is to celebrate the recognition of dependence, the discovery that one need not stand alone, and to accept the concept of mutuality in one's existence. Such a response uses strategies of cooperation, surrendering autonomy for the greater good of survival and prosperity. This response provides the impetus for comedy with its essential message that the community survives and, within its survival, individuals can prosper.

Given that these polar responses provide human beings with models for the forms of tragedy and comedy, where do the concepts of tragic and comic tone come from? The words *tragedy* and *tragic, comedy* and *comic* are clearly related, but they are, I would argue, quite distinct. After all, comic moments occur in plays that are clearly not comedies, while not all comedies are comic. One need only consider the comic porter's scene in the tragedy *Macbeth*, or the largely uncomic comedy *The Merchant of Venice*. The tragic view regards comedy as an incomplete tragedy: comedy is a stage of false reassurance on the way to the hero's betrayal and destruction. Ultimately the individual must fall, if for no other reason than mortality. Within tragedy, then, what is tragic is one's recognition that the world, as a closed system, is inevitably a tragedy.

Comedy treats other world views in a different way. Within the context of comedy, a tragic individual—i.e., one who believes that tragedy is inevitable or denies the possibility of trust and union— is finally a laughable (comic) figure. Ideally such a figure can be incorporated into the comedic model, but such incorporation need not occur for the model's existence. One can, after all, expel the discordantly tragedic character incapable of mutuality: such an expulsion happens to Malvolio, for instance, while in *As You Like It,* Jaques chooses to isolate himself as the comedy draws to an end.

Tragic and comic moments occur when someone, having accepted a particular model (tragedy or comedy) for understanding the world, tries to consider alternative views. Thus tragedy and tragic are generally congruent. Comedy and the comic need not be congruent at all. In tragedy, one acknowledges the possibility of an alternative view only during comic moments when the tragedy views itself from comedy's perspective. The conclusion of a tragedy, however, necessarily suppresses the comic (and comedy). Hamlet may laugh at the gravedigger's jokes, but the play quickly recalls the horror and inevitability of death and suppresses amusement. In contrast, comedy lacks tragic moments, because tragedy, a closed system, does not transgress into other forms, the existence of which would imperil tragedy's world view, and thus the whole system. In *The Merry Wives of Windsor*, Ford may consider himself a tragic hero cruelly betrayed by his wife, but within the form of comedy, his passion becomes comic, not tragic, because we can see not only his viewpoint, but also his wife's and Falstaff's. Comedy both recognizes the existence of other viewpoints and embraces them, seeking to incorporate them within its form.

Thus, comedy offers an optimistic model of the world; the comic moment deliberately employs the form of tragedy and marks its inadequacy by laughter. Tragedy looks at the world and sees the individual fall; the tragic moment occurs when a character considers the possibility of comedy and finds it inadequate. We are moved by the poignancy of that hope defeated. Comedy looks at the world and sees the individual become part of a community; the comic moment occurs when a character considers the possibility of tragedy and mistakenly finds it adequate. We laugh at someone who chooses not to fit in.

My discussion of comedy and comic moments, and tragedy and tragic moments, depends on the assumption that neither form has inherent superiority. Early writers discussing comedy and tragedy did not as a rule distinguish between comedy and the comic. Because they considered the closed system of tragedy as necessarily better than comedy, they believed that since tragedy and the tragic are congruent, comedy and the comic are as well. As a result, the great classical philosophers have little to say about what constitutes comedy, much less about what makes something comic. When Plato reaches the end of *Symposium*, he tells us that Socrates' talk about comedy put Aristophanes to sleep; and Harold Watts opens an essay on comedy with the sum of Aristotelian wisdom on the subject: "Aristotle is silent" (Watts 1981, 115). Nor do we need to hear what Plato or Aristotle would have said: what they say about tragedy implies quite clearly that it is the superior form, capable of evoking *catharsis,* however we interpret that term, and that comedy simply dramatizes a happy moment in the tragic existence of the hero as he struggles with the gods and his own mortality.

A series of other assumptions follow from the premise that tragedy is the master form. One, of course, is that we can discuss tragedy without discussing comedy, but we cannot do the reverse. Here we assume that comedy is subordinate and hence nonessential to tragedy, rather than assuming, as I have, that tragedy necessarily closes itself off while comedy remains open to other possibilities. Another assumption that may follow from the premise of tragedy as a master form is that a hierarchical universe exists in which both life and art are organized by hierarchies. That assumption leads one to speak of tragedy as a higher form; to insist that comedy focuses on the affairs of low people, as opposed to princes; and to regard laughter as a way of marking one's status. The intrusion of the comic into tragedy is often considered an artistic lapse by Renaissance commentators like Jonson and Sidney, for example, as Marcia McDonald explains in her essay. Finally, that assumption leads to the corollary that such hierarchies are natural, not fashioned, and immutable.

The essays that form this collection challenge each of these assumptions. They do so by focusing on the works of Shakespeare. His plays have been more intensively studied than any other dramatist's; moreover, he wrote successfully in several genres. Thus he offers a particularly rich body of material for anyone who wants to consider structure and characterization in comedy, why some comedies are not comic, why some tragedies use the comic, how culture marks some groups as marginal and whether that identification is comic or threatening, and so forth.

Essays that trace criticism of Shakespeare's comedies often begin by remarking that the comedies have been neglected:

> *Stanley Wells:* Although the comedies form the largest single group of Shakespeare's plays, criticism of them lagged behind that of the tragedies and histories except in relation to a few dominating characters, such as Shylock . . . a character of potentially tragic status.

> *Kenneth Muir:* It is surprising that, in spite of the overproduction of books on Shakespeare, so few should have been devoted to the comedies.

> *Laurence Danson:* Shakespeare's critics in the twentieth century have served his comedies less well than his tragedies.[5]

In the seminar discussion, participants seemed to be echoing these remarks on the lack of critical guidance. The history of criticism on Shakespeare's comedies is relatively spotty: not until this century were the comedies considered as a body of work comparable in value to the tragedies or even the histories. To be sure, individual essays contributed to understanding of the comic elements in Shakespeare: Maurice Morgann wrote one such essay on Falstaff, while Thomas DeQuincy wrote another on the porter's scene in *Macbeth*. (One notes, however, that neither wrote on the comedies, only on the comic.) But in the early part of the twentieth century, attitudes toward comedy changed. To some extent this shift began with thinkers like Sigmund Freud, Henri Bergson, or Johan Huizinga, who began an oxymoronically serious consideration of laughter. Furthermore, because of the plays and prefaces by such challenging dramatists as George Bernard Shaw and Luigi Pirandello, critics could no longer dismiss comedy as unimportant or unchallenging. The world of Shakespearean criticism began to turn its attention to the comedies and found a rich field for study. Few studies were comprehensive. Instead critics preferred to examine particular elements rather than to make any overreaching claims about the nature of either comedy or the comic. In the 1930s, for example, G. Wilson Knight focused on symbolic structures, particularly in the romances; H. B. Charlton concentrated on Shakespeare's use of comic conventions; while W. W. Lawrence took up the problem plays. Then came a fallow period in Shakespearean criticism as scholars, like the rest of the world, turned their attention to World War II.

In the late 1940s and the 1950s, three breakthrough works appeared. The first of these was Northrop Frye's *The Argument of Comedy* (1948), which became the third section of *Anatomy of Criticism*. From the work of classicists, anthropologists, and psychologists, Frye synthesized a coherent system that served not only to describe comedy but also to account for what was comic. In Frye's *Argument,* and in other studies, he developed the idea that comedy exists on a continuum with tragedy, satire, and romance. It employs recognizable archetypes to tell its tales of conflict between young lovers and old fathers, the lovers' flight into a green world, and their return to marriage and a re-formed society. In this theory comedy is a remarkably conservative form, which always reestablishes the cultural center in its closure.

Another major work is Suzanne Langer's *Feeling and Form* (1953), particularly its influential chapter on "The Comic Rhythm." While Langer has less to say about Shakespeare's comedy than about Continental thinkers and dramatists, she wants, like Frye, to create a coherent account of how comedy operates. In her view, comedy springs less from the impulse to map a social order than from a natural order. Comedy and laughter are as fundamental as breathing and movement to human beings. While Frye considers comedy intrinsically a form that comments on the social order in its reestablishment of the community in the closing moments of a play, Langer finds such insistence on the social or political unnecessary, although it is, as she acknowledges, a frequent accompaniment to the more fundamental task of the comedy: an assertion of life and its continued vitality.

A third major work appeared in 1957: C. L. Barber's *Shakespeare's Festive Comedy*. In it he develops ideas that he had been working with since the early 1950s. Like the works by Frye and Langer, Barber's study reaches beyond literature to pull together a coherent account of comedy. Unlike them, he focuses on the implications of his findings for Shakespeare's work, although he limits himself to a handful of the comedies. Frye considers comedy a conservative form, emphasizing the reestablishment of social order, the reinstitution of society's control of the individual. Langer feels less convinced that social order lies at the heart of comedy, arguing that the form recapitulates natural processes. Barber begins with some of the same sources as both Frye and Langer, but he reaches very different conclusions. For him, comedy illustrates the tension between natural desire for release and social desire for repression. He finds in rituals and festivals a model of how such tensions are channeled and released. Thus Barber emphasizes not the order at the end of a comedy, but rather the challenges to that order and the deliberate acting out of disorder that communities permit.

Shakespearean critics have used the work done by Frye, Langer, and Barber to generate a remarkable variety of studies, both of particular problems and of the comprehensive form of comedy. Some question whether we should speak of Shakespearean or Shakespeare's comedy. Others consider particular kinds of Renaissance comedy: problem plays, satires, or romances. Critics have concentrated on particular conventions, themes, and characters. Yet much work remains. Laurence Danson has sketched some areas that deserve further study:

[Audience-response criticism] is only one of many areas in which there is more work to be done. Under the influence of Frye and Wilson Knight, criticism has concentrated on the mythic dimensions of the comic plot, on the richness of image and symbol, on the quest for identity and self-knowledge. Psychoanalytic and feminist theories extend those emphases. . . . Critics will [also] want to ask about the relation of Shakespeare's comedy to his contemporary audience and to the life of his society as a whole: sociological theory informed by history can help. They will want to pay more attention to the theatrical dynamics of the plays, from the points of view both of audience and of actor. And while they continue to explore Shakespeare's comedies, they will also continue to explore the relation of the comedies to the histories and tragedies. (Danson 1986, 238–39)

The participants in the seminar varied in their ideas about what kinds of inquiry would be most useful to correct that neglect.[6] Some wanted to continue formal investigations of comic moments, but most made use of the newer approaches that Danson mentions in their examination of venerable problems. Some felt that performance analysis of "theatrical dynamics" offered the most effective way of understanding comedy, and some employed the methodology of cultural studies to see what "sociological theory informed by history" might offer. In addition to commenting on a lack of recent work on comedy, the participants found themselves dissatisfied with certain familiar assumptions about comic characters and situations in Shakespeare's plays. After the seminar ended, we reconvened for a symposium—in the original sense of that word—and I suggested that some of us continue our work by putting together this collection. In the seminar papers they did then, and that they have revised for this collection, the participants demonstrate that rejecting or modifying common assumptions about the comic enriches the plays significantly.

Since my essay on *Othello* began my interest, I include a revised version here to head the collection; it focuses on the duality of that play and how it uses stock comic types within a tragic matrix.[7] My involvement with the "Acting Funny" seminar and my work on this essay have shown me that one cannot discuss comic elements without considering pairs and pairing. While tragedies may be said to be unitary, comedies depend on duality. As Avraham Oz remarks:

One of the major points of difference between tragedy and comedy has to do with the ways each is pursuing dramatic fulfillment. If a linear, irreversible course of action is nearly always a hallmark of tragedy, comedy is usually marked by a sense of circularity that makes its progress highly conducive to repetitions, mirror effects, and variations on a theme. . . . (Charney 1980, 175)

Like Oz, Harry Levin remarks on the importance of doubles in comic plots and characters in a chapter he calls "Duplicities." The duality that Oz and Levin point out within comedy extends to discussions about comedy. While one can define tragedy without referring to other genres, virtually all definitions of comedy (including Oz's) have something to say about the relationship between comedy and tragedy. Even when one discusses comedy as a single sort of play, the discussion may well settle into a bifurcated analysis of whether a comedy tends toward either satire or farce. Discussing comic characters, the critic comments on the tension between pairs: men and women, young and old, high and low. Discussions of tragedy, in contrast, more often concern the tragic hero, a single and singular man.

Othello is arguably the least unitary of Shakespeare's major tragedies. The audience focuses its attention on the tragic hero, certainly, but in no other of Shakespeare's tragedies does a villain demand so successfully that the audience refocuses its attention on him and his plots. Indeed, a stage tradition of *Othello* productions is that the actors playing Iago and Othello trade roles from time to time in the course of the play's run. Given this dual interest, one can hardly be surprised to learn that this tragedy borrows freely from a comic tradition: the husband who becomes foolish because he fears cuckolding will make him foolish. Yet *Othello* is no comedy.

In a discussion of comic plots based on fear of a wife's adultery, Harry Levin remarks:

> Jealousy of sexual rivals would seem to be [a] . . . normal reaction, and one of its main components is the cuckold's apprehension of looking foolish. At the tragic level, this consideration does not affect Othello, who is more deeply and sincerely concerned with the vulnerability of his relation to Desdemona. It is the self-conscious question of reputation, the fear of what others might be saying about him, that so distresses Leontes in *The Winter's Tale* or Master Ford in *The Merry Wives of Windsor*. (Levin 1987, 107)

Such an evaluation, however, owes something to the common assumption that tragedy excels comedy, that its characters are "deeper" or "more sincere" and in some way less "self-conscious." Even if that evaluation is fair in this instance, it is not universally true.

Yet some critics do continue to assume that tragedy and tragic moments are more worthy of attention than plays that make us laugh. Our culture disapproves of frivolity, preferring to investigate more solemn moments. In Umberto Eco's *The Name of the*

Rose, disapproval of laughter leads Jorge of Burgos to burn the
scriptorium and destroy Aristotle's work on comedy. Traditionally,
critics have anticipated Eco's villain by their tendency to dismiss
puns or pratfalls except when such comic devices point to more
ponderous meanings.[8] This cultural fear of frivolity derives from
a number of sources, ranging from the puritanical tradition that
condemns idle pleasure as idolatrous, to an overdeveloped reverence for Aristotelian pronouncements,[9] to the existentialist attitude that life is a bleak business at the best of times. (Consider,
for example, the values implicit in Miguel de Unamuno's comment
that "Killing time is perhaps the essence of comedy, just as the
essence of tragedy is killing eternity" [Unamuno 1985].)[10] Perhaps
critics find the comic troubling because, unlike the tragic, it more
often includes marginalized characters. Tragedies often show the
death of a hero who defines a culture as that culture imagines
itself: daring, aristocratic, male. Comic moments, however, so
often part of a courtship, usually involve female characters, as
well as others outside the cultural mainstream. To be sure, comic
moments are not free of patriarchal attitudes or cultural stereotypes; but in Shakespeare's plays, they include women, Jews, the
Welsh and Irish, drunkards, servants, and so on—none of whom
convincingly belongs in the class of "tragic hero" as Western culture has defined it.

Paradoxically, a critic who privileges tragedy over comedy may
ignore comic elements in the tragedies. Yet ignoring such elements distorts one's understanding of the tragedies by setting
aside what happens when the comic invades tragedy. If Othello
is identified as a braggart soldier and Iago as his clever servant,
after all, what happens to the play? One possible reason for this
subversive use of comic type characters and plot elements in a
tragedy is that Othello himself is a character at the margin of
Venetian society, the kind of figure more usually handled in comic
than in tragic plays.

Related to this assumption about what sort of character has
heroic stature is the assumption that reading comic characters
hierarchically offers a consistent and useful strategy. As George
Puttenham observed in 1598:

[Comedy is] neuer medling with any Princes matters nor such high
personages, but commonly of marchants, souldiers, artificers, good
honest housholders, and also of vnthrify youthes, yong damsels, old
nurses, bawds, brokers, ruffians, and parasites, with such like, in

whose behauiors lyeth in effect the whole course and trade of mans
life. (Puttenham 1936)

Implicit in this quotation, and in mainstream critical practice,
is the idea that plays dealing with princes, heroes, or "high
personages" are more serious than those dealing with ordinary
"bawds," "brokers," and "parasites." A corollary notion is that
sorting out those categories in a comic play helps an audience
understand what is going on. Mary Free and Geraldo de Sousa
challenge this assumption. In *"All's Well That Ends Well* as Noncomic Comedy," Free reexamines how social categories complicate
the relationships among the characters in *All's Well That Ends Well*.
She considers, in a lucid discussion of marking, what happens
when we mark something off, how its "value" diminishes, how
marking controls. For instance, in *All's Well That Ends Well* Helena's acquiescence in marking herself as a subservient allows her
a place in a serious moral and linguistically sophisticated sphere,
while marking Bertram as foolish and verbally inadequate. Finally
Helena and the King of France have a greater affinity than Helena
and Bertram. Free's essay argues that such marking frustrates an
audience's expectations of the comic, yet allows the play to be
a comedy.

Using ideas developed by anthropologists to describe what
happens when cultures meet, de Sousa writes about *"The Tempest*,
Comedy, and the Space of the Other." In *The Tempest*, Sycorax
and Prospero can both be categorized as users of magic who
nurture their offspring. Furthermore, both occupy not only the
same geographical place, but also the same cultural position:
Prospero was the Other in Milan, just as Sycorax was the Other
in Argiers. On the island, therefore, Prospero works to reenter
Milanese society by remaking Sycorax as his own Other. Of
course, "remaking" implies an earlier process of "making," and
that process by its very nature is mutable, not stable. (Each layer
of categorization is superimposed on an earlier one, forming a
palimpsest of character.) When one considers Prospero's relation
to Sycorax as a fluid positioning and repositioning, one can no
longer accept claims that Prospero occupies a superior position
in a fixed hierarchy. As de Sousa argues, "To turn the tragic story
of his life into a comedy," Prospero must subvert that hierarchy.

Theorists have also been concerned with the sources of comic
laughter, and most discussions return to the perception of duality,
presuming that laughter releases the tension created by the perception of a dichotomy of some sort. D. H. Monro points to two

different explanations of laughter: laughter that grows out of perceived superiority—as described by Freud and first discussed by Hobbes—and laughter that grows out of perceived incongruity—as described by Bergson and first discussed by Kant.[11] Both kinds of laughter depend on establishing a central group that marks itself or is marked off from others: In one version, the central group laughs at (to deny) those who don't fit; in the other, someone in the central group laughs to assimilate those who are incongruously different.

Ejner Jensen, in "'Knowing aforehand': Audience Preparation and the Comedies of Shakespeare," challenges these assumptions about what makes audiences laugh. He demonstrates how key scenes in the romantic comedies achieve their comic triumphs by playing off audience expectations created earlier in the plays. His emphasis is on performance, for as John Marston wrote: "Comedies are writ to be spoken, not read. Remember the life of these things consists in action" (Marston 1965, lines 65–67). In *The Merchant of Venice, Much Ado about Nothing, Twelfth Night, The Merry Wives of Windsor,* and *Love's Labors Lost,* key scenes evoke laughter by comic tactics that demand careful preparation. The theater audience laughs because of the way that the joke has been set up,[12] but the subject of laughter need not be a character or situation that the audience has marked as inferior or incongruous.

Most discussions of comic structure assume that tragedies and comedies follow certain ascernible rules to achieve their ends, an assumption seldom questioned successfully. It is one of the oldest of our culture's beliefs about drama.

> The parts of a comedy are the same with a tragedy, and the end is partly the same. For, they both delight, and teach. . . . Nor, is the moving of laughter always the end of *Comedy,* that is rather a fouling for the people's delight, or their fooling. For, as Aristotle says rightly, the moving of laughter is a fault in Comedy, a kind of turpitude, that depraves some part of a man's nature without a disease (Jonson 1970, lines 2290–2300)

Ben Jonson, clearly the Renaissance dramatist most important to discussions of the comic, does two things in this comment: he insists that comedies have similar structures, very like those of tragedy; and he disdains laughter, suggesting that comedy is best when most like tragedy.[13] Other Renaissance critics, including Sidney, would have agreed.

Nor has this aesthetic died in our own day. Recent critics who write about the comedies as a genre often hold the "view that some kind of comic structure is common to all his comedies, and that this structure can be elicited and described" (Berry 1972, 3). Marcia McDonald's essay, "Bottom's Space," seeks to historicize comic theory and practice in her analysis of *A Midsummer Night's Dream*. Specifically, she challenges the idea that a socially indexed comic structure exists and that disdain of laughter can be understood outside of a specific social context.

McDonald discusses the way that subplot comedy, at least in *A Midsummer Night's Dream*, may come to dominate the main plot comedy. In watching the working class mechanicals' subplot, the audience laughs most freely, most communally. McDonald uses Mikhail Bakhtin's belief that laughter has a history that we can profitably study. Bakhtin has written:

> Rabelais, Cervantes, and Shakespeare represent an important turning point in the history of laughter. Nowhere else do we see so clearly marked the lines dividing the Renaissance from the seventeenth century and the period that followed. The Renaissance conception of laughter can be roughly described as follows: Laughter has a deep philosophical meaning, it is one of the essential forms of the truth concerning the world as a whole, concerning history and man; it is a peculiar point of view relative to the world; the world is seen anew, no less (and perhaps more) profoundly than when seen from the serious standpoint. Therefore, laughter is just as admissible in great literature, posing universal problems, as seriousness. Certain essential aspects of the world are accessible only to laughter. (Bakhtin 1984)

In *A Midsummer Night's Dream*, a scene like the Pyramus and Thisbe play provides the dominant comic voice in the play; the inset play overwhelms the ducal power of Theseus and his plot, forcing the audience to see the world anew, in Bakhtin's phrase.

Like McDonald, Alan Powers considers what draws laughter from audiences in different historical periods and how comic elements subvert cultural givens about social hierarchy. In "'Gallia and Gaul, French and Welsh': Comic Ethnic Slander in the Gallia Wars," Powers treats the ethnic humor in *Henry V*, using anachronism to read synchronistically: from our time to 1642, from the English civil war to Shakespeare's time, from Tudor England to Agincourt. Powers points out that *Henry V* uses ethnic insults to resolve division; jokes about others' groups become a way for each to identify himself as "English" while retaining his ethnic identity. As Powers argues, the play uses "a substitution of ethnic and dialect stage conflict for stage wars of nationality," a substitu-

tion that finally includes even the French, thanks to the closing scene between Henry and Katherine.

Powers reads backward through the history of British culture to explore its comic margins and the characters who live there. Critical assumptions about central comic characters are considered by Thelma N. Greenfield and Christy Desmet. In "Ethos and Epideictic in *Cymbeline*," Desmet challenges the idea that critics who want to talk about the formation of self in literature must use tragedy's characters in their investigations. Such critics either ignore characters in comedies or at best find them problematic. Taking a radically different approach to character criticism, she uses *Cymbeline* to show that the characters of a play quite often declare an individual's worth within an *ethos*. As she argues, "Perception alone will not reveal ethos because moral character is a construct, a fiction created from an individual's background and actions and ratified by society's judgment. Without the formal structures of rhetoric, moral character is not only inaccessible— it does not exist." When one considers "rhetoric" as an inevitable concomitant of dramaturgy, her point becomes even more important. Like Trinculo in *The Tempest*, a Shakespearean character might declare himself "a made man," for each is fashioned (to use a fashionable word), not only by the playwright, but also by the actor and the culture, to meet an audience's requirements— and the audience accepts what these forces say. Thus characters who evoke laughter or approval are constructed linguistically, not by the audience, but rather by the rhetoric of a play.

Desmet challenges critical assumptions about how characters are constructed; Thelma N. Greenfield challenges the idea that comic characters are laughable because they are ridiculously different from what an audience considers appropriate. Thomas Heywood posits that idea:

> And what is . . . the subject of this harmlesse mirth? either in the shape of a clowne to shew others their slovenly and unhandsome behaviour, that they may reforme that simplicity in themselves which others make their sport, lest they happen to become the like subject of generall scorne to an auditory; else it intreates of love, deriding foolish inamorates, who spend their ages, their spirits, nay themselves, in the servile and ridiculous imployments of their mistresses. (Heywood 1963, 227–28)

In "Falstaff: Shakespeare's Cosmic (Comic) Representation," Greenfield explains how Falstaff (or Ben Jonson's Ursula or a Rabelaisian character) differs from other comic characters because he forces the audience to recognize his fleshliness, his unconventional nature. Literary characters are controlled by the text in a way that Falstaff seemingly is not; they don't simply go to bed and die—as the audience must and as Falstaff does. Audiences find Falstaff so comic, then, because he ought to be literary, but is instead like themselves. Though his actions may be "slovenly and unhandsome," they do not spur an audience to reform, but rather to celebrate life and all of its slovenly, unhandsome pleasures.

The final assumption about the comic that this collection questions is the notion that our laughter is our own. Virtually every discussion of the comic suggests that comic moments do not fit well in serious (and hence worthy) art or translate easily from one culture to another.

M. Arogyasami considers comic lower-class characters in tragedies: the porter in *Macbeth*, the rural clown in *Antony and Cleopatra*, the gravedigger in *Hamlet*. Instead of using the usual critical formulae to explain why these characters are comic, however, Arogyasami employs the aesthetic theory of Indian philosopher Bharata Muni. The paper is of greatest interest to Anglo-American readers when describing, implicitly or explicitly, the characteristic assumptions about Renaissance culture that a non-Western reader might bring to the text. The fundamental conservatism with which such a reader views the class structure in the play, for example, is most emphatically embedded in a cultural matrix incongruous to late-twentieth-century Anglo-Americans.

The power of that cultural matrix appears in Susan Baker's essay. If a critical examination of comedy and the comic focuses on Shakespeare's plays, rich and various though those works may seem, it is necessarily affected by our culture's understanding of who Shakespeare is. Using reception theory, Baker looks at the role Shakespeare plays in other people's comedies. For there can be no doubt that the murder mysteries she writes about are comedies: we know them by their mistaken identities, their comic character types, and their inexorable happy endings. By turning away from Shakespeare's canon to popular narratives about murder, Baker neatly reminds us that our most fundamental assumption—that Shakespeare holds a special place in literary studies—largely depends on an unspoken agreement about who Shakespeare is. We are accustomed to Shakespeare's comedy in the theater or in the classroom, but when he indicates social value in a locked room mystery, we may well want to pause and ask ourselves why we think our approach to his work is more correct than that of someone who writes a murder mystery.

Nevertheless, we do recognize a difference between theatrical comedies and those in prose. The title of this collection marks that difference. How does an audience know when actors are acting funny? These essays suggest that recognition lies in performance, as much as in language or culture. Five essays draw on specific productions to support critical arguments about the plays; all the essays implicitly consider performance, particularly audience response.[14] Thus, this collection recognizes that plays are not art objects but rather scenarios for an art process. Stage-centered criticism, whether a central concern (as in Jensen's paper) or the "sauce to the mess" (to borrow a phrase from Arogyasami), informs any discussion of why acting funny makes an audience laugh. Whether a play creates a sense of superiority, incongruity, or a combination of those impulses, the audience responds to—marks, if you will—that sense by laughter. Precisely because laughter grows from instability of categories, comic moments are hard to pin down. Perhaps that difficulty leads critics to privilege tragedy over comedy: tragedy is a safer form, one that does not invite us to laugh at (and recognize ourselves in) Bottom, Falstaff, or even Bertram; one that does not celebrate a man's death in a bear's maw or a king who behaves inappropriately. The comic, and the plays that contain it—whether they be comedies, histories, romances, or even tragedies—make us laugh at ourselves acting funny.

Notes

1. Another play one could use in this grouping is *The Merry Wives of Windsor;* Free's essay discusses connections between *The Merry Wives of Windsor, Much Ado about Nothing,* and other romantic comedies.

2. The participants included the contributors to this volume and Ralph Berry, William Carroll, Irene Dash, Martha Kurtz, Cary Mazer, and Francis Olley. I very much appreciate the work that all of these participants did, both responding to one another's work and helping me think through the problems of putting this book together. I owe a special debt of gratitude to Ralph Berry for his sharp good sense. I also want to thank Nancy Hodge, Executive Director of the Shakespeare Association of America, whose assistance in setting up and running the seminar was invaluable; Susan Baker, who helped fill an important gap by agreeing to contribute an essay on the reception of Shakespeare; as well as Ben Teague, Anne Williams, and Margaret Dickey for lending a willing ear when I talked about this collection.

3. As most readers will recognize, I am using ideas associated with the British object-relations school of psychology. Nanette Jaynes introduced me to the

work of D. W. Winnicott and his followers in a very different context, and I want to acknowledge that debt. By choosing the object-relations school to anchor my discussion, I may seem implicitly to reject Freud's significant work on the comic. Rather, what I have to say is a modification: Freud is able to account for some kinds of laughter, but not all.

4. Nevertheless, the variety of responses is important to remember, for otherwise we find ourselves trying to operate within a falsely dichotomized paradigm. That false dichotomy is what students use when they try to separate all drama into rigid categories of tragedy and comedy; such pigeonholding is naive because most plays, like most of life, fall somewhere in between the ends of the range.

5. The first quotation is from Stanley Wells, "Shakespeare Criticism since Bradley," in Kenneth Muir and Samuel Schoenbaum, A New Companion to Shakespeare Studies (Cambridge: Cambridge University Press, 1971), 259; the second is Kenneth Muir in his introduction to Shakespeare: The Comedies (Englewood Cliffs, N.J.: Prentice-Hall, 1965), 1; the third is Lawrence Danson "Twentieth-century Shakespeare Criticism: The Comedies" in Stanley Wells, The Cambridge Companion to Shakespeare Studies (Cambridge: Cambridge University Press, 1986), 231. Muir's remark points to one of the few instances in which the tragic transgresses into a comedy.

6. Some recent studies have considered Shakespeare's comedies, but have had relatively little to say about comic elements per se, elements that can exist in noncomedic works. Others have considered both comic and comedic elements, but have ranged over all drama, not considering the special circumstances or problems of Shakespeare's plays. Obviously we have benefited from both studies of the comedic and of comic drama, but our range of inquiry is narrower: we explore comic and comedic structures and characters in Shakespeare.

Maurice Charney has written Comedy High and Low (New York: Oxford University Press, 1978) and edited Comedy: New Perspectives, New York Literary Forum 1 (1978) and Shakespearean Comedy, New York Literary Forum 5–6 (1980).

Robert Corrigan's Comedy anthologizes important essays on the subject. Harry Levin's recent Playboys and Killjoys (New York: Oxford University Press, 1987) is a delightful study, while T. G. A. Nelson's Comedy (Oxford: Oxford University Press, 1990) provides a useful overview of the issues.

7. My essay is based on an article, "Othello and New Comedy," published in Comparative Drama 20 (1986): 53–64. I am grateful to the editors of Comparative Drama for allowing me to reprint that material.

8. Dr. Jonson's famous animadversion on Shakespeare's wordplay—"A quibble was to him the fatal Cleopatra for which he lost the world, and was content to lose it"—moots the question of why Shakespeare takes such delight in comic wordplay. Cleopatra was, after all, attractive for good reason. In his essay, Alan Powers considers the importance of puns and insults in preliterate culture.

9. Aristotle is mentioned in the essays by Teague, Greenfield, and Desmet. Arogyasami's essay on the aesthetic theories of Bharata Muni reminds us that Aristotle with his work, so central to Westerners' understanding of literature, is far from the only ancient authority available.

10. Studies of antitheatricalism have discussed opposition to all plays, not only comedies. Jonas Barish's The Antitheatrical Prejudice (Berkeley: University California Press, 1981) is the fullest discussion of the phenomenon, while Margot Heinemann, in ch. 2 of Puritanism and Theatre (Cambridge: Cambridge Uni-

versity Press, 1980), provides a useful corrective to those who think all Puritans operated like Jonson's Rabbi Zeal-of-the-Land Busy. In this collection, Marcia McDonald discusses the importance of antitheatrical arguments most thoroughly.

11. See D. H. Monro's discussion in *The Argument of Laughter* (Notre Dame, Ind.: Notre Dame University Press, 1963).

12. Jensen is not the only critic to argue that laughter is created by technique as much as by attitude. In *Anatomy of Criticism* (Princeton: Princeton University Press, 1957), 168, Northrop Frye makes a similar point when he writes:

> The principle of the humor is the principle that unincremental repetition . . . is funny. In a tragedy—*Oedipus Tyrannus* is the stock example—repetition leads logically to catastrophe. Repetition overdone or not going anywhere belongs to comedy, for laughter is partly a reflex, and like other reflexes it can be conditioned by a simple repeated pattern. In Synge's *Riders to the Sea* a mother, after losing her husband and five sons at sea, finally loses her last son, and the result is a very beautiful and moving play. But if it had been a full-length tragedy plodding glumly through the seven drownings one after another, the audience would have been helpless with unsympathetic laughter long before it was over.

13. Jonson's works and characters are discussed in the essays by Geraldo de Sousa, Thelma Greenfield, and Ejner Jensen. None of Shakespeare's other contemporaries is mentioned this often.

For a fuller account of Renaissance comic theory, see Marvin Herrick, *Comic Theory in the Sixteenth Century* (Urbana: University of Illinois Press, 1984).

14. Those essays are by Free, Arogyasami, Jensen, Teague, and Powers.

ACTING FUNNY

Othello and New Comedy

FRANCES TEAGUE

Critics agree that *Othello* differs qualitatively from *Macbeth, Lear,* and *Hamlet,* and some would trace this difference to the play's fundamentally comic structure. One approach, for example, is to point out similarities in the plots of *Othello* (1604) and *Much Ado about Nothing* (1598–99). Susan Snyder takes a different approach in her fine analysis of how "comic success precedes tragic catastrophe" in *Othello* (Snyder 1970, 70).[1] That the elements of comedy help to create a difference in kind is an idea implicit in what M. R. Ridley says:

> In none of them [*Lear, Macbeth,* or *Antony and Cleopatra*] is there that implication followed by explication which Aristotle thought one of the features of great tragedy, and of which, incidentally, Shakespeare was himself a master in another kind of play. *The Merchant of Venice, Much Ado,* and *Measure for Measure* have all theatrically effective plots. But Shakespeare used this form only once in high tragedy, and this is where *Othello* differs in structure and in effect from the others. (Ridley 1958, xlvi)

Thus Ridley argues that Shakespeare uses what was for him a characteristically comedic structure to achieve tragic effect in *Othello.* Certainly a comedic structure would help to account for some elements that differentiate *Othello* from the other major tragedies: the lack of subplot, the smaller number of characters, and the lower social rank of those characters are all features more characteristic of comedy than of tragedy. To argue that the play uses a comedic structure does not, however, provide any answers to certain recurring critical questions.

When one studies the play, one puzzles over Iago's motivation, Othello's trust of his servant and distrust of his wife, and the play's time setting. When one watches the play in performance, however, such questions are moot. In fact, the play on stage discourages such questions so thoroughly that one does not protest about inconsistencies of time or character, but rather will direct any protest at the terrible inevitability of its ending. Thus in 1751, when the settlers in Williamsburg produced *Othello* to celebrate a treaty with the Cherokees, the play ended abruptly after "the Emperor and the Empress of the tribe sent their attendants to stop the killing on the stage" (Speaight 1973, 70). An audience accepts Iago's malevolence, Othello's credulity, and the play's double time in part because it has no chance to question these characteristics: *Othello* moves too swiftly. The pace of the play, however, does not completely account for the way that the audience accepts such inconsistencies. If one looks to Roman comedy for the dramatic techniques that give rise to problems with time and character, one may find other reasons for an audience's acceptance.

The sources of *Othello* are well-established.[2] My concern is not with the play's sources, but rather with its comic analogues in Roman New Comedy, the works that might have provided Shakespeare not with events of plot, but with dramatic technique. For example, the opening scenes of the play are disorienting. While the urban street setting may recall Shakespeare's Roman plays (*Julius Caesar*, for example, or *Coriolanus*), the setting may also allude to Roman New Comedy. Furthermore, the play's rapid pace is set by Shakespeare's use of double time, a ploy he might have learned from a classical source, Plautus' *Captivi*. Finally, the audience may accept the major characters because some part of its attention recognizes a situation familiar from farce and rooted in Roman New Comedy: the mistaken sexual jealousy felt by a soldier whose emotions are manipulated by a clever underling.

At first glance, the place and time settings of New Comedy seem to have no relationship to those of *Othello*. Plautus and Terence set their plays not in Senate chambers or on islands, but rather in Roman streets before several doors. Yet the opening scene of *Othello* does recall these urban settings of New Comedy: two men, one of whom serves the hero, talk in the street and rouse a *senex* who learns of his child's unsuitable marriage. Again in 1.2 the street is the setting as a servant deceives his master. *Othello* opens, then, as a Roman comedy might, though the setting quickly shifts to the Senate chamber or to Cyprus.[3] These opening scenes are important for establishing the play's tone, as David Bevington has pointed out:

> Daringly, Shakespeare opens this tragedy of love not with a direct and sympathetic portrayal of the lovers themselves, but with a scene of vicious insinuation about their marriage. . . . Subtle but imperti-

nent ways of doubting the motivations of Othello and Desdemona are thrust upon us by the play's opening, and are later crucial to Iago's strategy of mistrust.[4]

Certainly this atmosphere of mistrust helps to create the play's intensity. The errors in understanding between *senex* and *servus*, which Plautus and Terence resolve comically, lead to tragedy in *Othello*.

Shakespeare also uses his time setting to create intensity, and here again *Othello* and the Roman comedies seem to have little in common. The Romans carefully observe unity of time, while *Othello*, notoriously, uses long and short time. Yet Plautus and Terence must often condense time in their plays. Sometimes they use offstage action: a character will exit, then return two or three hundred lines later saying he has been away all day long. Or the playwrights may proceed more directly:

> *Milphio to audience:* I'll go in and inform my master of this. It would be sheer stupidity to call him out in front of the house and repeat here what you've just heard. (*Poenulus*, 920 ff.)

> *Eutychus:* Let's go in; this place isn't suitable. While we're talking, the people who pass by can learn about all your business.
> *Demipho:* That's a good idea, and at the same time the play will be shorter. (*Mercator*, 1005 ff.)[5]

In short, Roman playwrights are amusingly conscious of how difficult it is to handle the passing of dramatic time. The most memorable instance of a New Comedy playwright adjusting time to achieve unity occurs in Plautus' *Captivi*. Ostensibly the play covers the events of a single day, for, as the parasite Ergasilus repeatedly reminds us, he has fasted all day long until the homecoming banquet at the day's (and play's) conclusion. In that single day, Philocrates goes on a journey that would necessarily take several days. Plautus, in this play, invents double time.

Othello, in the Cyprus scenes, comes closer to observing unity of time than any of Shakespeare's other tragedies. Acts II through V seem to cover only thirty-six hours, although Othello suspects Desdemona of an adulterous affair that has lasted much longer than a day and a half. The speed of events leads to the final tragedy.[6] If, when Shakespeare decided to use double time, he had wanted a model, particularly a model that allowed him some flexibility in handling time, he might well have chosen the New

Comedy plays he had studied in school. Specifically, he might have used *Captivi*.

Othello and New Comedy share another element. I will not belabor the standard comic device of the unsuitable marriage. Nor will I discuss the uxorious husband as a New Comedy figure: George Duckworth points out about *Every Man in His Humor* that

> Kitely, the jealous husband, is included by some scholars among "the characteristic types in Roman comedy," but wrongly so, for nowhere in Roman comedy except in the *Amphitruo* (by no means a typical play) does a husband have cause for jealousy. (Duckworth 1952, 421)

In New Comedy, the wife, not the husband, is the jealous spouse.[7]

Instead of an unsuitable marriage or a jealous husband, the element from New Comedy that Shakespeare may use in *Othello* is the character of the *miles gloriosus*. The professional soldier, who combines a suspicious nature with gullible trust in a servant, is so commonplace a figure in Roman plays that he appears in seven of the twenty Plautus plays that survive. Plautus could simply title one of his comedies *Miles Gloriosus*, knowing that his audience would recognize this reference to a stock character; centuries later Evelyn Waugh would title a chapter of *Men at Arms* "Apthorpe Gloriosus" with the same confidence.[8] Unless one is a Thomas Rymer, associating noble Othello with a braggart like Pyrgopolynices seems outrageous, yet such an association might help account for the ease with which Iago seduces Othello. In *Curculio, Truculentus*, and *Miles Gloriosus*, a distinguished soldier ventures into civilian life. Each falls in love, each is deceived, and each loses his love—none is sympathetic. The Roman soldiers lack sympathy because all are braggarts; Othello follows the same pattern of action, but he is sympathetic.

Shakespeare has Othello explicitly deny that he enjoys boasting, although, in fact, he is willing to tell of his adventures. Thus at 1.2.20–21, Othello says that his exploits are unknown, "Which, when I know that boasting is an honor, / I shall provulgate." Clearly he disapproves of boasting, and he later insists to the senate: "Rude am I in my speech, / And little bless'd with soft phrase of peace" (1.3.81–82). He has, however, won Desdemona by telling her "the battles, sieges, fortunes, / That I have pass'd" (1.3.130–31); "She lov'd me for the dangers I had pass'd, / And I lov'd her that she did pity them" (1.3.167–68). The audience listens sympathetically to Othello's account of his wooing. What he calls "a round unvarnish'd tale" holds us (1.3.90), as it has held

Desdemona, and leads the Duke to comment accurately that "I think this tale would win my daughter too" (1.3.171).

Yet Iago, Othello's servant, views the general with contempt, as the servants of New Comedy view braggart soldiers: "Mark me with what violence she first lov'd the Moor, but for bragging and telling her fantastical lies" (2.2.222–24). Shakespeare intends the audience to reject Iago's cynical comment, yet the audience may also recognize that cynicism if they have any familiarity with Plautus. For example, in *Miles Gloriosus*, the servant Palaestrio tells the audience:

> illest miles meus erus
> qui hinc ad forum abiit, gloriosus, impudens,
> stercorus, plenus periuri atque adulteri.
> ait sese ultro omnis mulieres sectarier:
> is deridiculost, quaqua incedit, omnibus.
> itaque hic meretrices, labiis dum ductant eum,
> maiorem partem videas valgis saviis.
>
> (88–94)

> The soldier you saw just now
> Going off to the forum—he's my lord and master;
> He is also a dirty liar, a boastful, arrogant,
> Despicable perjuror and adulterer.
> He thinks all women are after him, but in fact
> Wherever he goes he's an object of derision.
> Even the girls who smile their allurements at him
> Are usually making mouths behind his back.[9]

In short, the Plautine soldier is a braggart and adulterer, who is loathed by women. The ideas and hyperbole in Palaestrio's speech are analogous to those used by Iago who also loathes his "lord and master." In 2.1, Iago claims that Othello enjoys "bragging and telling fantastical lies"; his master, "the lusty Moor," is supposedly an adulterer who "Hath leap'd into my seat"; though Othello enjoys Desdemona's love, soon she will "begin to heave the gorge, disrelish and abhor the Moor" (2.1.223–24, 295–96, 233). The difference, of course, is one of tone: Palaestrio finds the tales that Pyrgopolynices tells ridiculous, and the audience agrees; Iago hates Othello and his adventures, while Shakespeare's audience admires the man and "the dangers he has pass'd." In a tragic context, the audience does not accept the servant's judgment; the stock figure of the *miles gloriosus* becomes disturbing rather than comic.

Plautus uses the epithet *gloriosus* ironically, for there is no glory in his general, as anyone can see. Shakespeare inverts the comic stereotype for tragic effect. When Othello bids farewell to "glorious war," the irony is dramatic, for the soldier has allowed Iago to impose a false and twisted view of human nature. In this view, Desdemona is a slut and Othello a braggart soldier who deserves betrayal; the audience, however, knows better and rejects the potentially comic situation by responding to the tragedy implicit in Othello's renunciation of the truth. One reason that the audience knows better is its rejection of Iago's view of Desdemona as a slut, for since she is obviously honest, Othello is no cuckold (and not laughable) and Iago is treacherous.

Although Othello is a tragic inversion of the *miles gloriosus*, Desdemona has no analogue in New Comedy. The women in New Comedy fall into a limited range of types: the jealous, middle-aged wives; the prostitutes and music girls; and the young brides. Clearly Desdemona is unlike the matrons or the prostitutes. Nor is she like the brides, who are in some way unsuitable for the hero to marry. Their lack of virginity or of social standing becomes a Roman play's stumbling block that a hero must get over before he reaches the happy ending. In Shakespeare's play, on the other hand, it is Othello who is the unsuitable partner. Desdemona brings to her marriage both the social position and the unquestioned virginity that a New Comedy heroine lacks. The importance of Desdemona's role in this play is too easily overlooked and misunderstood. Among other things, she is an index to Othello's worth. Because Desdemona in no way resembles a New Comedy heroine, the audience recognizes that Othello is a tragic version of the *miles gloriosus*.

The braggart soldier, as critics have pointed out, is incomplete without a clever servant to trick him. (Hanson 1965, 66 ff.), and Iago is a tragic version of the *servus callidus*. In New Comedy plays, a clever servant plays a role. It is he who aids the *adulescens* to win the girl, he who invents plans on the spur of the moment and spins half-truths to deceive, he who tells others how to act and even lends them language. Despite his cleverness, the *servus callidus* is no hero. He ignores the finer points of ethics and has a weakness for wine and song. While Shakespeare draws on the morality figure of the Vice (an influence reflected in the language of the play) and may have used the improvisatory action of the *zanni*, he could also have had the prototype for the *zanni*—the *servus callidus*—in mind when he created Iago.[10] The *servus* helps a young man in love with a seemingly unsuitable woman. In this case, the "compliant and invertebrate" *adulescens* is Roderigo, who desires the unattainable Desdemona.[11] In addition to helping Roderigo, Iago is like the classical *servus* in that he also seeks eventual freedom from service to Othello. To achieve his ends, both of which mirror the motives of a New Comedy *servus*, Iago employs the usual techniques. He spins plots as he goes, trusting his luck to make all cohere. He uses half-truths, knowing that lies based on truth are more plausible than outright falsehoods. He directs Roderigo's and Othello's actions, telling them what to do and even what to say.

His machinations begin when he uses Roderigo to manipulate Brabantio into breaking off the marriage. His plan is quickly made and executed; they will simply tell the truth:

> Call up her father
> Rouse him, make after him, poison his delight,
> Proclaim him in the streets
>
> (1.1.67–69)

Roderigo does as he is told to do, and, when his voice is too weak, Iago adds his own. After this plan to halt the marriage fails, Iago finds a new one:

> Let me see now:
> To get [Cassio's] place and to plume up my will
> In double knavery—How? how?—Let's see—
> After some time, to abuse Othello's ear
> That he is too familiar with his wife.
>
> (1.3.392–96)

From this beginning, he turns all to account. When Cassio greets Desdemona gallantly, Iago remarks, "With as little a web as this will I ensnare as great a fly as Cassio" (2.1.168–69). He uses Cassio's gallantry to incite Roderigo; when Cassio is drunk and twitted by Roderigo, anger leads Cassio to chase the *adulescens* and even to attack Montano.

In this scene, Iago gives a perfect performance as a drunken singing servant. Like Pseudolus or the slaves in *Stichus*, Iago celebrates his master's marriage: "Well—happiness to their sheets! Come, lieutenant, I have a stope of wine, and here without are a brace of Cyprus gallants that would fain have a measure to the health of black Othello" (2.3.29–32). Pseudolus and other New Comedy servants get drunk, sing, and make jokes at the wedding feast. Iago too drinks, sings, and jokes about drinking habits.

And, just as a drunken *servus* may tell a dangerous truth without shame, Iago seems to tell Montano the truth about Cassio's drinking. As Othello investigates the attack on Montano, he hears this story as well.

The result of the drinking scene is Cassio's disgrace and Desdemona's attempt to help him. Using Desdemona's plea for clemency and her stolen handkerchief, Iago twists the truth as he talks with Othello: Michael Cassio was Othello's go-between to Desdemona and "I dare be sworn I think that he is honest" (3.3.100, 125); Othello may not know Iago's thoughts and should beware of jealousy (3.3.133–76); Desdemona tricked her father to wed Othello (3.3.206–11). Having told Othello these things, all true, Iago need only show Othello Cassio's meeting with Bianca to convince him of Desdemona's adultery. Iago does not lie directly, yet his ingenious shaping of the truth pulls all his plots together.

The end of his plotting is his complete control over Othello. The servant commands his master. Othello is unable to think or act for himself after watching Cassio; "How shall I murder him, Iago?" he asks and abides by Iago's decision. When Othello thinks of his wife, planning to "chop her in messes" or poison her, Iago stops him with the order to "strangle her in her bed" (4.1.207). This capitulation to a servant's will is not unique to *Othello;* Plautus has a similar moment in *Miles Gloriosus.* As one critic describes the scene:

> the miles begs [his servant] Palaestrio to . . . begin amorous negotiations on his behalf. The slave does so, and leads his master across the stage just as this great leader had earlier (line 78) directed his minions with a royal *sequimini, satellites* (line 1009):
>
> > *Palaestrio:* Sequere hac me ergo.
> > *Pyrogopolynices:* Pedisequos tibi sum.
> > *Palaestrio:* All right, follow me.
> > *Pyrgopolynices:* I'll be your follower.
>
> Now the eminent general not only tags dutifully after the footsteps of his own slave, *pedes sequitur,* but as he does so he unconsciously admits that he has been transformed into a *pedisequus,* a lackey, the meanest of menials. (Segal 1968, 127)

The Plautine moment is comic, Shakespeare's tragic, but the situation is the same in both. A clever servant has tricked a great soldier into humiliating surrender to the servant's will. Thus, Pyrgopolynices and Othello not only follow their servants, doing what they are told to do, but they also echo what their servants say.

> Palaestrio has also succeeded in putting his own words into the soldier's mouth. Three times the slave "instructs" his master on how best to get rid of the girl, Philocomasium, lines 980–982, 1099–1100, and 1126–1127. Finally, in lines 1203–1205, the soldier parrots his slave's advice as if it were his own idea.
>
> Much the same "saturnalian" phenomenon occurs in *Othello*, albeit on a far more sinister level. As Iago's control of his millitary master increases, the Moor begins to talk like his crafty subordinate. E.g., when Iago tortures Othello with animal images of his wife's supposed infidelity, "were they as prime as goats, as hot as monkeys . . ." (III iii 403), his description so overcomes the Moor that later, in greeting Lodovico, he suddenly blurts out, "Goats and monkeys!" (Segal 1968, 208)

Certainly the key word here is "sinister." If Shakespeare draws on Roman New Comedy in *Othello*, making use of the plays of Plautus and Terence for tragic effect, he does so by turning comic conventions into tragic grotesques. At some level, an audience may recognize that Othello and Iago correspond to stock comic figures, yet that they do not act or react in a comic way. The disjunction between comic type and tragic tone unsettles an audience because it heightens the tension that ends with Desdemona's death and intensifies the sense of loss at Othello's suicide. Thus the qualitative difference that critics have noted between *Othello* and the other major tragedies may come from *Othello*'s analogue, Roman New Comedy.

It would be a mistake to argue that comic elements in a tragedy are somehow improved or raised by that appropriation to an opposite form. When Shakespeare uses the comic to create a tragedy, he does not privilege one form over the other. Rather he appropriates the affective powers of comedy to heighten tragedy. If one accepts the notion that literature must fit into a hierarchy of value, a hierarchy in which one form is higher art than another, this case might suggest that tragedy, because it is enhanced by the affective power of comedy, is inferior to it. Yet such an argument is ultimately grounded in an inadequate model of value. A more adequate model would point to the mutuality of comedy and tragedy, breaking down formal categories through attention to how a work achieves its affective power.

Unrealistic time and place settings amuse us in a comedy because they suggest an artistic world in which physical laws may be safely broken. To perceive the play's world as one that is fashioned, one has to make the assumption that such a world is constructed, controlled, and controllable. In a tragedy, such a setting is disturbing, suggesting that "chaos is come again" to an anarchic world that has slipped beyond control. The figures of the Roman *miles gloriosus* and *servus callidus* entertain in comedy because they are anarchic and hyperbolic; yet an audience expects such figures to be brought under control by the comedy's conclusion. In a comedy, the threat posed by such figures is dissipated by our expectation of a happy ending for the young lovers. But in *Othello,* the *miles* is no braggart, the *servus* serves himself, and the lovers are destroyed. The threat of anarchy is realized. A comedy begins in discord and ends in union; *Othello* begins with marriage and ends in murder.

Because *Othello* is tragic, the characters and events in it that recall comedy disturb us by recalling comedy's alternative world of order and love only to show how it is frustrated and destroyed. If the affective power of comedy comes from sanctioned anarchy, with its implicit promise that such disorder will be controlled, tragedy that breaks its bounds to appropriate the comic also breaks that promise.

Notes

1. Ray Heffner says in "Hunting for Clues in *Much Ado About Nothing*" that John Russell Brown and Rosalie Colie first observed that *Much Ado* is "a comic rehearsal for the tragedy of *Othello*" (212). In "Shakespeare Inferred," John Velz juxtaposes the two plays (30–31). Both essays are in *Teaching Shakespeare,* ed. Walter Edens, et al. (Princeton: Princeton University Press, 1977).

The dating and all quotations from *Othello* are from *The Riverside Shakespeare,* ed. G. Blakemore Evans (Boston: Houghton Mifflin, 1974).

2. Geoffrey Bullough in *Narrative and Dramatic Sources of Shakespeare* (New York: Columbia University Press, 1975), 7:193–265, does not discuss the argument that Iago is modelled on the *zanni* of *commedia dell'arte.* Advanced by Barbara de Mendonça, "Othello: A Tragedy Built on a Comic Structure," *Shakespeare Survey* 21 (1968), 31–38, and René Fortin, "Allegory and Genre in *Othello*," *Genre* 4 (1971): 153–72, this theory is the closest approach that I have found to the argument that Iago is a Renaissance version of New Comedy's *servus callidus.*

3. One could, of course, argue that the trial scene and island setting are comic, though they need not come from Roman comedy. The trial scene recalls similar moments in *The Merchant of Venice* and *Measure for Measure;* the island setting is used for young lovers in *The Tempest.* While trials and islands do not occur explicitly in New Comedy, the fate of a romance turns on a question of law in *Phormio, Rudens,* and *Pseudolus,* and seacoast settings are essential in

Rudens and *Menaechmi.* Cf. George Duckworth, *The Nature of Roman Comedy* (Princeton: Princeton University Press, 1952), 27n and David Konstan, *Roman Comedy* (Ithaca: Cornell University Press, 1983), 75–77, 91–92, 116–18. I need not point out the classical association of Cyprus and Venus.

4. See David Bevington's introduction to the play in his 1980 edition of Shakespeare's *Works* (Glenview, Ill.: Scott, Foresman, 1980), 1121–22.

5. These examples, only a few of many, and their translations are from Duckworth 1952, 130.

6. A similar case of condensing time for dramatic effect occurs in *Romeo and Juliet,* in which the nine months of Shakespeare's source become five days.

7. Although, as Duckworth says, *Amphritruo* is atypical, it *is* a play that Shakespeare seems to have used, specifically in creating the twin servants in *Comedy or Errors.* Shakespeare could not have known Menander's work, in which the jealous husband is a commonplace figure; otherwise I would discuss *Perikeiromene,* a play introduced by the goddess Agnoia. In it, a jealous soldier wrongs his faithful lover by his suspicions of unfaithfulness. This superficial coincidence of plot between *Othello* and a play that Shakespeare could not have known illustrates the dangers of seeing too great a resemblance to New Comedy; for Menander, see Philip Vellacott's translation of the *Plays and Fragments* (Baltimore: Penguin, 1967). Let me emphasize that I am discussing analogues, not sources, for Shakespeare's tragedy.

8. See John Arthur Hanson, "The Glorious Military," in T. A. Dorey and Donald R. Dudley, eds., *Roman Drama* (New York: Basic Books, 1965), 51, 54.

9. The Latin text is from the Loeb Library edition of Plautus, ed. and trans. P. Nixon (Cambridge: Harvard University Press 1916–38); the translation is by E. G. Watling from *The Pot of Gold and Other Plays* (Baltimore: Penguin, 1965).

10. Whether Iago is more like a Vice or a devil is not my concern here, but those who wish to explore the issue should consult Bernard Spivak, *Shakespeare and the Allegory of Evil* (New York: Columbia University Press, 1958), or Leah Scragg, "Iago—Vice or Devil?" *Shakespeare Survey* 21 (1968): 53–65.

11. The descriptive phrase is from Watling's translation, 150; the connection to Roderigo is my own.

All's Well That Ends Well
as Noncomic Comedy

MARY FREE

The title of *All's Well That Ends Well* suggests potential for mistaken identity, intrigue plot, thwarted romance—the stuff that makes comedy and the comic—and in its way the play fulfills those potentials. All does end well at least in the sense that girl does get boy despite all obstacles.[1] In gross structure and plot, *All's Well That Ends Well* also conforms to comedy's basic outlines as they appear in other Shakespearean plays. Bertram's flight from authority figures—King, Countess, Helena—and their rules and dictates to pursue the Florentine wars echoes flight to the saturnalian green world. His abandoning the woman he scorns along with his later pursuit of one who scorns him has precedent in both *The Two Gentlemen of Verona* and *A Midsummer Night's Dream*. Proteus and Demetrius forswear their former vows ("In number more than ever women spoke" as Hermia prophetically reminds us, 1.1.176)[2] to woo Silvia and Hermia respectively. Silvia in *The Two Gentlemen of Verona* is a worthy predecessor to Diana in *All's Well That Ends Well;* the dogged devotion that Julia *(The Two Gentlemen of Verona)*, Hermia *(A Midsummer Night's Dream)*, and Helena *(A Midsummer Night's Dream)* display toward the sometimes unworthy objects of their adoration anticipates Helena's in *All's Well That Ends Well*. This late play's conclusion also fits the comedic prototype by bringing together those admired with those shamed; everyone reenters the community—even Parolles with his "scurvy" curtsies—which creates "a movement towards harmony, reconciliation, happiness: the medieval idea" (Nelson 1990, 2).

These conformities to formulae notwithstanding, *All's Well That Ends Well* provides less pleasure, amusement, or even laughter than either the relatively weak *The Two Gentlemen of Verona* or the comedically superior *A Midsummer Night's Dream*. Throughout

All's Well That Ends Well's progress we, as theater-goers or critics, become aware—to our growing discomfort—that "ending well" does not in and of itself guarantee the presence of the comic within comedy. Two factors help to hold the comic at bay in this play: first, the placement and use of marriage as an expression of power; and second, the metalanguage of power that distinguishes the marked hierarchies of noble/commoner, public/domestic, and maturity/foolishness that the play presents.

Marriage as an Expression of Power

Marriage is a central element in the construct of Renaissance comedy. In the Shakespearean canon, a number of the comedies include marriages, placing them (or implying that they impend) close to or at the plays' ends as a reaffirmation, restoration and promise for the continuation of society.[3] Other comedies deal with married women as in *The Comedy of Errors* and *The Merry Wives of Windsor;* or they move the marriage forward, thus foregrounding it and making it precipitate further action in the main plot as in *The Taming of the Shrew* and *Much Ado about Nothing.* What makes *All's Well That Ends Well*'s foregrounded marriage unique is the undeniable fact that Bertram does not want Helena regardless of how much she wants him or how much the members of the nobility—most notably the King, the Countess, and Lafew—want him to want her. Further, in its institution, its mixing of high personages with low, and the alliances between social groups, the foregrounded marriage in *All's Well That Ends Well* subverts the comic by creating discomfiting inversions in the play's social spheres. While the concept of marriage as regenerative force via Helana's pregnancy obtains in principle at the end, when the "broken nuptial" comes together,[4] no wonder we, along with the King in the epilogue, feel little if any delight: things but "seem" well; we have no guarantees. We cannot be certain even there that Bertram truly wants her.

A distinction that contributes to my thesis is that *All's Well That Ends Well* stands apart from the Shakespearean comedic mainstream in that Helena and Bertram, however estranged their relationship, remain the single couple in the play.[5] Elsewhere Shakespeare provides us with sets of couples: twins who marry and woo in *The Comedy of Errors* and *Twelfth Night,* two men in pursuit of one woman in *The Two Gentlemen of Verona* and *A Midsummer Night's Dream,* two married women who plot to outwit one man and teach another a lesson in *The Merry Wives of Windsor*, Rosalind and Celia with their loves in *As You Like It*, and a triad of lovers in *The Merchant of Venice*. Even *Measure for Measure*, the play most often closely linked to *All's Well That Ends Well*, provides us pairings. *All's Well That Ends Well* gives us two widows, a virgin, and a wife in name only. While all these pairings deal with power in relationships, they do not constitute the exact marked hierarchies of power that *All's Well That Ends Well* presents to us.

The foregrounded marriage in *All's Well That Ends Well* differs from those in *The Taming of the Shrew* and *Much Ado about Nothing* in origination and ordination. While Kate in *The Taming of the Shew* has no more choice than does Bertram about whom each marries (Baptista and Petruchio merely strike a bargain as do the King and Helena), Petruchio and Kate as a pair remain this play's focal point. We observe the battle of wit and will between them, and the entire fourth act centers on them. Whether we grant or disallow the concept of mutuality of consent,[6] whether the production relies on Zefferellian horseplay or a more restrained production concept, *The Taming of the Shrew* provokes laughter[7]— the *sine qua non* of the comic—because of the physical and verbal interaction between the principal characters. The same holds true for *Much Ado about Nothing*. Like Kate and Petruchio, Beatrice and Benedick command our attention, their wit and wordplay amuse and distract us, and they are more interesting to us than the play's other couple Claudio and Hero. Even in that relationship, the comedy of *Much Ado about Nothing* remains more comic than does *All's Well That Ends Well*. Claudio and Hero agree to marry, an important distinction between their relationship and that of Helena and Bertram. The distasteful circumstances of the broken nuptial notwithstanding,[8] the separation between Claudio and Hero fails to disrupt wholly the play's overall comic spirit for two reasons: first, we know Dogberry and the Watch hold the key to reconciliation; second, as well as more important, the comic Beatrice and Benedick remain our primary focal point.

Helena and Bertram appear on stage together in but five scenes. Their exchanges generally indicate the dynamic of power in their relationship as Helena oozes subservience to her lord and master, while Bertram, until the final scene, plays his superiority, both of class and gender, for all it's worth. In three scenes where they appear together, they speak to or about one another but engage in no dialogue. In 1.1 Bertram in one and a half lines commands that Helena, "Be comfortable to my mother, your mistress, / And

make much of her" (76–77). In 2.3 she subserviently offers herself
to him in two and a half lines:

> I dare not say I take you, but I give
> Me and my service, ever whilst I live,
> Into your guiding power
>
> (2.3.102–104)

The remainder of this scene has them each talking to the King,
but not to one another. In a third scene (3.5), Helena merely views
Bertram from a distance as the army passes and asks about him.
Only two scenes have them exchanging dialogue. In 2.5, comprising thirty-five lines, Bertram, without having consummated the
marriage and refusing Helena's modest request for a departing
kiss, dismisses his bride by sending her back to Rossillion. His
language is primarily in the command form, hers acquiescent.
She comes "as [she] was commanded from [him]" (2.5.54). She
declares herself Bertram's "most obedient servant" in a scene that
allows for no possible irony (2.5.72). Even when she musters the
courage to hint at a parting kiss, she hesitates and stumbles as a
young woman very much in love and unsure of herself. In 5.3,
the reconciliation, they exchange two lines each, and arguably
Bertram's "If she, my liege, can make me know this clearly / I'll
love her dearly, ever, ever dearly" is addressed more to the King
than to Helena. These two encounters comprise but thirty-nine
lines all told.

All's Well That Ends Well remains a comedy in structure, yet
Helena's agency in the enforced marriage, as well as the subsequent separation and ploys, distances us from the comic. Other
elements distance us as well. When the Countess learns that Helena loves Bertram, we have the perfect occasion for a traditional
blocking figure, but no. The Countess not only enjoys, but also
encourages Helena in her aspirations. No witty bantering about
sex, love, fidelity in wedlock—that which might create the comic
within the matrix of comedy—takes place between Helena and
Bertram, the play's only couple. Certainly some comic playfulness
occurs within the play. No one will deny its presence in the virginity dialogue between Helena and Parolles, nor in the choosing
scene as Helena walks from budding youth to budding youth
before "giving" herself to Bertram, nor in Parolles's humiliation.
Nevertheless, what lightness exists remains apart from the focal
couple. Of added significance is how little of the playfulness associated with earlier comedies takes place among the women.

Beyond the Countess' hope for Helena's love, her brief acknowl-
edgement of her own past, and her teasing in the "I say I am your
mother" dialogue (1.3), women's dialogue as they assess man's
fecklessness has a more brittle edge than do similar assessments
given in the earlier comedies.

Helena's actions set her apart from her Shakespearean sisters.
Other independently-acting heroines—Viola, Rosalind, Portia—
play at their love-games and are, in some cases, willing to leave
Time to fadge things out. They also employ masculine disguise
to effect the amount of control or empowerment they enjoy. Helena does what she does without disguise. In some respects Helena and Portia are the most closely akin. Portia is willing to
comply with her father's will; Helena is willing to submit herself
to Bertram's.[9] Both work purposefully to achieve their goals. However close that kinship, differences obtain. Allies from the play's
outset, Portia and Nerissa plot to test true love's faith; Helena,
who must create her allies, has yet to gain mere acceptance as
wife. To achieve her goals, she acts with what Western culture
sees as male prerogatives. As A. P. Riemer has said, she acts with
a "male purposefulness" (Riemer 1975–76, 54). In order for her
to succeed undisguised, she must perform these actions in a way
that the empowering male structure (i.e., the King and Lafew as
members of the *ancien régime*) fails to recognize as violating sex
or class differences.

In *All's Well That Ends Well* Helena follows Bertram to Paris.
There she originates the marriage by striking a bargain with the
King and curing him. Unlike the other pairings and marriages in
the comedies, however, no tacit nor overt mutuality exists between this nuptial pair. Here the King must ordain an enforced
marriage of his ward Bertram to comply with the terms of the
bargain. Such ordination violates the usual circumstances that
we find in the festive comedies.[10] In those comedies, ordination,
directed against a woman, may initiate the flight from authority
into the saturnalian world of comic license.

Bertram's response to the King's command is like that of Silvia
or Hermia: forced into marriage ordained against his will, a marriage that is originated by a spouse who is not loved, he runs
away, as do the heroines. Bertram's running away to Florence
offers a different kind of escape from that of the heroines. Not
only is his escape to a city but to one associated with sexual
licentiousness. The King himself warns his courtiers against
"Those girls of Italy." When Helena discovers Bertram in Florence,[11] she entraps him by means of the bed trick, which inverts

predicated male-female sex roles just as "girl gets boy" inverts what we would recognize as the clichéd phrasing. Her action substitutes the legal for the licentious. Helena entraps Bertram a second time as well in 5.3 by her further employment of Diana before the King. Even the King becomes confused as Helena employs her skills. What allows everyone to escape prison is Helena's ability to use the language of empowerment without disturbing the status quo.

Metalanguage of Power

Since Renaissance cultural and sexual politics determine that only males have the possibility of an unbounded (or "unmarked") scope of action, Helena's behavior—both her actions and linguistic powers—marks her. Marking is a means of classifying, of categorizing differences that exist within orders. To be marked is normally negative because a marked group is set apart to be evaluated on a special scale, one generally lower than the universal scale of the unmarked whole. Hence critical study often uses a lesser scale to evaluate minority authors or marginalized works (such as the problem comedies).[12] The group that is unmarked thus controls the discourse used to evaluate; that group establishes the hierarchical ranking. To reproduce a marking system is to reproduce a form of hierarchy under the guise of "natural" reality. Significantly, to maintain a classification scheme, we learn to believe that principles of difference are *natural* principles inherent in given structures. This naturalization is a social process effected by a particular discourse that reproduces structures in a consistent manner. When something violates these classificatory principles, it disconcerts. As a problem comedy, *All's Well That Ends Well* provides a case in point. Comedy by its classification should be comic. When it's not, we begin marking it, setting it off from its parent class. As we do so, we find ourselves referring to an anomalous work negatively and mask, or "background," its historical provenance, making the work lie beyond normal reflection.[13] Hence what doesn't fit takes precedence over what does. But understanding the process does more than just clarify how the work is marked vis-à-vis the canon. That understanding also offers a way of accounting for what happens within the play.

All's Well That Ends Well works on three pairs of well-known marking distinctions. First, writers from Engels on have stressed the importance of the distinction between the domestic sphere of marriage and family, the main arena of women (and the structural principle of comedy), and the public sphere dominated by males (the world of tragedy). The public sphere activities of production are the activities that maintain social institutions defined as important by leaders and politicians—"to busy giddy minds with foreign wars," and by merchants and businessmen—to have "argosies [that] overpeer the petty traffickers." At the same time they appear routine and relatively empty of interesting human drama, save when they become disrupted by such male passions as revenge (*Hamlet*), ambition (*Macbeth*), and violence (*Coriolanus*), when they become the stuff of tragedy. The activities of reproduction in the domestic sphere are always marked by human drama even if often trivial drama. To oversimplify, in the domestic sphere the "image" of public legitimacy does not have to be maintained, so the discordant details of human relations can be revealed. From Shakespearean comedy to modern sitcom, the domestic sphere and its activities, because they are marked, are routinely more entertaining, even comic, than public activities, but they are also less "real," less significant in their impact than the activities of the male-dominated sphere. The extra information that makes domestic activities more interesting also assures us that they are in the less important domestic sphere. In *All's Well That Ends Well* the major concerns are about the domestic institutions of marriage and sex; public institutions of power and war are in the background.

Second, in *All's Well That Ends Well* the characters divide into fools—Bertram, Parolles, Lavatch—and sincere, mature people—the King, Lafew, and all of the female characters. The marking of fools is analogous to the marking of the domestic sphere in that the fools are more interesting (or perhaps irritating is a better choice of word in Bertram's case), but are less involved in important things. The Florentine wars as war, after all, figure little in the plot, and Parolles's loss of the drum parodies heroic action. Because most of the play's fools are male and most of the sincere, mature people are female, the things attended to by the serious people are things of importance to women, in this case, principally marriage. Significantly, this fact places the King as an ally with the women in their concern for marriage, a fact especially crucial in understanding the King's decision to help Diana to a husband at the play's end. Despite the Renaissance prohibition that comedy should not mix King with commoner, this alliance not only establishes the play as comedy, it reinforces the King's role as "father" (with its implications for marital status) and the dominant patriarchal figure in society—a role Bertram must also learn to play in order for society to work.

Third, the characters are divided into nobility versus common-ers. The latter group includes Helena and Parolles along with Diana and the Widow. In *All's Well That Ends Well* noble/common fits the same unmarked/marked pattern as the other two distinc-tions (i.e., public/domestic, mature/fool). The Widow alludes to having lost a former higher status and states her aspirations for Diana. Helena's common birth makes her love for Bertram appear hopeless, something she strives to overcome. Both Helena and Parolles seek to climb the social ladder, yet nothing in the text supports a reading of her as mere social climber. She is no would-be Count Malvolio. Parolles, by way of contrast, is the play's true social climber who gets his just deserts in public humiliation. Helena is marked because the normal marriage arrangements among the nobly born, public spectacles and often dynastic alli-ances, are unavailable to her. Thus, she must undertake a series of interesting but unusual activities (travel, linguistic magic, the bed trick) if she is to gain the ceremony of formal marriage, which in turn posits comedy, and the domestic intimacy of consumma-tion, which in the play's inverted sexual manipulation denies the comic.

Helena's decision to leave Rossillion to go to Paris and her later decision to become Saint Jaques's pilgrim indicate her indepen-dence and self-reliance. Those attributes do not guarantee her success. To achieve her goals, she must insinuate herself into the world of power, the world of the nobility that figures so impor-tantly in this play. Her means is linguistic. (Arguably that linguis-tic skill in the sense of language of power is part of the legacy her father has left her and facilitates her success with the King.) Other heroines control language as game, as play; Helena does not often play at comic wit. She dominates Parolles in the dia-logue on virginity; she wins the Countess's favor and the King's trust on the basis of language. As the play builds her power in allying her with the King, so Helena uses that power in allying Diana and the Widow with herself. At the same time that the play allows Helena power via language, Helena's professed view of herself calls attention to her subordinate position in the domes-tic sphere. As Joan Larsen Klein argues for Lady Macbeth as a good huswife, so could we for Helena in her desire to wed, bed, produce offspring, and be subservient to her lord.[14] Unlike Lady Macbeth, Helena becomes the embodiment of power via her preg-nancy.

Helena's skill in language will not work with Bertram, however, because he fails to understand it, as his alliance with Parolles suggests. Parolles also attempts to violate the noble/commoner distinction but fails. His attempts to move into the public world end in cowardice and shame, for Parolles lacks the linguistic superiority associated with other Shakespearean rogues. The ultimate irony of the unmasking scene lies, I believe, in the language of command the lords choose: doubletalk. Unlike Helena and the King, Parolles—despite his name—never controls language and, therefore, remains powerless: a victim easily undone by a plot concocted by those who do control the language of power. His final line, "I will not speak what I know," underscores that powerlessness. In contrast, however much humiliation Falstaff suffers at the Windsorites' hands, he maintains his comic dignity by recognizing his folly. Lafew may take Parolles home to sport, but the latter's curtsies remain "scurvy ones." While the unmasking action comprising Parolles's comeuppance is the most comic in the entire play, it remains unsuccessful because he has never mastered the original linguistic game and because it profits nothing for Bertram. Bertram must undergo his own linguistic education before an even higher court.

The (mis)alliance between Bertram and Parolles differs from earlier dramatic models. The play never convincingly shows Parolles misleading Bertram in the classic morality or prodigal son format. Were he to do so, the action would empower him. Instead Parolles tends to parrot Bertram's views. Parolles as parrot helps to point out that Bertram doesn't know how to control language either. Bertram offers clichés or denies the significance of the language of power when the King says that "I can create the rest" referring to his ability to bestow a title on Helena (2.3.143). Such a failure suggests an inability to understand the larger game wherein the words signify, a failure potentially far more dangerous than the Florentine wars. Because of that lack of knowledge, Bertram mistakenly chooses *commoner*—in his alliance with Parolles, or his haste to the Florentine wars—an inversion that cannot obtain ultimately in the world of comedy. Only through his humiliation, as he is caught in a linguistic trap of Helena's devising, can Bertram fulfill the comedic formula of reconciliation. Although Diana speaks the riddling verse, Helena originates it, and it bears similarity to her incantatory charming of the King. Helena's inventions work, but Bertram's fail. While the aspirations for Helena, Parolles, and Bertram differ in degree, these inversions, given the construct of this play, strike the audience as illegitimate and unpleasantly manipulative be they male or female. As such the inversions violate and deny the comic.

It might appear that the dramatic structure of *All's Well That Ends Well* would be a parallelism of these three distinctions: public/domestic, mature/fool, and noble/commoner. But what is dramatic about the play is its inversion of public/domestic and mature/fool. This inversion takes place because the power of the king/subject distinction supplants that of the more generic noble/commoner one. The King can write new rules for the game. He can alter the standards at will to ordain the marriage of his unwilling ward, raise Helena in status, condemn and forgive both Diana and Bertram, promise yet another female commoner one of "This youthful parcel / Of noble bachelors [who] stand at [his] bestowing" (2.3.52–53). The language of power is almost always unobtainable for those in the marked class because the holders of power can change the language at will, thus changing the rules. Helena is an exception.

The play still fundamentally does not oppose male hegemony and the marked nature of the domestic sphere, however. What Helena wants—along with her Shakespearean sisters—is marriage (that she actually wants Bertram remains a disappointing reality for most of us). She wins in the end through her use of intelligence and through the inversion that places her in the serious moral and linguistically-sophisticated sphere and Bertram in the arena of the foolish and verbally inadequate. But the inversion takes place initially because Helena cures the King. From then on the King, the ultimate symbol of male controlling power, is on her side. What the play's end restores is marriage and the domestic sphere "the way it should be" in a comedy.

Viewed dialectically, both the King and Helena have different roles from the other characters in the play. For the others, distinctions such as male/female, noble/commoner are givens (preattentive distinctions); they assume that these distinctions are normal and thus cannot manipulate them or even understand why they are so. The King, on the other hand, understands and can manipulate the metalanguage of power. After Helena cures him, the King cancels for her not only the effect of commoner birth, but also female lack of power in the prerogative of marriage choice by means of the foregrounded and ordained marriage. Helena does not have the King's power, but she does have (perhaps) an even greater understanding of the metalanguage. What she understands is that when a woman can mobilize the solidarity of other women, as she does with the Countess, Diana, and the

Widow, she can succeed—*if* the males do not notice any sex or class differences being violated; hence Helena's acquiescing to a subservient role. It is thus fitting that Bertram is such a weak character; in the dialectic of the play the King is Helena's true partner. And it is no wonder that he, along with us, is left trying to puzzle this comedy out in the Epilogue.

Notes

1. The fact that "girl gets boy" reverses the usual phrasing. What that reversal encompasses in the play's action helps to contribute to the noncomic atmosphere in *All's Well That Ends Well*, a point I take up later in the body of the essay.

2. All Shakespeare quotations are from *The Riverside Shakespeare*.

3. See Northrop Frye, *Anatomy of Criticism*, or C. L. Barber, *Shakespeare's Festive Comedy* for extended consideration of the function of marriage in comedy.

4. The phrase is from Leo Salingar, *Shakespeare and the Traditions of Comedy* (Cambridge: Cambridge University Press, 1974) and Carol Thomas Neely, *Broken Nuptials in Shakespeare's Plays* (New Haven: Yale University Press, 1985).

5. Robert Ornstein comments on the implications of this feature, which Shakespeare appropriated from his source, Boccaccio's tale of Giletta and Beltramo; see his *Shakespeare's Comedies: From Roman Farce to Romantic Mystery* (Newark: University of Delaware Press, 1986), 173–78.

6. I agree with Irene Dash that while the play "throws both ideas [forced marriage vs. 'good consent'] out to the audience . . . the comedy offers a remarkably mature affirmation of the potential for understanding between a man and a woman" (Dash 1981, 35, 64). *The Taming of the Shrew*'s plot contains that potential, while *All's Well That Ends Well* ends with a series of conditional "ifs" and "seems."

7. Notable exceptions are Charles Marowitz's 1975 adaptation and the Royal Shakespeare Company's 1978 production; cf. David Bevington, "*The Taming of the Shrew* in Performance," in *Shakespeare: Four Comedies* (New York: Bantam, 1988), 12.

8. Certainly one could argue that Claudio and Bertram are close kin in rejecting their brides. Claudio's accusation, however, breaks that nuptial before the ceremony is complete. Bertram must perforce go through the rite. He then vows not to consummate the marriage, which means it will remain a marriage in name only until Helena can meet his demands. Furthermore, in *Much Ado about Nothing* Hero remains offstage until the reconciliation while we must attend to Helena's actions in *All's Well That Ends Well*.

9. The question of Portia's and Helena's "submission" is beyond the focus of this study. Richard A. Levin's recent *Love and Society In Shakespearean Comedy* (Newark: University of Delaware Press, 1985) examines Portia's motivations while Bertrand Evans's *Shakespeare's Comedies* (Oxford: Clarendon, 1960) and Howard C. Cole's *The "All's Well" Story from Boccaccio to Shakespeare* (Urbana: University of Illinois Press, 1981) remain classic statements on Helena's assertive behavior.

10. For the way in which enforced marriage of a ward violates the guardian's responsibilities, see the discussion of *All's Well That Ends Well* in Marilyn Williamson, *The Patriarchy of Shakespeare's Comedies* (Detroit: Wayne State University

Press, 1986), 59–64, or the analysis of what such considerations meant to women in Lisa Jardine, *Still Harping on Daughters* (New York: Columbia University Press, 1989), 79–85.

11. I am not concerned here whether her arrival is by plan or happenstance.

12. Joanna Russ's *How to Suppress Women's Writing* (Austin: University of Texas Press, 1983) is relevant here.

13. My discussion is grounded in the work of Peter Berger and Thomas Luckman, *The Social Construction of Reality* (New York: Anchor, 1967).

14. See Joan Larsen Klein, "Lady Macbeth: 'Infirm of Purpose,'" in Carolyn Lenz, et al., eds., *The Woman's Part* (Urbana: University of Illinois Press, 1980), 240–255.

The Tempest, Comedy, and
the Space of the Other

GERALDO U. DE SOUSA

T*he Tempest* echoes such New World materials as William Stra-chey's *A True Repertory of the Wracke and Redemption of Sir Thomas Gates* (1610) and *A True Declaration of the Estate of the Colonie in Virginia* (1610); whether Shakespeare intended the play as a com-mentary on European expansionism has long been debated.[1] Re-cently several critics have attempted to ground *The Tempest* in colonial discourse.[2] The play seems to share with the age of dis-covery the central image of the European man who is cast into a new world that he must describe and map in order to bring it into the domain of ethnography and history.[3] Seizing upon this image, a number of critics have argued that Prospero represents the European colonizer who subjugates Caliban, the defenseless native.[4] This interpretation would suggest that the play is far from being a comedy: Prospero, the protagonist as oppressor, becomes a bully determined to control or destroy what he finds. To see the play in this way, however, ignores the basic fact that Prospero, like Sycorax, came to the island not as the oppressor but the op-pressed.

A more productive way to examine *The Tempest* in relation to European expansionism might be to focus on one culture's en-counter with its Other. The model for my discussion derives from such travel and ethnographical descriptions as Hans Staden's *The True History of His Captivity* (1557), Jean de Léry's *Histoire d'un voyage faict en la terre du Brésil* (1578), and Gabriel Soares de Sousa's *Tratado descriptivo do Brasil*, or *Noticia do Brasil* [*News from Brazil*] (1587)—all of which focus on European men who confront their culture's Other.[5] Numerous travelogues share a common struc-ture, akin to that of comedy, which Michel de Certeau ably identi-fies in Jean de Léry's journey:

In 1556 Jean de Léry is twenty-four years old. Published twenty years later, his *Histoire* casts the movement of departure that had gone from over here (in France), to over there (among the Tupis), into circular form. It transforms the voyage into a cycle. From over there it brings back a literary object, the Savage, that allows him to turn back to his point of departure. The story effects his return to himself through the mediation of the Other. (Staden 1928, 213)

Similarly, Prospero's voyage takes him to the fringes or the outer limits of his society, into the space of the Other. I will argue that his return to use de Certeau's terminology, is "instituted in the space of the Other" (Staden 1928, 210). My argument, however, radically departs from treatments of colonial discourse in The *Tempest;* I will argue that Prospero himself might be a tragic figure: rejected and expelled from his culture, he occupies—at least temporarily, provisionally, if not permanently—the space reserved for the Other. By his voyage into the space of the Other, Prospero transforms the potentially tragic story of his life into a comedy.

Prospero arrived on the island as an outcast, not an emissary from the colonial powers. As an exile and outcast, he resembles the witch Sycorax, expelled from her home country in Northern Africa. He and his infant daughter were abandoned aboard a small boat to die at sea. To be sure, colonial powers frequently sent undesirables to their new colonies, and such undesirables became—paradoxically and ironically—the ambassadors of their culture.[6] But Milan has no grand colonial dreams: the Italians seem little interested in an uninhabited island, and Prospero was not a prisoner left in a penal colony. At the end of the play, we are to infer, no colony will remain behind. *The Tempest* is less about Shakespeare's views on Italian or English colonialism than about the encounter and interaction of different cultures and subcultures.

Prospero is driven to the margins of his culture, or in Victor Turner's phrase, "to inhabit the fringes and interstices of the social structure" of his time, to occupy that "liminal space." His expulsion came after a period of seclusion, meditation, and study.[7] If we are to believe Prospero's assessment, Milanese society, much like our own, privileges and rewards action over contemplation (studies), thus marginalizing intellectualism. Perhaps because of his alienation from his culture, Prospero misjudged the reaction to his isolation. A difference and a distance arose between himself and his culture; hence he perhaps unwittingly rejected his culture, and his culture staged his expulsion. He wandered off into a dangerous region that delineates the margins of power; therefore, instead of epitomizing colonial power, Prospero represents the battleground of a culture made uncomfortable when it senses the presence of its Other. However one gets to those margins, the relationship to the centers of power is similar, as a contemporary example makes clear: a town in Florida turns on its water sprinklers at night to drive away the homeless from the benches of the community park. In our own culture as in *The Tempest*, we find abundant examples of such displays of force whose sole purpose is to dehumanize and displace into the fringes and interstices of the social structure.

Feminization of Prospero

Prospero's potential tragedy begins with his exile. To understand his expulsion from his culture, I turn to an example from anthropology. Unlike Europeans, some aboriginals, such as the Mehinaku, institutionalize the encounter with the Other. For the present purposes, the Mehinaku provide not a source for *The Tempest*, but an analogue to help explain how it becomes a comedy.[8] The Mehinaku live in a male-dominated society, not different from the larger, Portuguese-based, Brazilian society. Under clearly defined conditions, however, the Mehinaku stage the collapsed difference between man and woman. "*Couvade*," anthropologist Thomas Gregor explains, "is an institution that requires a father to imitate some of the behavior of his wife at the time of childbirth" (Gregor 1985, 194).[9] In many indigenous societies, "[the *couvade*] varies from literal acting out of the woman's labor to relatively informal observances of food taboos" (Gregor 1985, 194).[10] Most interestingly, "the father's movements are restricted, much like a woman in an advanced stage of pregnancy; all of his activities have an impact on the well-being of his child; and, analogous to a woman who has recently given birth, he assumes the taboos appropriate for the postpartum flow of blood" (Gregor 1985, 195).[11] Lasting about a year, the Mehinaku *couvade* ensures the father's return to a position of domination.

I suggest that in societies—such as the one in *The Tempest*—that do not practice the *couvade*, the collapsed difference between man and woman is politicized and not tolerated. In fact, Stephen Orgel suggests that although Prospero's wife is "missing as a character," "Prospero, several times explicitly, presents himself as incorporating the wife, acting as both father and mother to Miranda, and, in one extraordinary passage [1.2.155–58], describes the voyage to the island as a birth fantasy" (Orgel 1986, 54).[12] The absence of the wife casts Prospero into the role of a woman—the role of the Other—as I hope to demonstrate. Therein may lie the source of his problem.

For reasons unexplained, Prospero withdraws from his public life, a space traditionally occupied by males, into a domestic world, the space of females (and of comedy). His movements are restricted as his masculine, decisive brother takes the reins of government, not only overpowering Prospero, but also setting "all hearts i'th'state / To what tune pleased his ear" (1.2.84–85).[13] Prospero defines his "trust" in his brother as a woman giving birth to an unruly offspring:

> and my trust,
> Like a good parent, did beget of him
> A falsehood in its contrary as great
> As my trust was.
>
> (1.2.93–96)

I take "trust" to be the conceiving female, and Antonio to be the male, although the passage presents cruxes that modern editors have simply ignored.[14] The brother is further described as aggressive: "He [is] thus lorded, / Not only with what my revenue yielded / But what my power might else exact" (1.2.97–99). Like a mother, Prospero, on the other hand, had to protect and nurture his infant daughter and was perhaps prevented from actions that would defend himself and his throne:

> A treacherous army levied, one midnight
> Fated to th' purpose, did Antonio open
> The gates of Milan; and i' th' dead of darkness,
> The ministers for th' purpose hurried thence
> Me and thy crying self.
>
> (1.2.128–32)

For Miranda, the experience can only be described as a second birth, for expelling the weeping child from the body politic seems analogous to expelling the newborn from the mother's womb. But this time there is a parturient father, not mother, as the gates of Milan open and Miranda is born again, not into a world of lights, but into the "dead of darkness." Her comment seems appropriate, "Alack, what trouble / Was I then to you!" (1.2.151–52).

Prospero responds in terms reminiscent of those of a mother who has gone through the pains of labor:

> O, a cherubim
> Thou wast that did preserve me! Thou didst smile,
> Infused with a fortitude from heaven,
> When I have decked the sea with drops full salt,
> Under my burden groaned: which raised in me
> An undergoing stomach, to bear up
> Against what should ensue.
>
> (1.2.152–58)

As the play's prehistory unfolds, Prospero assumes the role of a woman caring for an infant daughter in the space of the Other, a space that he eventually must share with Sycorax, Ceres, and other females who occupy the margins of their cultures.

Female Shadows: The Space of the Other

The desolate island where Prospero and Miranda landed after being expelled from Milan was the tragic space into which Algerian society sent its undesirables. The island had been conquered and ruled by Sycorax, a woman/witch/exile who had become Algiers's Other. Sycorax's problem seems at first the opposite of Prospero's. Prospero was feminized through his withdrawal into a domestic world; Sycorax was masculinized through her display of magical power.[15] Curiously, two exiles representing unacceptable subcultures occupy the same space. Upon his arrival, Prospero records the ethnographical history of the island, a history that he has pieced together apparently from two contradictory sources: Ariel, Sycorax's slave, and Caliban, her infant son. The data Prospero collected may be unreliable, although some facts become apparent. Sycorax tamed and enslaved the autochthonous inhabitants (spirits) and established succession on this island through the female line, as Caliban points out: "This island's mine by Sycorax my mother" (1.2.331).

Prospero reports, although he does not reveal the source of the information, that Sycorax pursued her "art" in Algiers:

> This damned witch Sycorax,
> For mischiefs manifold, and sorceries terrible

> To enter human hearing, from Argier,
> Thou know'st, was banished.
>
> (1.2.263–66)

The statement begs the question, assuming that all reasonable, civilized people share a common understanding of "mischiefs manifold, and sorceries terrible." Prospero notes that because Ariel refused to obey her "earthly and abhorred" commands (1.2.273), she took a "cloven pine" within which rift / Imprisoned thous didst painfully remain / A dozen years" (1.2.276–78). In fact, "moody" Ariel at first also rejects Prospero's commands and complains of "more toil." Apparently, Ariel finds servitude to Prospero no worthier than servitude to Sycorax. Only after Prospero threatens to punish Ariel as Sycorax did, does the spirit become "correspondent to command." Later Prospero describes Sycorax to the royal party: "[Caliban's] mother was a witch, and one so strong / That could control the moon, make flows and ebbs, / And deal in her command without her power" (5.1.269–71). One assumes that some of these comments are Prospero's—and apparently Ariel's—attempts to vilify Sycorax, and perhaps to make her more powerful than she really was.

What she did in Algiers can only be inferred; clearly, however, her powers could not stop the punishment that she eventually received. Because she was pregnant, the Algerians did not put her to death: "This blue-eyed hag was hither brought with child / And here was left by th'sailors" (1.2.269–70). As a witch, Sycorax was the Algerian savage Other; as an expecting mother, she reminded the Algerians of her humanness. She was powerless to change her fate; in fact, she proved quite human: within a dozen years, she died (1.2.279). Although Prospero offers no evidence for his assumptions that Sycorax's crime was not only witchcraft but also adultery, he suggests that Caliban was "got by the devil himself / Upon thy wicked dam" (1.2.319–20). Caliban, however, refers to Setebos as his mother's god, not as his father. One culture's god might be another's devil.[16]

Witches, devils, savages, and society's undesirables inhabit the space of the Other, a barren island lost in the Mediterranean of the mind. Deposed from his throne in Milan, Prospero chances upon Sycorax's barren kingdom and locates himself in her shadow. This matriarchy represents what has been relegated to the outer limits of Algerian and Milanese societies. Prospero seems unaware that Sycorax, like himself, was the victim of male aggression.[17] Their lives have run parallel courses. While Prospero does not mention whether Antonio accused him of witchcraft in Milan, several points—his study of old texts there, his command of knowledge on the island, and the association between his magic and the book he finally gives up—all clearly imply that his study of magic was one reason he was expelled from Milan. Indeed, that connection between Prospero's study and his expulsion may help to explain his brother's hostility. E. E. Evans-Pritchard concluded that "the operation of witchcraft beliefs in the social life are also closely connected with the kinship system, particularly through the custom of vengeance" (Evans-Pritchard 1951, 102).[18] Macfarlane observes that witchcraft accusations "made by the young against the old trend to be provoked by desire for change" (232).

Further, Prospero explains the origin of his estrangement in vague terms: "The government I cast upon my brother / And to my state grew stranger, being transported / And rapt in secret studies" (1.2.74–77). Through his secret studies, Prospero became an outsider: he "grew stranger" (i.e., belonging to another country; foreign; belonging to another person or place).[19] "Rapt" (from Latin *raptus*, to seize or to rape, *OED*) suggests being "carried away by force; raped." His "studies" were "secret," kept from public knowledge and also "kept from the knowledge of the uninitiated" (in the 1526 usage recorded in *OED*). Prospero's mistake was not only to transfer the government to his untrustworthy brother, but also to keep his knowledge to himself, not to share it with his subjects. His subjects may have perceived his studies as a threat.

Later in a soliloquy overheard by Ariel but by no mortals, Prospero reveals other particulars about his "rough magic," in terms that seem too "terrible to enter human hearing":

> I have bedimmed
> The noontide sun, called forth the mutinous winds,
> And 'twixt the green sea and the azured vault
> Set roaring war; to the dread rattling thunder
> Have I given fire and rifted Jove's stout oak
> With his own bolt; the strong-based promontory
> Have I made shake and by the spurs plucked up
> The pine and cedar; graves at my command
> Have waked their sleepers, oped, and let 'em forth
> By my so potent art.
>
> (5.1.41–49)

The parallels to Sycorax—and other witches—are indisputable.[20]

As Keith Thomas explains, the 1604 Act of Parliament, repealed only in 1736, made it a felony "to take up a dead body in whole or part for magical purposes," and to "'consult, covenant with, entertain, employ, feed, or reward any evil and wicked spirit to or for any intent or purpose'" (Thomas 1971, 443).[21] According to the Act, Prospero would have committed a felony. In this context, "rough" acquires a very specific meaning. "Rough," according to the *OED*, originally signifed, when referring to persons, "having the skin covered with hair, hairy, shaggy" and, when referring to the ground, "difficult to traverse, uneven, broken, uncultivated, wild." To engage in "rough magic" can imply a state of wildness, of savagery. One has the impression that Prospero's "rough magic" is precisely the kind of *maleficium* for which Sycorax was almost put to death in Algiers and many were hanged in England.[22] Savagery and witchcraft seem to go hand in hand in the European and Algerian mind.

In the world of the play, Sycorax was the first to practice "rough magic." In *Daemonology*, King James addresses the question as to why there are so many female witches: "What can be the cause that there are twentie women giuen to that craft, where ther is one man?" (James I 1597/1966, 43): "The reason is easie, for as that sexe is frailer then man is, so is it easier to be intrapped in these grosse snares of the Deuill, as was ouer well proued to be true, by the Serpents deceiuing of *Eua* at the beginning, which makes him the homelier with that sexe sensine" (James I 1597/1966, 44). As practitioner of his "art," Prospero follows a career whose parameters a woman first defined and imitates her actions. He takes possession of Sycorax's island and adopts some policies of her "masculine" matriarchy: he enslaves the indigenous inhabitants (the spirits) and later her son. He exercises his rule with an iron fist and does not tolerate dissension. To keep his subjects pliable and obedient, he sends spirits to torment Caliban and threatens Ariel with Sycorax-like punishments. No matter how much he may want to distance himself from the Other, he inhabits the space that a woman and a witch once occupied. Remnants of her rule and her absent presence are everywhere.[23] On the island, Prospero seems unaware that he has been cast into the space of the Other; yet he constantly chooses feminine agents to speak for him and to mediate between himself and the royal party from Italy, and in fact he relies on female agents to bring about his return to Italy. As Prospero's agent, carrying out Prospero's wishes, Ariel presents three female roles—a water nymph, a harpy, and the goddess Ceres. Prospero instructs Ariel: "Go make thyself like a nymph o'th'sea. Be subject / To no sight but thine and mine; invisible / To every eyeball else. Go take this shape / And hither come in't" (1.2.301–4). Obviously, if Ariel remains invisible, the "shape" he takes should not matter, but Prospero wants to create the image of a young, beautiful, amorous, non-threatening woman to allure the Neapolitans to the island.

The sexually attractive, apparently harmless sea nymph invites the royal party to a banquet into which coalesce several cultural fantasies, dreams, and fears. Several "strange Shapes" bring in food, dance about it, and salute the royal party. Sebastian and Antonio both agree that they now believe that unicorns and the phoenix really exist. Antonio remarks: "Travellers ne'er did lie, / Though fools at home condemn 'em" (3.3.26–27). Gonzalo wonders about how people back home will react to his report: "If in Naples / I should report this now, would they believe me / If I should say I saw such islanders? / (For certes these are people of the island)" (3.3.27–34). The fantastic tales that Gonzalo heard as a boy seem to be true:

> When we were boys,
> Who would believe that there were mountaineers
> Dewlapped like bulls, whose throats had hanging at 'em
> Wallets of flesh? Or that there were such men
> Whose heads stood in their breasts? which now we find
> Each putter-out of five for one will bring us
> Good warrant of.
>
> (3.3.43–49)

Independently, Gonzalo recognizes the island as the space of the Other, a *tabula rasa*—in Paul Brown's words, "an empty space to be inscribed at will by the desire of the coloniser" (Brown 1985, 56).[24] We recall that this is the same space where the medieval and Renaissance imagination placed the monstrous races—headless men, cannibals, Amazons, and all sorts of both real and imaginary alien races.[25] Inevitably, in this space of the Other, the nymph's body becomes monstrous and threatening to the "three men of sin." As Orgel points out, harpies had the faces and breasts of young women, the wings and bodies of birds, and talons for hands.[26] Their leader was Celaeno, a witch, who controlled them. By presenting the Celaeno-like harpy, Ariel may be creating a representation of Prospero, the "witch," behind the banquet. The sea nymph—the epitome of the male dream—transforms into a frightening monstrous harpy, half nymph, half beast—the epitome of collective male fear.

Ariel also presents the goddess Ceres in the masque: "I presented Ceres," he says (4.1.167). But unlike the banquet, staged for male eyes, depicting a male nightmare, the masque is above all a male version of what a female fantasy about fertility, abundance, and "hourly joys" ought to be. Males are excluded from the masque. Juno, the Queen of the skies, assisted by Iris, and Ceres bless Miranda's betrothal to Ferdinand:

> Honor, riches, marriage blessing,
> Long continuance, and increasing,
> Hourly joys be still upon you!
>
> (4.1.106–7)

But also like the banquet scene, the masque contains a threatening side. The female dream contains a nightmare, enacting the fear that the male will be a rapist. The masque focuses on a subtext of a mother, Ceres, lamenting the fate of her daughter Prosperine:[27]

> Tell me, heavenly bow [i.e., Iris],
> If Venus or her son, as thou dost know,
> Do now attend the Queen [Juno]? Since they did plot
> the means that dusky Dis my daughter got,
> Her and her blind boy's scandalled company
> I have forsworn.
>
> (4.1.86–91)

Ceres alludes to Proserpine, abducted and raped by "dusky Dis" (Pluto), god of the underworld. Angry with Venus and Cupid, who conspired with Dis, Ceres suggests that perhaps the tragedy happened recently. Like Prospero, whose daughter was almost raped by Caliban (1.2.345–48), Ceres is concerned with her daughter's well-being; but unlike Miranda, Proserpine has already been violated. Rejoicing in Miranda's happiness, Ceres cannot forget her personal tragedy. She knows that both Cupid and Venus pose a real threat to Miranda. Within the masque lies the tragic story of a mother's suffering over her daughter's abduction, and "whenever [Prospero] contemplates Miranda's happiness, a demonic representation of her rape lurks out of the 'dark and backward and abysm' of his subconscious, where Prosperine—Miranda's double and foil—is forever lost" (de Sousa 1987, 47).

This fear of violation reflects on Prospero, whose "raptus" in secret studies and political rape by his own brother are deeply imprinted in his perception of reality, and it may even be behind the rapture with which he pursues a happy resolution later in the play. We recall that Prospero has no male heir; by deposing him, Antonio has violated not only Prospero himself but also Prospero's heir. In fact, Antonio posed the first threat to Miranda's honor and integrity. "A threat against Miranda's honor lurks out of the past; for a moment present hopes and past fear coalesce in chaotic, antimasque-like fury. The dusky underground, where Pluto has taken Proserpine, opens up; in the antimasque world, Miranda's betrothal turns into the nightmarish rite of Prosperine's rape" (de Sousa 1987, 47).

Cultural Paradigms

The space of the Other subsumes cultural assumptions about the devilish nature of difference and estrangement. "The devil speaks in him" (5.1.130), says Sebastian as Prospero reveals himself as "the wronged Duke of Milan." A little later Alonso adds that "these are not natural events" (5.1.227). Sebastian's, and Alonso's, words get lost as Prospero rapturously rushes to turn the tragic story of his life into a comedy. He quickly proceeds toward the long-awaited happy resolution and promises to forgive all. But cultural paradigms resist change. Sebastian repeats a pattern that we see Prospero himself following. Like Sebastian, Prospero demonizes Sycorax and Caliban, distancing himself from their diabolic and savage nature, forging an antithesis that validates his actions. He suggests that Sycorax's lover was the devil, a frequent charge against witches, equating Caliban's devilish nature with his alleged bastardy. Prospero calls Caliban a "demi-devil / (For he's a bastard one)" (5.1.272–73), and Miranda refers to him as a "savage."

Prospero at first may have felt sympathy for the orphan he found on the island. Caliban recalls a gentler Prospero, who was more accepting of difference:

> When thou cam'st first,
> Thou strok'st me and made much of me; wouldst give me
> Water with berries in't; and teach me how
> To name the bigger light, and how the less,
> That burn by day and night; and then I loved thee
> And showed thee all the qualities o' th'isle.
>
> (1.2.332–37)

The relationship ended when Caliban attempted to violate Miranda:

> I have used thee
> (Filth as thou art) with humane care, and lodged thee
> In mine own cell till thou didst seek to violate
> The honor of my child.
>
> (1.2.345–48)

Caliban, however, gloats on what he could have accomplished: "I had peopled else / This isle with Calibans" (1.2.349–50). This line seems to be a strange reply that suggests conquest by mere replication.[28] Prospero assumes that Caliban, like the perfidious brother Antonio, does not share the principles of civility and gratitude that Prospero lives by. In fact, as Miranda remarks, Caliban is perceived as a "savage," belonging to a "vile race" (1.2.355, 358). One wonders, however, whether the demonizing process is retrospective: knowing Sycorax's mistreatment of Ariel and Caliban's vile nature and acts, Prospero concluded that Sycorax was a witch and Caliban the bastard son of the devil; knowing what Antonio had done to him and Miranda, Prospero concluded that Caliban represented the subhuman in Antonio.

Caliban's attempted violation of Miranda can be seen as a political as well as a physical act of violence. Knowing that Prospero has no male heir, Caliban can conquer the island through the daughter. Caliban seems to imply that he has a power that Prospero does not. He can replicate himself and thus colonize the island with little Calibans; Prospero, however, has no little Prosperos but only a female "version" of himself—a small, vulnerable Miranda. As Lawrence Stone explains, "The three objectives of family planning [in the early modern period] were the continuity of the male line, the preservation intact of the inherited property, and the acquisition through marriage of further property or useful political alliances" (Stone 1979, 37). This policy could be partly accomplished by "restricting the claims of the children on the patrimony through primogeniture" and by "excluding younger sons and daughters from the bulk of the inheritance" (Stone 1979, 37–38). Obviously, in a patriarchy without a male heir, such as Prospero's Milan, the role of the female heir becomes problematic. To continue the dynasty, Miranda must marry; in so doing, she brings in a male who will perpetuate his line at the expense of the monarchy's dynastic interests. Antonio may have been aware of this as he decided to overthrow his brother; later believing that Ferdinand has drowned, he encourages Sebastian to bypass Claribel's claim to the Neapolitan throne. A male heir perpetuates the dynasty in the male image; a female heir creates problems not easily resolved. In a patriarchal society, a father/king with a female heir presides over the extinction of the male line and—ironically—becomes a substitute for the female Other until she herself is displaced by the husband. Such is the fate of Prospero and could be the fate of Alonso if Ferdinand had died in the wreck. In this specific, political sense, the feminization of Prospero—which Caliban astutely perceives—had begun before he studied in secret.

Family politics and the politics of gender uncannily coalesce in Prospero's displacement. This displacement is grounded in a discourse that operates within his society and depends upon gender antagonism.[29] Curiously, Shakespeare simultaneously situates his island in two different places, the Mediterranean and the New World. Milanese society as depicted in the play used the "model of the power relationship between men and women" to articulate the expulsion of Prospero from the mainstream of society.[30] His rule over the island rests upon a foundation built by a female witch, and his shadows—expressive of his fears, assumptions, and desires—often assume the form of women. One wonders why Prospero works so hard at turning Sycorax into his Other when their lives are so parallel. A witch, powerless to change the course of events in Algiers and now dead, cannot be much of a threat to Prospero.

Paradoxically, to regain his dukedom, Prospero depends upon the mediation of the Other, but at the same time, to be accepted back, he must abjure the rough magic, break the staff, and drown the book—emblems of his and Sycorax's Otherness. His power to protect Miranda from a rapist Pluto or Caliban or from an ambitious, ruthless man like Antonio will eventually end. She cannot be allowed to become a harpy or a witch; however, the renunciation of his magic does not solve the political problem of having a female heir—an aspect of his Otherness that he cannot change. Only through Miranda can Prospero have a political identity, but she too represents the death of his dynasty: "And thence [I will] retire me to my Milan, where / Every third thought shall be my grave" (5.1.310–11). Miranda will, in all likelihood, move to Naples and rule Milan through her husband.

Temporarily in Sycorax's shadow, Prospero asserts masculine rule over a matriarchy, but even here his predicament becomes apparent. Caliban instinctively recognizes that he has more power than Prospero to people the island with Calibans. In this space of the Other, Prospero learns to accept Miranda's future husband's dominance and Neapolitan primacy, which at the beginning of the play he referred to as Milan's "ignoble stooping" (1.2.116). A masculinized, assertive Miranda with magical powers to control men like Antonio would be no more acceptable in Milan than Sycorax's displays of power were in Algiers. Whether Prospero and Antonio like it or not, succession to the throne of Milan will be through the female line, in the space of the Other. Algiers thematized Sycorax as an Amazonian hag who threatened masculine hegemony; Antonio thematized Prospero and his female heir as the threatening Other that could be imprinted with prejudices about the nature of a feminized monarchy—a permanent *couvade* from which Prospero cannot emerge.

Like *The Tempest*, Ben Jonson's *The Masque of Queens*, presented at Whitehall on 2 February 1609, stages a fantasy of displacement and replacement. As part of this courtly entertainment, Jonson devised an antimasque of twelve witches, a "spectacle of strangeness" that represented an overt attempt to subvert courtly order (Jonson 1969, 123). The hags fail, however, and are displaced and replaced by Perseus, *"expressing heroic and masculine virtue,"* who proudly presents his "daughter, then, whose glorious house you see" (Jonson 1969, 134–35). To effect his return to Milanese society, Prospero must forge a myth of an evil witch and a benign magician who "has done nothing but in care of thee, / Of thee my dear one, thee my daughter" (1.2.16–17). In a sense, his regime can do nothing but in care of a female heir, whom he has educated outside the realm of witchcraft and magic and who embodies the Creole dream of reintegration into her culture. Unable to be a tragic hero when he is placed in his culture's space of the Other, Prospero has apparently taught himself to be a comedy father and to accept the masculine rule of Naples, something that ironically Antonio had already prepared Milan to accept.

Notes

1. In a recent article, Meredith Skura poses a fundamental question: "How do we know that *The Tempest* 'enacts' colonialism rather than merely alluding to the New World?" (Skura 1984,47). Skura notes several problems with the colonial readings of the play. She remarks that there were other "Prosperos" in Shakespeare's earlier works: the exiled dukes in *As You Like It* and *Measure for Measure* for example, who find their own Calibans (Jaques, Lucio). "In the case of all of these 'Prosperos'," she writes, "it is hard to see the attack on 'Caliban'

as part of specifically colonialist strategy, as a way of exploiting the Other or of rationalizing illegitimiate power over him rather than over what he represents in 'Prospero' himself" (Skura 1989, 63). She places the play in the larger context of "an ideology of political exploitation and erasure" and "in the psychological aftereffects of having experienced the exploitation and erasure inevitable in being a child in an adult's world" (Skura 1989, 69). In his introduction to *The Tempest* (Oxford: Oxford University Press, 1987), Stephen Orgel discusses the question of the New World material, 31–39.

2. A hegemonic tendency characterizes colonial discourse. At the time of the discoveries, Europe was making its transition from the medieval to the Renaissance, but the view of the Other was apparent even in chivalric romance:

> The paradigmatic conception here is that of the quest in romances of chivalry in which the adventurous knight leaves Arthur's court—the realm of the known—to encounter some form of otherness, a domain in which the courtly values of the Arthurian world do not prevail. The quest is brought to an end when this alien domain is brought within the hegemonic sway of the Arthurian world: the other has been reduced to (more of) the same. The quest has shown that the other is amenable to being reduced to the status of the same. And, in those few instances where the errant knight—Lohengrin, for example—does find a form of otherness that he prefers to the realm of the same from which he came, this otherness is interpreted—by contemporary critics as much as by medieval writers—as the realm of the dead, for it is ideologically inconceivable that there should exist in otherness of the same ontological status as the same, without there being immediately mounted an effort at its appropriation. (Godzich 1986, xiii)

In *The Conquest of America*, Tzvetan Todorov remarks on Western Europe's attempt and success to "assimilate the other, to do away with an exterior alterity" (Todorov 1984, 247); this is partly due to the Europeans' "remarkable qualities of flexibility and improvisation which permit them all the better to impose their own way of life" (Todorov 1984, 248).

3. This is the age of what Peter Hulme calls the "polytropic man" in "Polytropic Man: Tropes of Sexuality in Early Colonial Discourse," in Francis Barker and Hulme, eds., *Europe and Its Others* (Colchester: University of Essex, 1985), 2: 19–20.

4. In "Shakespeare's Indian," *Shakespeare Quarterly* 39 (1988): 137–153, Alden Vaughan traces the development of the connection of *The Tempest* to the New World. He notes that the connection of Caliban to American Indians is a very late development. Vaughan writes that "in response to changing intellectual fashions, [Caliban] evolved generally and gradually from a drunken beast in the late seventeenth century, to a fishy monster in the eighteenth, to an apish missing link in the nineteenth" (138). Only in the nineteenth century did critics begin associating Caliban with the American aboriginals.

Other articles focusing on colonialism include Barker and Hulme, "Nymphs and Reapers Heavily Vanish" in John Drakakis, *Alternative Shakespeares* (London: Methuen, 1985), 91–205; Philip Brockbank, "*The Tempest*: Conventions of Art and Empire," in J. R. Brown and B. Harris, eds., *Later Shakespeare* (London: Edward Arnold 1966), 183–201; Paul Brown, "'This Thing of Darkness I Acknowledge Mine,'" in Jonathan Dollimore and Alan Sinfield, eds. *Political Shakespeare* (Ithaca: Cornell University Press, 1985), 48–71; Thomas Cartelli, "Prospero in Africa: *The Tempest* as Colonialist Text and Pretext" in Jean Howard and Marian O'Connor, *Shakespeare Reproduced* (New York: Methuen, 1987), 99–115; Bruce Erlich, "Shakespeare's Colonial Metaphor: On the Social Function of Theatre in *The Tempest*" *Science and Society* 41 (1977): 43–65; Charles Frey, "*The Tempest* and the

New World," *Shakespeare Quarterly* 30 (1979): 29–41; Trevor R. Griffiths, "'This Island's Mine,'" *Yearbook of English Studies* 13 (1983): 159–80; Hulme, *Colonial Encounters* (London: Methuen, 1986); Hulme, "Hurricanes in the Caribbees," in Barker and Hulme, *1642* (Colchester: University of Essex, 1981), 55–83; and Orgel, "Shakespeare and the Cannibals," in Marjorie Garber, ed. *Cannibals, Witches, and Divorce* (Baltimore: Johns Hopkins University Press, 1987), 40–66.

5. Bullough (1975, 8: 238–74) discusses Shakespeare's indebtedness to travel literature. Modern editions of sixteenth-century travel literature include Hans Staden, *The True History of His Captivity* (London: Routledge, 1928); Jean de Léry, *Le Voyage au Brésil* (Paris: Payot, 1927) and *Viagem à Terra do Brasil* (Rio de Janeiro: Biblioteca do Exército, 1961); and Gabriel Soares de Sousa, *Noticia do Brasil* (Sao Paulo: Livraria Martins, 1939). An equally fascinating work is *Cartas do Brasil* by Jesuit missionary Fr. Manuel da Nóbrega, written 1549–60 (Rio de Janeiro: Academia Brasileira, 1931). For a cogent discussion of Léry, see chapter 5, "Ethnography: Speech, or the Space of the Other: Jean de Léry," of Michel de Certeau's *The Writing of History* (New York: Columbia University Press, 1988). Clifford Geertz discusses the travelogue/ethnographical text *Tristes Tropiques*, by Claude Lévi-Strauss, in *The Interpretation of Cultures* (New York: Basic Books, 1973), 345–59), which provides interesting parallels to earlier travel literature. Emmanuel Lévinas writes: "But already, in the very heart of the relationship with the other that characterizes our social life, alterity appears as a nonreciprocal relationship—that is, as contrasting strongly with contemporaneousness. The Other as Other is not only an alter ego: the Other is what I myself am not. The Other is this, not because of the Other's character, or physiognomy, or psychology, but because of the Other's very alterity"; *Time and the Other* (Pittsburgh: Duquesne University Press, 1987), 83.

6. After much debate Pedro Alvarez Cabral, the commander of the Portuguese fleet that "discovered" Brazil in the spring of 1500, opted not to take any native prisoners but rather to leave two young convicts behind to learn the "manner of living and customs" of the natives (7), perhaps the most insidious way of intervening in another culture; John H. Parry and Robert G. Keith, New York eds., *New Iberian World* (New York: Time Books, 1984) 5: 7–9.

7. See Victor Turner, *The Ritual Process* (Ithaca: Cornell University Press, 1977), 145. Seclusion as an institution practiced among aborigines stages a distance between individual and culture. The Mehinaku of central Brazil, for example, practice various types of seclusion: "varying in duration from one month to three years, seclusion is a period of isolation during which a villager lives behind a partition set up in his house for the purpose" (Gregor 1977, 224). Gregor, who has lived among the Mehinaku and carefully studied their customs, reports the various types of seclusion that mark important moments in a person's life: birth, adolescence, parenthood, mourning, becoming a shaman, ear piercing (Gregor 1977, 225). Among the Mehinaku, seclusion marks a period of privacy but also assures the eventual reintegration into the community.

8. Many anthropologists have used a similar methodology to draw conclusions about other cultures. Among others, Clifford Geertz uses Indonesian aboriginals for some of his theories about the nature of cultural anthropology, and E. E. Evans-Pritchard derived from his study of the Azande conclusions about magic and witchcraft in *Witchcraft, Oracles and Magic among the Azande* (Oxford: Clarendon, 1968).

9. *Couvade* comes from the French *couver*, "to hatch or incubate." Gregor's earlier book, *Mehinaku: The Drama of Daily Life in a Brazilian Indian Village*, is a

fascinating study of Mehinaku culture as drama. I found Gregor's ideas to be most stimulating.

10. Functions of *couvade* for the Mehinaku include "dramatizing paternity," "dampening the expression of resentment toward the newborn child," and "the nature of the father's connection to his offspring" (Gregor 1985, 195).

11. Gregor points out that "Bruno Bettleheim and Ruth and Lee Munroe and John Whiting have proposed a theory of the *couvade* that centers on its sexual implications. Bettleheim maintains that the *couvade* is an expression of a hidden but universal male desire 'to find out how it feels to give birth'. The Monroes and Whiting trace this wish to the father's latent feminine identity" (Gregory 1985, 195).

12. That there is no wife in *The Tempest,* as there is no wife in *Lear,* is not altogether remarkable given the high mortality rate of women in childbirth; Lawrence Stone, *Family, Sex, and Marriage in England 1500–1800* (New York: Harper Colophon Books, 1979), 48.

13. All citations are from the Pelican edition of *The Tempest,* ed. Northrop Frye (New York: Penguin Books, 1981).

14. In the Arden edition (London: Methuen, 1954), Frank Kermode cites the proverb, "Trust is the mother of deceit," which would support my reading, but he does not explain the meaning of "beget of him." Northrop Frye, in the Pelican edition, takes "good parent" as an allusion to the proverb cited by Miranda: "Good wombs have borne bad sons" (1.2.120). Orgel, in the Oxford edition, assumes that the passage poses no difficulties and offers little help.

15. Sycorax apparently dared to affirm an identity that neither marriage nor Algerian values could subsume. In fact, as Alan Macfarlane notes, "Case histories show that women accused [of witchcraft] have usually shown unusual independence." See chapter 18, *Withcraft in Tudor and Stuart England* (New York: Harper and Row, 1971), 226–39. In *The History of Witchcraft and Demonology* (New York: University Books, 1956), Montague Summers devotes a chapter to "The Witch in Dramatic Literature" (276–313). In *Witchcraft and Religion* (Oxford: Blackwell, 1984), Christina Larner observes that "the stereotype witch is an independent adult woman who does not conform to the male idea of proper female behaviour. She is assertive; she does not require or give love (though she may enchant); she does not nurture men or children, nor care for the weak. She has the power of words—to defend herself or to curse. In addition, she may have other, more mysterious powers which do not derive from the established order" (Larner 1984, 84).

16. Caliban inherits his mother's kingdom but not her supernatural powers. Left all alone, he had to fend for himself, like a savage; and, therefore, he had to learn about the island's resources in order to survive. His knowledge is, in fact, remarkable. He showed Prospero "all the qualities o' th'isle, / The fresh springs, brinepits, barren place and fertile" (1.2.337–38). Mistaking Trinculo for a powerful god who will help overthrow the tyrant who holds sway over the island, Caliban promises Trinculo: "I'll show thee the best springs; I'll pluck thee berries; / I'll fish for thee, and get thee wood enough" (2.2.156–57). He will help Trinculo find the crabs, pignuts, nimble marmosets, filberts, and young scamels (2.2.163–68). Caliban is also attuned to the natural noises, sounds, sweet airs, and the twangling instruments, and voices:

> That, if I then had waked after long sleep,
> Will make me sleep again; and then, in dreaming
> The clouds methought would open and show riches

Ready to drop upon me, that, when I waked,
I cried to dream again.

(3.2.132–41)

Having to survive on his own, Caliban apparently never acquired a native language, and only later was he taught Italian by Miranda, as she explains:

I pitied thee,
Took pains to make thee speak, taught thee each hour
One thing or other: when thou didst not, savage,
Know thine own meaning, but wouldst gabble like
a thing most brutish, I endowed thy purposes
With words that made them known.

(1.2.352–58)

From her teachings, Caliban brags, "I know how to curse" (1.2.363–64). Curiously, Miranda—like Prospero—assumes that Calibran's short-comings derive not from the conditions of Calibran's upbringing but rather from the ethnic characterisitcs of his "vile race" (1.2.358).

17. In "The Stuff that Dreams Are Made of," *Newsweek,* 14 August 1989, Sharon Begley notes that some researchers have concluded that "dreams also bear the unmistakable stamp of gender" (Begley 1989, 42). She quotes Dr. Milton Kramer, director of the Sleep Disorders Center of Greater Cincinnati, as saying: "Dreams of American women have more in common with those of Aboriginal women than they do with those of American men." The content of dreams is apparently different, although this difference is beginning to disappear and both sexes are having more "androgynous" dreams: "In the past, women dreamed more of interior, homey scenes; men of the outdoors. Women's dreams featured more conversation and emotion, and portrayed the dreamer as a victim of aggression. Men's dreams tended toward mechanical images" (Begley 1989, 42).

18. For a detailed anthropological study of witchcraft beliefs among the Azande, see E. E. Evans-Pritchard, *Witchcraft, Oracles and Magic among the Azande.* 1937. Rpt. Oxford: Oxford University Press, 1968.

19. See C. T. Onions, *A Shakespeare Glossary* (Oxford: Clarendon Press, 1986), 269–70.

20. Prospero raises the sea storm that causes the shipwreck of the Neapolitans, a power attributed to witches. Larner (1984) points out that during the trials for treason by sorcery that took place in Scotland from November 1590 to May 1591, "it was alleged that over 300 witches had gathered at various times to perform treason against the king. They were supposed to have raised storms, while the King and his bride were at sea, to have attempted to effect his death by melting his effigy in wax, to have indulged in hitherto unheard of obscene rituals in the kirk of North Berwick in the physical presence of their master, the Devil" (Larner 1984, 9). James VI went to Denmark to fetch his bride in fall 1589. "When at last the Scottish party set sail in the spring of 1590 they had a very rough passage and one of the attendant ships was lost" (Larner 1984, 10). Both in Scotland and Denmark, witches were apprehended "on charges of storm-raising against the King of Scotland" Larner 1984, 11).

21. As Geoffrey Scarre points out, in *Witchraft and Magic in 16th and 17th Century Europe,* even white witches from the lower classes "ran some risk of being taken for black," and those in higher status were less in danger; "some hard-line opponents of magic, such as Bodin or King James, thought that the

more knowledgeable magicians were, the more they deserved punishment, for the more fully aware they should be of the iniquity of their activities. For such theorists, Shakespeare's Prospero would have been a more objectionable figure than the three weird sisters from *Macbeth*" (Scarre 1987, 31). In *Daemonology*, King James argues that all magicians and witches "ought to be put to death according to the Law of God"; no one, regardless of sex, age or rank, should be spared (James I 1597/1966, 77).

22. Summers says that Prospero's "rough magic" is indeed a "delicate situation to place before an Elizabethan audience" (Summers 1956, 289).

23. Anthropology has taught us that assumptions about Otherness were so deeply ingrained in the culture that they escape the *consciousness* of most of the culture's followers. As Hayden White has suggested, "the vitality of any culture hinges upon its power to convince the majority of its devotees that it is the sole possible way to satisfy their needs and to realize their aspirations. A given culture is only as strong as its power to convince its least dedicated members that its fictions are truth" (White 1978, 153).

24. Paul Brown cites Eden's translation of Peter Martyr's *Decades* (1555): "The Amerindians are 'Gentiles' who 'may well be likened to a smooth, bare table unpainted, or a white paper unwritten, upon the which you may at the first paint or write what you list, as you cannot upon tables already painted, unless you raze or blot out the first forms'" (Brown 1985, 56). An interesting parallel to this is Pero Vaz de Caminha's letter to the King of Portugal reporting the discovery of Brazil in April 1500. Caminha notes the remarkable similarities between the Europeans and the Indians. He points out twice, for example, that the Indians "were not circumcised" (Parry and Keith 1984, 7); in fact, "none of them were circumcised, but all were as we were" (8). Through this encoded message, he was telling his king that the natives were not Moors—Portugal's defeated Other—but rather creatures that could be imprinted with Portuguese culture. A *cacique*, he tells the king, "was well decked with ornaments and covered with feathers stuck to his body, so that he looked pierced with arrows like Saint Sebastian" (8). On the body of the *cacique*, Portugal can imprint its image. Caminha further remarks that "for it is certain this people is good and of pure simplicity, and there can easily be stamped upon them whatever belief we wish to give them" (13); "these people in order to be wholly Christian lack nothing except to understand us, for whatever they saw us do, they did likewise" (14). The remarkable feature of this encounter was Indian empathy and power of representation "for whatever they saw us do, they did likewise." It was construed by Caminha and subsequent explorers that the Indians were a *tabula rasa*. On a certain level, the Moors and the Indian *caciques* occupy the same space on the borders of the Portuguese world; it was just a matter of time before Portugal saw the Indians as a threat to Portuguese colonial ambitions.

25. See, for example, John Block Friedman, *The Monstrous Races In Medieval Art and Thought* (Cambridge: Harvard University Press, 1981); Rudolf Wittkower, "Marvels of the East: A Study in the History of Monsters," *Journal of the Warburg and Courtauld Institutes* 5 (1942), 159–97; and Marie-Helene Huet, "Living Images: Monstrosity and Representation," *Representations* 4 (1983): 73–87.

26. Orgel writes: "The episode is based on *Aeneid* iii.225 ff.: Aeneas and his companions take shelter on the Strophades, the islands where the harpies live. The Trojans prepare a feast; but, as they are about to eat, the dreadful creatures swoop down on them, befouling and devouring the food. The sailors attempt

to drive the harpies off, but find them invulnerable, and their leader, the witch Celaeno, sends Aeneas away with a dire prophecy" (Shakespeare 1987, 166n).

27. I have made this argument in "Closure and the Antimasque of *The Tempest*," *Journal of Dramatic Theory and Criticism* 2 (1987): 41–51.

28. Frances Teague brought this to my attention.

29. Edward W. Said addresses the feminization of the Oriental in his book, *Orientalism* (New York: Random House, 1979) and in his article, "Orientalism Reconsidered," in Barker and Hulme, *Europe and Its Others*, 14–27.

30. See Helen Carr, "Woman/Indian: 'The American' And His Others," in Barker and Hulme, 46–60. Carr (1985), suggests that "From the first contact with the New World, the model of the power relationship between men and women been used to structure and articulate the relationship of the European to the New World inhabitants: here and in other colonized territories the difference man/woman provided a fund of images and topoi by which the difference European/nonEuropean could be politically accommodated" (Carr 1985, 46).

"Knowing aforehand": Audience Preparation and the Comedies of Shakespeare

EJNER J. JENSEN

Some years ago at Ontario's Stratford Festival, I attended a production of *The Merry Wives of Windsor*. At the close of the performance, two spectators seated a row or two behind me rose from their seats still applauding and, moved by the play's comic energy, launched into a celebration of the skills of its author. At a pause in this chorus of praise, one suddenly asked the other, "When did Shakespeare live?"

Her friend replied, "In the fourteenth century, I think."

"No," said the first, "I think it was the fifteenth." After a series of such assertions, queries, and guesses, the initial poser of the question brought such irrelevancies to an end by cutting through to the key matter. "Well," she said, "it doesn't matter; he's still as funny as he always was."

On that matter, my fellow spectator was, I think, on target. Shakespeare is still as funny as he always was. Sometimes, though, twentieth-century critics have asked him to bear a larger share of our burdens of anxiety than is quite fair and have made his comedies, even the most joyous among them, no laughing matter.[1] But this is a familiar story, and most of us recognize the impulses that have led critics to render nearly all of the comedies problematic and (more or less) dark. Less familiar is the curious phenomenon that results from the encounter between stage-centered criticism and the comedies of Shakespeare.

The emergence and nearly universal acceptance of stage-centered criticism has generated a wide variety of effects. One of the more common and, on the surface, more trivial of these has been the ubiquity of the phrase, "but in the theatre." We all know what follows the phrase: an assertion about how some matter that seems to be less than well managed comes to theatrical life

72

with no trace of a problem, or a contention that some glaring inconsistency simply disappears in the sweep and excitement of performance, or a confident claim about the wondrous magic that a skilled actor can effect with even the most stubbornly knotty role.

Ordinarily the assumption behind these arguments is available to us and even clearly stated. Those who believe that Shakespeare was, above all else, a writer for the stage want us to see that a reading of the plays attentive to their theatrical qualities will clarify difficulties, cause apparent inconsistency to disappear, and bring the plays to new and robust life. Such a reading, in other words, will restore to us what Shakespeare intended.

When critics turn their attention to the comedies, however, the assumption seems to undergo a shift that is subtle enough to go unattended. Skillful actors, the argument goes, can bring the comedies to life. If *Love's Labor's Lost* has passed beyond retrieval for today's readers, a sprightly performance can bring new vigor to the play on stage, giving point to its witty exchanges and a stylish energy to its turns of plot. But somehow the process being described is not a matter of the restoration of the Shakespearean score to its rightful performance platform; rather, it is a matter of inventive actors supplying something no longer available to a modern audience in the Shakespearean text. What we have, to put a rather crude gloss on it, it is not so much a resuscitation as a transplant.

My argument in this essay, therefore, is both straightforward and narrowly focused. I look to a few comic texts in an effort to show how Shakespeare himself guarantees the continuing life of his plays. He does so, I believe, by creating within the plays the very conditions of our response. As we read any of the great comedies, we may see how key scenes again and again satisfy us and achieve their comic triumphs by playing off expectations created earlier in the play's unfolding. In many ways this experience has elements in common with stand-up comedy and with our experience of familiar comic figures in our popular culture. The difference, of course, is that Shakespeare achieves his effects within the limited time available for the staging of a single play.[2]

My examples are drawn from a few plays chosen rather arbitrarily: I like them. But I think that I could make the same case with nearly any of the comedies in the canon. Comic preparation is a tactic within the larger, more encompassing, strategy of Shakespeare's comic designs, but it is a central tactic and a key to the plays' success. Shakespeare the comic dramatist is the best guarantor of the comedies' continuing life in the theatre; and a close look at his comic tactics makes clear why this is so. Most modern criticism of the comedies has attended chiefly to their structure, throwing light on matters of overall comic design. But the actual working of comedy is primarily a matter of tactics, and it is in this realm that Shakespeare achieves his master strokes. Preparation is the key matter here, the means by which Shakespeare orders events in a way that focuses and in large part defines our response.

In *The Merchant of Venice*, comic preparation focuses our perspective on scenes of testing and helps to create throughout the play a tone of joyousness. In *Much Ado About Nothing*, the same technique, employed somewhat differently, enables Shakespeare to repeat a single convention with no loss of effect in the twin spying scenes. In *Love's Labor's Lost* and *Twelfth Night*, the playwright employs the tactic variously to shape our responses to characters, emphasize central moments in the design of his plot, and reinforce similarities among comic events.

Let me begin with *Love's Labor's Lost*, the earliest of these plays and the source of my most straightforward example. Berowne, with flourishes of wit and rhetoric that are the hallmarks of his character and finally, no doubt, with a flourish or two of his pen, subscribes to the oath, "Not to see ladies, study, fast, not sleep" (1.1.48).[3] His agreement, however, hedged with conditions and delivered in tones that mock the courtiers' enterprise, ends in the same spirit with an appeal for relief: "But is there," he asks, "no quick recreation granted?" (1.1.161). The King offers immediate assurance, and he goes on to describe in considerable detail "a refined traveller of Spain, / A man in all the world's new fashion planted, / That hath a mint of phrases in his brain" (1.1.163–65). This account of Armado, concluding with the King's resolution to use the Spanish knight "for my minstrelsy" (1.1.176), gets further emphasis in the action that follows. Dull, stumbling over the Spaniard's name, delivers a letter to the King; and the document itself, unread but apparently a potent sign of the writer's character, prompts the courtiers to anticipatory merriment. The letter itself, a magnificent hors d'oeuvre to the feast of language the play as a whole provides, is a final element in the elaborate preparation that Shakespeare employs to set up the character of Armado.

Shakespeare wastes no time in exploiting that preparation, for 1.2 opens with Armado and his page in a scene that combines elements of vaudeville-like repartee, far-fetched classical allusion, and (at its close) a wonderful solo turn by the love-struck knight. I want to emphasize the closeness of preparation and performance here, the way that Shakespeare no sooner gives us the "character" of Armado than he delivers the character itself, acting out the previous description with a precision that allows us as spectators to share in full measure the mocking pleasure that the courtiers have already taken in their recollection of the knight's excesses. We are right to imagine that Shakespeare here wants an immediate return on his investment or that he is less confident than he will be on later occasions in his ability to fix in his spectators' minds the images that he wants to turn to account later in the unfolding of a comic design.

Nevertheless, the return is there in good measure in the second scene; and as a comic practice it represents a kind of success that Shakespeare will continue to achieve with this tactic throughout his caeer. What the first scene of *Love's Labor's Lost* provides is a pattern of expectation communicated to us through characters whose values and whose judgments we are invited to share. As the King and his fellows talk of Armado, we find ourselves responding to their jokes and, in the theatre (that phrase again) perhaps watching them mimic the Spaniard's gestures, or posture, or intonation. Thus when he appears on stage we have no doubt of his identity; and his behavior, far from opening new dimensions of his character, is successful precisely because it is limited to and thus deeply confirms what we already know. Our pleasure in this first encounter with Armado, then, is the pleasure of spectators who can be gratified by being given what they have been taught to expect.

The actor playing Armado is thus in a position not unlike that of any of our popular comics. Like them, he has the benefit of a ground of expectation from which he can work, secure in the knowledge that some of his lines are almost certain winners because his audience has been primed to respond to them. I used to tell my students at this point that they should think of how Jack Benny had only to mention money, or going to the bank, or (an extreme example) paying the check to have his audience in chuckles. Like all such allusions, that one is dated, and Jack Benny seems to have gone the way of other icons of our cultural past. But I have confidence that most readers of this essay could pass one of Professor Hirsch's quizzes and thus offer my example without the worry of searching for a more telling contemporary instance. Having made that connection, I want to invite attention to the ways in which 1.2 then becomes less a stage in the play's plot development than a performance space for Armado. From his opening query to Moth, "Boy, what sign is it when a man of great spirit grows melancholy?" through "O well-knit Sampson, strong-jointed Sampson! I do excel thee in my rapier as much as thou didst me in carrying gates. I am in love too," to "Assist me, some extemporal god of rhyme, for I am sure I shall turn sonnet. Devise, wit, write, pen, for I am for whole volumes in folio," Armado trades on the expectations established in 1.1, delighting us with a comedy as welcome as it is familiar.

Comic preparation in later plays becomes a more elaborate matter and, in some cases, a more significant part of the comedy's overall design. In *The Merchant of Venice*, the casket scenes owe a great deal of success to this tactic; and though they are built on the same ground, they manage to develop a wide range of comic effects. The scenes with Morocco and Arragon, though they ask for far different treatments in the theatre, may be discussed together. Morocco's attempt to choose the right casket (2.2) is especially well prepared for. Shakespeare mentions him first in 1.2, when Portia responds to news of his impending arrival with a racial remark: "if he have the condition of a saint, and the complexion of a devil, I had rather he should shrive me than wive me" (1.2.129–31). Act Two, scene one is a short scene, given over to formal exchanges between Morocco (who enters with his followers) and Portia (with Nerissa and other attendants). It allows Shakespeare to spell out the conditions that the suitors must accept, but more significantly it allows him to illustrate Portia's scrupulous attention to the terms of her father's will. She is gracious and polite to Morocco, assuring him that the man who wins her, whatever his color, "then stood as fair / As any comer I have look'd on yet / For my affection" (2.1.20–22). Yet at Morocco's subsequent appearance (2.7) and at the trial of Arragon (2.9), neither the harshness of the will's conditions nor Portia's willingness to stick to her share of the bargain have the dominant effect on our perception. Instead, the primary shaping forces of our view are Portia's earlier satiric descriptions of the retiring suitors and the mingled attitudes of Portia and Nerissa, compounded of mockery and trepidation, as they watch each suitor approach the caskets and attend to the logic that will direct his choice. Certainly the influences I have just described control most stage versions of these scenes. The Morocco in Olivier's National Theatre production was only an extreme version of the ethnocentrism and racial stereotyping that customarily define the character's role. Arragon, often a mustachioed dandy, may be asked to lisp his way through a thicket of "s's" in the schedule he finds in the silver casket. But it is not merely theatrical tradition that leads us to see the scenes in this way; a more fundamental cause is Shakespeare's use of comic preparation in a way that both shapes and determines the scenes' tones and directs our judgment.

Preparation for the comic dimension of the two casket scenes begins in 1.2 with Portia's catalogue of the unwelcome suitors: the Neapolitan prince, the County Palentine, the French lord, Monsieur le Bon, Falconbridge, the Scottish lord, and the Duke of Saxony's nephew make up a gallery of stereotyped portraits. While the Neapolitan prince is obsessed with his horse, a creature that provides his sole source of converse and value, the French suitor is devoid of ideas and so given to mimicry that he has no character at all. The young baron of England borrows his clothing from all the countries he visits but seems incapable of gathering even a scrap of their language. Each figure has the faults of his country, and Portia ends her comic analysis with the drunken German, telling Nerissa in mock horror, "I will do any thing, Nerissa, ere I will be married to a spunge" (1.2.98–9). Thus when the unwelcome suitors, Morocco and Arragon, come to take their chances in choosing a casket, Shakespeare has already provided a context in which to judge them. In 2.7, Portia says little; she seems content to direct Morocco in his task, open the golden casket once he makes his choice, and express her relief at his departure. The bulk of the scene is taken up with Morocco's speeches: his lengthy process of decision making, and his reading and response to the scroll. But the scene enacts a contest, even a kind of ritual, witnessed by the trains of Portia and the prince. As observers of that contest, Portia and Nerissa watch the performance put on by Morocco. Shakespeare gives us few verbal clues to their behavior, yet it seems clear that the combination of earnest concern and mockery seen in 1.2 operates in this instance as well. Portia's derisive account of her earlier suitors prepares for her attitudes toward Morocco here, and though that mockery is not articulated verbally, it has full opportunity for nonverbal expression during the ponderous and heavily rhetorical self-questioning of the prince. John Styan suggests that "The ceremonial of the three fairy-tale casket-scenes in *The Merchant of Venice* . . . may have matched the rhetoric of the foreign princes' speeches with suitably exotic splendour" (Styan 1967, 134). This is undoubtedly the case, but that splendor is itself necessarily viewed in the context of the xenophobic jesting of 1.2 and the byplay allowed to Portia and Nerissa as Morocco enacts his laborious decision making.

While Morocco's scene is well prepared for both by the comments of 1.2, which provide a context of mockery, and by his arrival in 2.1, Arragon's casket scene (2.9) is a hastier affair. Yet it takes advantage of the same dramatic preparation that governs our view of Morocco's performance. If the earlier suitor offers a target for ridicule in his self-important oratory, a comic Othello expending rhetorical riches in a little room, Arragon provides an even more inviting mark in his boasting self-righteousness. Distracted easily by the appeal of simile ("like the martlet," 2.9.28 ff.), he loses his way like some doddering figure from Chekhov when a didactic point claims his attention:

> Let none presume
> To wear an undeserved dignity.
> O, that estates, degrees, and offices
> Were not deriv'd corruptly, and that clear honor
> Were purchas'd by the merit of the wearer!
> How many then should cover that stand bare?
> How many be commanded that command?
> How much low peasantry would then be gleaned
> From the true seed of honor? and how much honor
> Pick'd from the chaff and ruin of the times
> To be new varnish'd? Well, but to my choice.
>
> (2.9.39–49)

And Portia, her mocking judgment confirmed, pronounces finally on both unsuccessful suitors:

> O, these deliberate fools, when they do choose,
> They have the widom by their wit to lose.
>
> (2.9.80–81)

Bassanio's casket scene (3.2) is another matter altogether. One of Shakespeare's great gifts as a comic writer is a sure control of tone. Here that gift is revealed in the strikingly different atmosphere of a scene that we have already witnessed twice. Mockery is behind us. Gratiano and Nerissa, great talkers both, keep silence. Portia, having declared her love, but having declared too her commitment to the terms of her father's will, sends Bassanio to the contest:

> Live thou, I live; with much, much more dismay
> I view the fight than thou that mak'st the fray.
>
> (3.2.61–62)

Suspense joined to mockery defined the tone of the earlier casket scenes. Now the tone is suspense and a sort of constrained joyousness that struggles for release. Portia is emotionally with Bassanio in his deliberations; and Nerissa, formerly her partner in mockery, is now one with Gratiano, silently hoping for a choice that will ratify their own election. The performance of Bassanio, enriched by the music Portia calls for at line 43, is a meditation on that most familiar of Shakespearean themes, appearance and reality. Dismissing "ornament" from the beginning, Bassanio moves inexorably to choose the leaden casket and, by his choice, to release in Portia the joy that is the consequence of his right determination:

> O love, be moderate, allay thy ecstasy,
> In measure rain thy joy, scant this excess!
> I feel too much thy blessing; make it less,
> For fear I surfeit.
>
> (3.2.111–14)

The comedy of this third casket scene, then, once again works through the device of comic preparation joined to another tactic that is a constant in the casket scenes, the use of an onstage audience. Here, the primary effect is not mocking laughter; indeed, nothing in the scene grows out of that dimension of the comic experience that involves our superiority as audience. This is a kind of participatory comedy in which we share the characters' elation.[4]

Much Ado About Nothing affords comic pleasures different from those available in *The Merchant of Venice,* pleasures less tinged with near-sadness and free from that nervous exultation that still holds an awareness of dangers narrowly avoided. But they are, like the delights of the earlier play, still derived from the skillful use of comic preparation. Before nearly every major event of *Much Ado,* and preceding most of its significant comic moments, Shakespeare prepares his audience for what they are about to witness.

Benedick's introduction affords the first illustration of the tactic in this play. After twenty-seven lines of dialogue between Leonato and the messenger, during which time Hero and Beatrice presumably register to each other and to the audience their reaction to the news, Beatrice inquires, "I pray you, is Signior Mountanto return'd from the wars or no?" (1.1.30–31). Why Beatrice should identify Benedick in this way remains unclear, though the usual explanations—"fencer, duellist" (Arden), "from Italian montanto,

a fencing term meaning blow or thrust" (Riverside)—seem less
than persuasive. But Hero knows full well that "My cousin means
Signior Benedick of Padua" (1.1.35–36) and Leonato, excusing his
niece's mocking, explains to the messenger that "There is a kind
of merry war betwixt Signior Benedick and her; they never meet
but there's a skirmish of wit between them" (1.1.61–64). Somewhere between Beatrice's account of Benedick as boaster, coward,
trencherman, and affliction and the messenger's report of a "good
soldier" and one who "hath done good service . . . in these wars"
(1.1.48–49) exists the Benedick who will emerge later in the play.
But for the moment, and for the sake of his audience's immediate
pleasure, Shakespeare gives us a Benedick whose entire function
is to fulfill the expectations set up for him at this point in the play.
How completely this is so appears in the fact that it is Leonato, not
Beatrice, who first exploits the preparation of the scene's opening section.

When Benedick chirps up in response to Leonato's somewhat
hackneyed but incongruous joke about his wife's fidelity—Hero's
mother "hath many times told" him that he was Hero's father,
says Leonato, and Benedick follows this with "Were you in doubt,
sir, that you asked her?"—the old man delivers a smart verbal
counterblow: "Signior Benedick, no, for you were then a child"
(1.1.105–108). But if Leonato's remark is the first to capitalize on
Shakespeare's well-prepared expectations about Benedick, it
stands as the briefest preliminary to Beatrice's fuller exploitation
of the audience's receptivity. As Don Pedro and Leonato "talk
aside,"[5] leaving Claudio and Balthazar to amuse themselves, Don
John to chafe at the affability that surrounds Leonato's reception
of his brother, and Hero to discover her own response to the
"young Florentine called Claudio" who "hath borne himself beyond the promise of his age" (1.1.10–14), Beatrice throws out one
of the surest winning lines Shakespeare ever provided a female
comic character.

The energy of that line, its saucy assurance, impels the whole
of the Beatrice-Benedick connection and defines its character: "I
wonder that you will still be talking, Signior Benedick, nobody
marks you" (1.1.116–17). With its utterance, we recognize that the
preparation for Benedick's entrance was necessarily entrusted to
Beatrice; for, however telling Leonato's retort may seem, the quint-
essential Benedick appears only after he engages fully with "Lady
Disdain." Like other great comic pairs, they nourish one another,
and it makes little difference whose serve it is in this game of
wit. Hal and Falstaff, creations of the same period, function in

the same way, striking sparks off one another, energized by their playful antagonism.

As the comic action of *Much Ado* unfolds, the ground prepared in the play's opening scene serves effectively to give other comic episodes the same energy and vividness it provides for the initial encounter of the two witty lovers. Especially in the spying scenes (2.3, 3.1), with their brilliant challenge to the notion that "art abhors duplication," Shakespeare gives his spectators full measure of comic enjoyment. I haven't the space here to explore in detail the working of those scenes; but I would assert, and invite others to test that assertion, that in them Shakespeare brings to triumphant maturity the tactic I have been describing in this essay. Not the least of the pleasures afforded by the spying scenes is the range of their comedy. That range is defined in part, of course, by the plotters, both the men and the women; but Benedick and Beatrice themselves reveal its full extent: "The world must be peopled"; "Benedick, love on, I will requite thee."

I want to come to my last example indirectly, by way of Ben Jonson, and particularly by way of *The Alchemist*. Coleridge, of course, praised Jonson's play for its plot; and the overarching plot of the comedy, with its attention to the demands of the unities, is undeniably masterful. But a critic intent on discovering the sources of pleasure in Jonson's play would not find them in plot considered as overall design. Instead, such a critic would locate Jonson's primary achievement in his plotting, comic preparation that leads to ends predictable to an audience or reader, but hidden at least from some of the play's characters. Even such a minor matter as Mammon's entrance in 2.1 affords an instructive example, for its effect is to a very great extent dependent on Subtle's description of him in the preceding scene:

> Methinks I see him, entering ordinaries,
> Dispensing for the pox and plaguy houses,
> Reaching his dose; walking Moorfields for lepers;
> And off'ring citizens' wives pomander-bracelets,
> As his preservative, made of the elixir;
> Searching the spittle, to make old bawds young;
> And the highways for beggars, to make rich:
> I see no end of his labours. He will make
> Nature asham'd of her long sleep: when art,
> Who's but a step-dame, shall do more than she,
> In her best love to mankind, ever could.
> If his dream last, he'll turn the age to gold.
>
> (1.4.18–29)[6]

Having enjoyed this preview of the character, we are primed for Mammon's imaginative and linguistic excesses as he enters with Surly: "Come on, sir. Now you set your foot on shore / In novo orbe" (2.1.1–2).

Almost any of Jonson's plays could supply a similar incident. What *Twelfth Night* shares with Jonsonian comedy is an abundance of such comic events subsumed to the requirements of the play's major action, but generating an energy that makes them almost independent episodes. I want to focus on just one instance of plotting of this kind. It is, like Jonson's comic preparation for Mammon, a matter of introducing a character, in this case, Olivia. But, as with most comparisons of Jonson and Shakespeare, the differences are instructive. Subtle's speech has a vivid particularity about it. He captures Mammon's habits of imagination, joining a view of alchemy as art beyond nature with the action of "Searching the spittle, to make old bawds young" (1.4.23). Further still, Jonson's construction of the speech encourages the actor playing Subtle to treat the audience to a physical parody of the knight's figure and gestures before Mammon himself appears: "Methinks I see him." Finally, the payoff in *The Alchemist* is immediate. After Subtle has given the audience a lesson on how to read Mammon, the knight himself appears, palpable and transparent. In many ways, Jonson's management of the tactic here resembles Shakespeare's introduction of Armado.

Shakespeare's introduction of Olivia develops differently, and it does so in a way that reinforces the play's connection with the Feast of Epiphany; Sebastian is not alone in making a miraculous appearance in *Twelfth Night*. In the play's opening scene, we learn of Olivia through Orsino, who gives first an unprompted view of her magical powers—"O,when mine eyes did see Olivia first, / . . . / That instant was I turn'd into a hart,"—and then an interpretation of Valentine's report, in which Orsino chooses not to see a rejection of his suit but "a heart of . . . fine frame" (1.1.18, 20, 32). The next three scenes of the play continue this line of plotting. Shakespeare never lets us forget Olivia's importance, and through the use of a marvelous dramatic retard he increases our eagerness to see her even as he increases the demands on the actress playing the role. She must meet the high expectations the playwright has set for her in scenes one through four. In this respect, Shakespeare exploits the experience of delayed gratification, with the attendant risk of disappointing his audience, while Jonson, in the case of Mammon at least, is so eager to please that he unwraps his comic gift immediately.

Twelfth Night's fifth scene is the culmination of this plotting line considered as a discrete episode. Shakespeare unveils Olivia at last. But even here the retard continues, for the scene begins with Feste and Maria, who warns the clown, as she had earlier warned Sir Toby, of her lady's displeasure. Olivia's initial verbal jousting with Feste performs two functions: it helps to separate her from the earnest solicitude of Malvolio, and it prepares her for the whimsical act of admitting the messenger, that figure described by Malvolio as "between man and boy," one who is "very wel-favor'd," "speaks shrewishly," and looks as if "his mother's milk were scarce out of him" (1.5.159–62). Defeated in her contest with Feste, she chooses to continue the sport with a competitor who promises to be less skillful. What follows, of course, is one of the great comic confrontations in all of Elizabethan drama. As comic preparation, the whole of Act One, up through 5.26, works magnificently to establish a context for Olivia's appearance. When she does at last enter, she ought to be both as wonderful as Orsino suggests and more real than the creature of his delicate imaginings. She does not disappoint us. At once removed from the world and in it, she jokes with Feste and pronounces her authoritative judgment on Malvolio: "You are sick of self-love." Then she turns, or Shakespeare turns her, to enact yet another miraculous appearance, this time to Orsino's clamorous messenger.

The examples I set out here constitute a very small selection from just one tactic in Shakespeare's comic repertoire. They suggest, I hope, his mastery of the tactic; but they also suggest the range of comic responses he could generate through this single means. It seems useful to recognize that Shakespeare is just as funny as he always was; it seems equally useful to recognize the variety of ways in which he could be funny.[7]

Notes

1. See Richard Levin in *New Readings vs. Old Plays* (Chicago: University of Chicago Press, 1979).

2. Although some of the points I make here are related to his idea of "discrepant awareness," my focus is not on the matters treated by Bertrand Evans in *Shakespeare's Comedies.*

3. My text is the *Riverside Shakespeare.*

4. We need to be more attentive than we ordinarily are to comedy of this sort, a comedy that invites us as spectators to share in the delight of the characters.

5. This stage direction is supplied in the Arden edition, ed. A. R. Humphreys

(London: Routledge, 1981). Though it has no textual authority, appearing in neither quarto nor folio, it does describe the scene accurately.

6. My text is the Revels edition, ed. F. H. Mares (Cambridge: Harvard University Press, 1967).

7. Parts of this essay appear in my book *Shakespeare and the Ends of Comedy* (Bloomington: Indiana University Press, 1991).

Bottom's Space: Historicizing Comic Theory and Practice in *A Midsummer Night's Dream*

MARCIA McDONALD

"This palpable-gross play hath well beguil'd / The heavy gait of night" (5.1.353–54). With this benediction, Duke Theseus dismisses the artisan players who have made their dramatic offering for the nuptial festivities of the Athenian court. As unflattering to the actors as the compound adjective "palpable-gross" may be, Theseus' phrase represents the effort of the aristocrat to categorize the theater he has just experienced.[1] Theseus' efforts are circumscribed by *A Midsummer Night's Dream* itself, the theatrical experience of which he is merely a part. Theseus' efforts do reflect, however, the play's engagement with issues of genre, of theatrical effects, and of interpretation. The play makes no particular claims to uphold the Thesean aesthetic or social attitudes; on the contrary, as a dramatic experience its "power base" may be located in Bottom, the social "bottom" of the scale. Bottom's theatrical power—his power to create a laughing community out of the various individuals composing the audience—offers a challenge to the primacy of Theseus' power derived from social rank and its consequent privileges of interpretation.

This internal dialogue is situated in an external dialogue particularly heated in London in the mid-1590s: the controversies swirling around the use of and the effect of the stage. The debate between London civic authorities and the crown is conducted in the midst of competing definitions of the stage and its effects from these authorities, as well as from literary critics and from polemicists. *A Midsummer Night's Dream* is a seminal text in this debate, a text that ultimately widens the parameters of what the stage could be in and for Elizabethan England. Shakespeare places *A Midsummer Night's Dream* within the debate through specific, even textual, connections with discourses in literary criticism, most notably Sidney's *Defence of Poesie;* puritan polemic, exemplified in Stephen Gosson's antitheatrical pamphlets; and regulation of the stage.[2] As a result, *A Midsummer Night's Dream*'s well-known "self-reflexivity" or "metatheatricality" dramatizes the inability of theoretical or regulatory discourse to account for the social and cultural place of the stage and for the effects of theater.

These discourses identify comedy as a particular point of anxiety because of its tendency to consider matters of love and State and to transgress moral bounds. As a stage clown and an artisan attempting to enact the role of "lover" in a court theatrical, Bottom embodies almost every element essential to comedy, the very elements also identified as threatening to social order and "abused" by playwrights. Bottom's impudence is not contained or explained by his role as clown, though, of course, a clown's license to speak and misspeak is essential to his role. Indeed, his role, and that of his cohort mechanicals, dramatizes the competing social/cultural constructions of the concept of theater and comedy in Elizabethan England. It is in this production of the process of theatrical representation that *A Midsummer Night's Dream* constructs a new—that is, politically and socially unsanctioned—space for the theater.

Sidney and the Debate over the Stage

A common interest in harnessing the powerful effects of comedy on an audience pervades the three kinds of discourse about the stage, and stage comedy in particular: literary critical, exemplified by Sidney's *Defence*; antitheatrical writings, exemplified by Gosson's pamphlets; and the declarations of the London aldermen. Though each discourse has distinct concerns, all address the content and the effect of theatrical representation and suppose the potential of those representations to disorder the commonweal. This debate and dissension informs the representations of theater in *A Midsummer Night's Dream*.

The rise of a persistent antitheatrical "lobby," evident in the pamphlets against the stage from 1577 until its closing in 1642, signals the power of the theater, power the pamphleteers argue leads England to social and moral decay. Though individual polemicists vary in the details and vehemence of their arguments, their case can be aptly represented by Stephen Gosson, whose dedication of *The Schoole of Abuse* (1579) drew a perhaps unwilling Sir Philip Sidney into the debate. Gosson's appeal for patronage may have been motivated by his perception of Sidney as an international symbol of Protestant erudition and his effort to garner aristocratic endorsement of his project.[3] Though he succeeded in gaining Sidney's private scorn and not his patronage, Gosson also succeeded in constructing images of the theater and definitions of its function that other pamphleteers echo well into the seventeenth century.[4]

Gosson moves from some toleration of the most moral of stage plays in *The Schoole of Abuse* to complete denunciation of them in *Playes Confuted in Five Actions* (1582). In both pamphlets he challenges the argument for the power of the stage to inculcate wisdom, especially through the negative examples provided by comedies. To those who claim the English stage has reformed Latin comedy, changing "force, to friendshippe; rapes, too mariage" (Kinney 1974, 87), Gosson answers that if we seek moral instruction at the theaters, "wee shall have a harde pyttaunce, and come to shorte commons" (Kinney 1974, 89).[5] Gosson praises plays with clearly enunciated morals but condemns even his own comedies: "I haue sinned, and am sorry for my fault" (Kinney 1974, 97).

By 1582, Gosson cannot admit even the most moral of stage plays to be performed: *stage Plaies are not to be suffred in a christian comon weale"* (Kinney 1974, 150). His grounds are the space— literally the theater itself, morally the behavioral license—they give to "carnall delight" (Kinney 1974, 186). The stage, and particularly stage comedy, releases the severe restraint necessary for personal and social control:

> But Comedyes make our delight exceede, for at them many times wee laugh so extreemely, that striving to bridle our selues, we cannot; . . . where such excesse of laughter bursteth out . . . there is no temperance . . . where no temperance is, ther is no wisdome, nor use of reason; when we shew our selues voide both of reason, and wisedome, what are we then to be thought but fooles? (Kinney 1974, 186)

The very dialectic between sorrow and delight that justifies the place of delight in life is a false logic, Gosson claims, used to "shake off the yoake of severer discipline" and to "forc[e] upon life a certaine necessity of carnall delyght, to set up . . . Comedies" (Kinney 1974, 185). It is this carnal delight in particular that Gosson sees reenacted at the theaters. The stage images are not translated into lessons in virtue but the theater itself *is* the "market of bawdrie" for the citizens of London (Kinney 1974, 92, 194). Though Gosson adapted his descriptions of London theater activities from Ovid, his descriptions form part of the rhetoric of his attack.[6] For the continuing debate over the theater in Elizabethan London, the accuracy of his description is less important than the absoluteness with which he connects social behavior to stage representation and social disorder to the existence of the public theaters. The persistence of Gosson's arguments in pamphlets by Anthony Munday, *A Second and Third Blast of Retrait from Plais and Theaters*; Philip Stubbes, *The Anatomie of Abuses*; William Rankins, *A Mirrour of Monsters*; and others well into the seventeenth century attests to the influence of his images.

Gosson's pamphlet about the particulars of the English public theater may have in part (through its dedication) generated Sidney's *Defence of Poesie*. Sidney is concerned with "Poesie" in a much broader sense than is Gosson, but he is nonetheless compelled to address the current state of English letters, which inevitably includes the stage. Sidney also addresses Gosson's issues of the effect of poetry, the place of literature in a commonweal, and the audience responses of "delight" and "laughter," but uses different arguments and draws different conclusions. Sidney's comments about comedy are shaped by his overall thesis that literature ultimately serves virtue: "as vertue is the most excellent resting place for all worldly learning to make his end of, so *Poetry* being the most familiar to teach it, and most Princely to move towards it, in the most excellent worke, is the most excellent workeman" (E3^{r-v}). To make the case for poetry's superiority in this purpose, Sidney sets forth the premise that the "delight" in poetry is integral to its "teaching." In the initial sections of the *Defence*, such a discussion of poetic effect is relatively unproblematic:

> for indeed Poetrie ever sets vertue so out in her best cullours, making fortune her well-wayting handmayd, that one must needs be enamoured of her. . . . And of the contrary part, if euill men come to the stage, they ever goe out . . . so manicled as they litle animate folkes to follow them. (D4^v)

Likewise, the poet "doth not onely shew the way, but giveth so sweete a prospect into the way, as will entice anie man to enter into it" (E^v). In this initial discussion, the moral character of poetry is invested in its content: poetry "sets virtue out," it "entices" the reader toward virtue.

In the confirmation, Sidney's effort to align the various genres with this purpose prompts a comment on contemporary English stage comedy and perhaps a notice of Gosson's pamphlet: "No perchance it is the *Comick,* whom naughtie Play-makers and stage-keepers, have justly made odious. To the arguments of abuse, I will after answer" (E4^r). The comment, however, is puzzling in its use of "justly." Are the play-makers "just" in showing the comic repulsive (i.e., are they teaching by negative example)? If so, why are they "naughty"? Are their comedies so offensive that they in turn render judgment on the genre? The sentence is ambivalent in locating the responsibility for comic effects: does it lie with the author or the genre? He defines ideal comedy in terms of content and effect:

> . . . an imitation of the common errors of our life, which he [the poet] representeth in the most ridiculous & scornfull sort that may be: so as it is impossible that any beholder can be content to be such a one. . . . so in the actions of our life, who seeth not the filthinesse of evill, wanteth a great foile to perceive the bewtie of vertue. (E4^{r-v})

As was true of his comment on the "naughty play-makers," however, Sidney's description of the actual working of comic effect is also ambivalent:

> And litle reason hath any man to say, that men learne the evill by seeing it so set out, since . . . there is no man living, but by the force truth hath in nature, no sooner seeth these man play their parts, but wisheth them *in Pistrinum,* although perchance the sack of his owne faults lie so behinde his backe, that he seeth not himselfe to dance the same measure: whereto yet nothing can more open his eies, then to see his owne actions contemptibly set forth. (E4^v)

Sidney's nod towards the "sack of his owne faults" hints at the difficulty of validating audience response; the complexity of human psychology may not allow for the quick rejection of vice. In this section, Sidney allows the complications to surface. Audience response is essential to complete comedy's purpose; however, individuals, because of their own evasions, may not be able to "dance the same measure" as the poet "sets forth." What seems a syntactical awkwardness here heralds a larger issue that Sidney must address: the place of audience response in the defense of poetry's function of inspiring virtuous action.

This issue Sidney meets head on in his effort to reconcile poetry and Eros, an effort occasioned by the third of the "imputations laid to the poore *Poets*" that poetry "is the nurse of abuse, infecting us with many pestilent desires, with a *Sirens* sweetnesse, drawing the minde to the Serpents taile of sinfull fansies; and herein especially *Comedies* give the largest field to eare, as *Chawcer* saith" (F4^v). The word *abuse* in this sentence connects this discussion to Sidney's previous one on comedy and perhaps to Gosson's *The Schoole of Abuse*. Sidney takes up the charge that poetry lures to lasciviousness; in Gosson's phrasing, "Poets in Theaters" create "effeminate gesture, to ravish the sence; and wanton speache, to whet desire too inordinate lust" (Kinney 1974, 89). Sidney's defense on this point is a pivotal one for the *Defence* as a whole: "not . . . that *Poetrie* abuseth mans wit, but that mans wit abuseth *Poetrie*" (G2^r). Ferguson notes that "this reversal signals a shift in Sidney's definition of poetic power" to a "circuit of energy which goes from author to work to reader" and a shift in the definition of poetry's moral value from its "representational content" to "authorial intention and the interpreter's response" (Ferguson 1983, 147). To illustrate just such a shift and to propose a means of rehabilitating the grosser tendencies of man's wit is the purpose of Sidney's page devoted to the contrast between "delight" and "laughter."

The familiar "mingling kings and clowns" passage heralds a lengthy discussion of "delight" and "laughter," which Sidney must address because "our Comedients thinke there is no delight without laughter, which is verie wrong" (1^v). Though Sidney claims "that they may goe well togither," he separates their origins: "for delight wee scarcely doo, but in thinges that have a conveniencie to our selves, or to the generall nature: Laughter almost ever cometh of thinges moste disproportioned to our selves, and nature" (I^v). He also separates their effects: "Delight hath a joy in it. . . . Laughter hath onely a scornfull tickling" (I2^r). Laughter is associated with disproportion, scurrility, doltishness, wretched beggars, and beggardly clowns, a catalogue that aligns laughter with a class perspective and that underscores Sidney's courtly perspective. Such a perspective would not wish to encourage those responses, as laughter, that emphasize differences of degree and authority in the social structure.[7] Sidney's balance in phrases and sentences, a syntactical strategy he maintains through the three paragraphs on the subject, would seem to undergird an argument for a balance of these two comic effects. But his goal is to accommodate laughter within the purpose of "delightful teaching": "that all the ende of the Comicall part, bee not uppon suche scornefull matters as stirre laughter onelie, but mixe with it, that delightfull teaching whiche is the end of *Poesie*" (I2^r). The playwright achieves such ends by using stage types, a "busie loving Courtier, and a heartlesse threatening *Thraso*; a selfe-wise seeming Schoolemaister, a wry transformed traveller." These types evoke "delightfull laughter, and teaching delightfulnesse" (I2ᵛ). This last phrasing of delight and laughter couples more than the two effects; Sidney also sets out a progression from the forms of comedy (the catalogue of stage types) to the audience's response ("delightfull laughter") to the fulfillment of poetry and comedy's purpose ("teaching delightfulnesse"). This phrasing with its balanced inversions of "teach" and "delight" also makes the audience/reader's response mirror authorial intent, rehabilitating "man's wit," guilty of the abuse of poetry.

Though Sidney, like Gosson, sets up a dichotomy between laughter and delight, Sidney's purpose is not to banish laughter but to create a hierarchy of effects. Gosson rejected the strategy of dichotomy because it could be used to justify "delight," an effect that cannot escape the carnal; Sidney sets up a "contrarietie" in order to arrive at his own formulation, which at least momentarily reconciles form, intent, and effect in the context of a genre "pittifully abused" (I2ᵛ).

The complexities of Sidney's text emerge even in this isolation of a single point in his *Defence*. The problematic status of comedy among Sidney's classical and Renaissance authorities may contribute to his struggles with the genre.[8] The dominance of comedy in Gosson's attack may account for his need to answer to abuses. His effort to privilege a courtly set of attitudes and responses may require his demotion of laughter and scurrility and his scornful tone.[9] One of the most striking and significant elements of Sidney's treatise, however, is its irony and self-depreciation. A particularly courtly stance,[10] Sidney's self-conscious irony and self-depreciation, most evident in his opening and closing passages, surround the proclamations of the *Defence* with a recognition of the limitations of absolutist discourse. Such a tone may owe something to Sidney's tenuous position at court in the 1580s and to inherent complexities in a courtier's discourse.[11] It also allows him to place himself in his discourse as mediator[12]—as the self-conscious interpretive voice—between forms and effects, between Eros and virtue, an arbiter in the dilemmas that have always faced efforts to "defend" poetry, an arbiter in the dilemmas that face English poetry, created especially by stage comedy. Such is not the role played by Shakespeare's version of the courtier/critic in Duke Theseus, although he has some Sidneyesque phrases.

Together Sidney and Gosson's comments on "abuse," "delight," and "laughter" frame the argument and establish the language used in the debate over the stage conducted in various versions— despite the fact that Sidney did not live to see the full flowering of the stage and that Gosson seems to have spoken his final words on the subject in his 1582 pamphlet. Though their solutions differ, both aristocrat and polemicist see the same need for surveillence of the stage and especially comedy to harness its representations of love and wantonness, vice and scurrility, to circumscribe bold laughter and deflect or defeat its potential to encourage perception of social disarray or participation in social disorder.

As the pamphleteers echo Gosson, so other literary critics and rhetoricians advance formulas for comedy similar to Sidney's. Thomas Wilson in his *Arte of Rhetorique* (1553), after an extensive discussion of the value of humor to engage an audience, advocates a median position between delight and laughter, a cicumscribing strategy, anticipating Sidney (Wilson 1553/1562, 70–71). Webbe in *A Discourse of English Poesie* (1586) locates the moral judgment in comedy in the reader, not the writer; comedy, which originated in communal ritual, now requires the clear judgment of the reader to effect its moral value (Dii[r]-iiii[r]). Puttenham in the *Arte of English Poetrie* (1589), ties comedy's "good amendment of man by discipline and example" to the use of stage types (Puttenham 1936, 32), not unlike Sidney's formula to achieve "delightful teaching." Puttenham, more forcibly than Sidney, outlines the potential of the theater to be an agency of effective government and social regulation.[13] Harington's "Preface" to his translation of *Orlando Furioso* (1591) summarizes Sidney on comedy and adds a significant narrative of the censorship of a comedy of state that was resolved in the play's favor based on the assumption of its corrective potential.[14] In "The Teares of the Muses" (1591) Spenser has Thalia, the muse of comedy, complain of the "scoffing /Scurrilitie, / And scornfull Follie," the "shameles ribaudrie / Without regard, or due Decorum kept" upon the stage.[15] These writers, and others, amply demonstrate comedy's ambivalent status in Elizabethan England and show the persistence of the issues of representation, effects, and moral purposes. Though tragedy comes in for serious discussion, it does not seem to provoke the particular anxieties about scurrility and sedition that comedy does. The tie between social behavior and stage representation is made by the London mayor and aldermen in their effort to regulate the stage.

Under Elizabeth, the same concerns of the pamphleteer and literary critic informed the city magistrates' texts related to the theater. The 6 December 1574 Act of the Common Council of London links social disorder to depiction of "unchastitie and sedition":

> Whearas hearetofore sondrye greate disorders and inconvenyences have benne found to ensewe . . . by the inordynate hauntynge of greate multitudes of people . . . to plays . . . namely occasyon of ffrayes and quarrelles, eavell practizes of incontinencye . . . the publishinge of unchaste uncomelye and unshamefaste speeches and doynges. . . . from henceforth no playe, Commodye, Tragidye, enterlude, nor publycke shewe shalbe openlye played or shewed . . . whearin shalbe uttered anie wourdes, examples, or doynges of anie unchastitie, sedicion, nor suche lyke unfytt and uncomelye matter. (Chambers 1923, 4:273–74)

Though it is the pamphleteers who argue the psychological effects of wanton subject matter in this phase of the debate, the City regards the subject matter as simple realism: seditious, unchaste words are not fictions but facts. The actor who speaks them is subject to imprisonment.

In the mid-1590s, the Council is still deferentially petitioning the Privy Council (13 September 1595):

> for the suppressing of the said stage playes . . . that neither in policye nor in religion . . . ar to be permitted in a Christian Common wealthe, specially being of that frame & making as usually they are, & conteyning nothing but profane fables, Lascivious matters, cozonning devizes, & other unseemly & scurrilous behaviours, which ar so sette forthe, as that they move wholy to imitacion & not to the avoyding of those vyces which they represent. (Chambers 1923, 4: 318)

In the eyes of the City, the "aesthetics of correction" does not work; representation has proved politically threatening:

> which wee verely think to bee the cheef cause, aswell of many other disorders & lewd demeanors which appeer of late in young people of all degrees, as of the late stirr & mutinous attempt of those fiew apprentices and other servantes, who wee doubt not driew their infection from these & like places. (Chambers 1923, 4: 318)

That weavers and other artisans and apprentices led these "late stirr[s]" of the summer of 1595 is crucial to recognizing the ties between *A Midsummer Night's Dream*, especially the mechanicals' scenes, and the years of its composition and performance.[16] The riots, some involving crowds as large as 1,800 artisans, appren-

tices, husbandmen, and vagabonds, focused on the high prices
of food and on the Lord Mayor's harsh justice. Both Crown and
City were anxious to restore order. Leaders of the riots were executed, though not quite as rapidly as the Privy Council would
have liked (Manning 1988, 209). Though no riot spills over into
rebellion, the riots and punishments do suggest an increasingly
"fragile relationship between rulers and ruled in early modern
England," and London in the mid-1590s offers plenty of "social
and cultural signs of unusual, economic distress" (Walter 1985,
95).[17] As the document above indicates, the London Council implicated theaters in this distress. Advocating closing the theaters
as a means to restore order, the council does not limit its com-
plaint to "sedition" shown on stage. The entire range of stage
representation is regarded as politically threatening and socially
disruptive.

The mid-1590s project of stifling the theaters and the mid-1590s
project of enhancing the reputation of Sir Philip Sidney may seem
to have little connection. Yet the publication of the *Defence* in 1595
brings into circulation Sidney's ideas about a literary culture in
service to virtue. As Gosson's pamphlet may have drawn Sidney's
attention to the stage in the late 1570s, so Sidney's *Defence* draws
a context of literary issues for the mid-1590s version of the debate
over the stage. Howard notes that in the antitheatrical contro-
versy: "debates about the inherent morality of the theater reveal
themselves as political debates about who will control the theater
and whose theatrical practices will be considered legitimate"
(Howard and O'Connor 1987, 165). Sidney, Gosson, and the London aldermen all define "legitimate." *A Midsummer Night's Dream*
invokes these definitions in the comedy of Bottom and company,
playing out what the discourses offer, and offering a much
broader, more fluid set of definitions in return.

Shakespeare and the "Palpable-gross" Play

Turning to *A Midsummer Night's Dream* within this context, we
can recognize it as a complex text in the debate over a comedy
suitable for the English commonweal. Its relevance is obvious: the
play of "Pyramus and Thisbe" becomes an occasion for a comic
yet serious discussion of the role of theater in a hierarchy. Shakespeare heightens the social tensions by making the artisan players
contend with a courtly aesthetic. Shakespeare further complicates
matters by dramatizing a variety of love plots: not only is "Pyra-

mus and Thisbe" about "lascivious matters" and played in a manner that fully exploits its bawdy, but so are the plots involving the four lovers, and Bottom and Titania. All the means whereby stage comedy creates its effects, evokes the anxiety of city officials and pamphleteers, and proves difficult for the literary critics like Sidney—audience response, representation, purpose of comedy, character types—Shakespeare produces in *A Midsummer Night's Dream*, most particularly in the scenes with the artisan players.

We meet Bottom, Peter Quince, and company at rehearsal. Though we are made quite conscious of the issues of theatrics as Bottom tries out every role, we are also made aware of a group of newly literate artisans struggling to read and interpret a play script. David Cressy's study of literacy shows that weavers, joiners, carpenters, and tailors all fell close together in the scale of literacy for 1550 to 1650.[18] In particular, tailors and weavers became more literate in the 1570s and 1580s as schooling became somewhat more accessible (Cressy 1980, 149). Thus, the likes of Bottom and company working with a play script is not without some plausibility in Elizabethan life. Shakespeare may be inviting his audience to watch a group experiment with its newly acquired literacy, as indeed had been the case each time an audience viewed actors from the ranks of artisans in the newly established public theaters.[19] The artisans in *A Midsummer Night's Dream* have one foot in the territory of the literate in their effort to be faithful to the demands of the text, and one foot in a communal, preliterate realm in their solutions to the challenges the text presents.

Though Bottom and company are able to read the script in 1.2 (with a few exceptions here and there), their biggest challenge is how to *represent* the script. They know that staging *"realizes"* the words of the text in ways that do not allow the script or them to escape the historical contingencies of their actions. While these scenes are often highlighted as evidence of the mechanicals' ignorance about the theater, the scenes actually reveal an awareness of the "facts" of the stage for the mid-1590s: handling swords and the icons of State (lions and moonshine) could quite likely arouse someone's attention. In the first rehearsal, the "lion's part" galvanizes their concern; if they "fright the duchess and the ladies," they fear being hanged, a fate that echoes like doom through the next lines (1.2.70–76).

The issue of the proper representation for their performance becomes more complicated in the next rehearsal scene, as concerns of violence resurface. The three problems they take up are killing with swords, the lion (again), and moonshine.

> *Bottom.* There are things in this comedy of Pyramus and Thisbe
> that will never please. First, Pyramus must draw a sword to kill him-
> self; which the ladies cannot abide. How answer you that?
> *Snout.* Byrlakin, a parlous fear.
> *Starveling.* I believe we must leave the killing out, when all is done.
> *Bottom.* Not a whit; I have a device to make all well. Write me a
> prologue, and let the prologue seem to say we will do no harm with
> our swords, and that Pyramus is not killed indeed; and for the more
> better assurance, tell them that I, Pyramus, am not Pyramus, but
> Bottom the weaver. This will put them out of fear. (3.1.8–20)

The fear of offending aristocratic "ladies" and of threatening
"harm with their swords" is met with the solution of literacy: we
will write an explanation that will accommodate our performance
to our sense of aristocratic taste and that will diffuse aristocratic
anxieties.[20] These anxieties about swords in the hands of weavers
were particularly real in the mid-1590s, as riots, several key ones
led by weavers, plagued London especially in 1595–96. As Leinwand notes, "their specific fears are resonant because they have
to do with more than theatrical decorum" (Leinwand 1986, 13).
They have to do with social relationships and saving themselves
from hanging. The artisans suspect the Duke's audience will
"read" a sword much as the London aldermen do—as a weapon,
not a prop—and that they, as citizens and not actors, will be
responsible for the consequences of drawing that weapon.

The lion and moonshine, too, present their difficulties. Both
were icons of State, symbols of Crown and of Elizabeth in particular. The marginal literacy of the artisans leads them to debate the
choices they have in representing lion and moonshine, but not
to consider the aristocratic iconography. Thus, their debate and
solutions throw into relief the scaffolding of court iconography,
exposing its rarefied symbols. To the mechanicals, the lion is a
"fierce wild-fowl," and like the sword, may make the ladies, as
well as Snout, fear for their lives (3.1.39–43). The strategy is to
make the lion into a partial mask, whose "maskness" is unmistakable, and again to add to the prologue. But "moonlight in a chamber" is a little trickier problem of representation, for moonlight is
both an emblem of Elizabeth,[21] and a central image in *A Midsummer Night's Dream*. As an emblem of Elizabeth, moonlight is an
issue of state, fraught with difficulty for the dramatist. John Lyly
in *Endimion*, a play that some claim as a source for *A Midsummer
Night's Dream*, brings moonlight into a chamber by a full re-crea-
tion of the cult of Cynthia through Endimion's extended paean to
her. Endimion's speech reconciles the negative and positive physi-

cal qualities of the moon in order to sustain an iconography that idealizes and compliments and inspires courtly devotion:

> *Endimon.* O fayre *Cynthia,* why doe others terme thee vnconstant, whom I haue euer founde vnmoueable? Iniurious tyme, corrupt manners, vnkind men, who finding a constancy not to be matched in my sweete Mistris, haue christned her with the name of wauering, waxing, and waning. Is shee inconstant that keepeth a setled course, which since her first creation altereth no one minute in her mouing? . . . What thing (my Mistris [Cynthia] excepted) being in the pride of her beauty, & latter minute of her age, that waxeth young againe? (1.1.30–36, 49–50)[22]

Endimion's verbal habilitation of the various natural aspects of the moon to the virtues of the sovereign prepares for Cynthia's entrance as a character who revives and reinstates her loyal suitor. In all her appearances Lyly maintains decorum, never "disfiguring" Cynthia. A similar process of presenting the Cynthia/moon iconography can be traced in Spenser's *Mutabilitie Cantos,* Raleigh's poem to Cynthia, and various entertainments for and portraits of Queen Elizabeth (Strong 1977, 48–52; Strong 1987, 124–29; Wells 1983, 147–56). This iconography seems to have been at its height in the post-Armada years through the 1590s (Strong 1987, 128).

Shakespeare's evocation of this problem of "representing moonshine," in the context of the other problems of staging that are politically resonant, serves as a way to situate his play in relation to the court and court ideology. What Lyly, Spenser, and others do, Shakespeare undoes. Instead of building up an idealized figure, Shakespeare lets Quince and company "disfigure" moonshine. Their first impulse is to treat it literally, to "look in the almanac," a popular document no less, that would tell precisely what the iconography seeks to hide: the mutability of the moon. The almanac is also the vehicle that seeks to interpret patterns of nature for the needs of community production and daily life. In that sense it is the pragmatic inversion of the court iconography that depicts Elizabeth as the beneficient sovereign and the ordering force in nature.

Quince, however, is not satisfied with this solution, and he opts for "disfiguring" moonshine in the person of folklore, an iconography that predates the courtly Cynthia/moon symbolism. In evoking the folkloric man in the moon, Quince opens the way for the parody of the aristocratic strategy of iconologizing; no idealization crosses the stage when Starveling enters with dog, lantern, and thorn bush. The artisan actors empty the icon of its aristocratic resonance, accomplishing in their dialogue and staging what Shakespeare does elsewhere in his play.[23]

The issue of representation, especially of moonlight, is not the only one that ties "Pyramus and Thisbe" and the actors to the rest of the text of *A Midsummer Night's Dream* itself and to the external dialogue on comedy; the artisan actors who struggle both with and in the text are the site of struggle over the concept of comic type. As with the issues of representation, the artisan actors both project an understanding of *type* and empty the concept of its meaning and function. Sidney and others who address the issue of comedy identify the fidelity to types as the essential mechanism of comedy's instruction. It is this predictability, the faithfulness of comic representation to circumscribed types that ensures "delightful teaching."

Bottom seems to affirm the rules of genre; the "true performing" (1.2.21) of Pyramus's role will be determined by whether he is a "lover, or a tyrant," and Bottom is prepared to enact the proper gestures of whatever Pyramus turns out to be. Bottom's willingness to enact all parts is also a capacity predicated on the understanding of theatrical representation as proceeding by types. Though his "chief humor" may be for a "tyrant," he knows the gestures for romance heroines and lions as well, a point that underscores their coding for the stage in Elizabethan England. The logic of types could lead to the didactic—teach and delight— conclusion, and as such was a cornerstone for the claim for comedy's teaching by "negative example." It is, however, this very logic that the City officials reject after the sequence of artisan-led uprisings in 1595: "they move wholy to imitacion & not to the avoiding of those vices which they represent" (Chambers 1923, 4: 318).

A Midsummer Night's Dream, too, rejects this logic not just by calling attention to it in the artisans' rehearsal scene, but by the way the characters are constructed. Bottom and his fellows are the particular case in point. Their "roles" have an double denomination in the quarto and in the folio texts as particular names and as "clowns."[24] The clown, of course, is a stage type par excellence, a type that certainly embraces the variety of dimensions of Bottom's role—and that carries with it associations of class, the country bumpkin, and the long-standing license in England to speak with impunity to the monarch. This artisan-clown acquires more roles as he moves through the play: ass, lover, even visionary— each role carrying with it a multitude of literary, social, and cultural connections. This collection of roles defies any effort to distinguish and classify comic effects by correlating stage type to audience response.

The mechanicals are also designated "the rabble" in the Quarto stage direction in 4.2: "Enter Quince, Flute, Thisbe, and the rabble" (G2^r). "Rabble" is cited as evidence for Shakespeare's foul papers as the quarto copy-text; thus "rabble" is his shorthand designation: "a delightful specimen of author's language" (Brooks 1979, xxiii). However, given the unstable nature of a play script,[25] we might draw back from judgments about Shakespeare's particular attitudes and instead contemplate what the stage direction tells us about the intersection of stage and world, of stage type and social type. By this term, the stage roles of the artisans translate directly to the "rabble" of Elizabethan culture, associating these stage artisans with the street rabble that stirred up trouble for the City and Crown. The "rabble" of the stage direction seems to confirm the London authorities' fears that players and playgoers are the same thing: "the refuse sort of evill disposed & ungodly people about this Cytie have oportunitie hearby to assemble together & to make their matches . . . being also the ordinary places for all maisterles men & vagabond persons that haunt the high waies to meet together & to recreate themselves" (Chambers 1923, 4: 318). *Rabble, vagabond*—these words are a familiar part of the documents regulating the acting profession in Tudor England. "Rabble" in the quarto momentarily re-places Will Kemp and his fellows—and their stage alter egos, Bottom, Quince, Flute, and all—back into their marginal, unstable social context. Though one may argue that this word *rabble* is merely a textual, not a stage, issue, it stands as a marker, a sign—whatever its origin—of the continuum between stage and society, and as one among many signs in *A Midsummer Night's Dream* that defeats the efforts to idealize the play out of its historical context, to simplify its effects and to read it as operating by conventions, in particular the convention of type.

The issues of representation, stage type, and theatrical effect that range through the rehearsal scenes are brought together in 5.1 in the performance of "Pyramus and Thisbe." This scene provides the encounter between all that has been unstable in the rehearsals and the stable interpretive voice of the aristocrat. Theseus makes his desires known: he wants theater as entertainment, to "ease the anguish of a torturing hour" and "beguile the lazy time," a form of entertainment tolerated by Court and City alike. What Theseus gets in the selection of "Pyramus and Thisbe" is entertainment, but not the kind that he can categorize. Philostrate does warn him what effect "Pyramus and Thisbe" has, a warning that may also serve as a guideline to the playing of the scene: "Which, when I saw rehears'd, I must confess / Made mine eyes water; but more merry tears / The passion of loud laughter never shed" (5.1.68–70). Philostrate admits to laughter as the response, a laughter he identifies as extreme, more than he has ever experienced before, and sounding suspiciously like the laughter Gosson so fears and that Sidney would harness to delight.

Ignoring Philostrate's comments, Theseus assumes that he can appropriate whatever meaning he wishes from the offering of the artisans. To claim his point, Theseus recounts his ability to appropriate "a welcome" from "Love, therefore, and tongue-tied simplicity" (5.1.100, 104). It is almost as if he is geared up for the Sidneyan interpretive role, having opened the act with a rehearsal—in a simplified form—of a few concepts from the *Defence*. But Theseus presents these comments without the irony and diffidence enveloping Sidney's treatise. Shakespeare's version of the aristocratic literary critic is one devoid of irony and self-consciousness, and thus one without a shield against challenges to the totality of his judgment. By flattening the portrait, Shakespeare creates a figure whose self-assured opinions are ripe for challenge. After the play is underway, Theseus maintains his prerogative to appropriate the theatrics of Bottom and company to his own aesthetic as he claims the "worst are no worse, if imagination amend them," which Hippolyta notes is "his" imagination (5.1.208–10). However clever and effective this aristocratic strategy of presuming to interpret good intents from the actions of one's social inferiors, it simply does not operate in *A Midsummer Night's Dream*.

In light of Theseus's expectations to be able to "read" the play and harness its meaning, perhaps he should have attended to the Prologue's comment "All for your delight, / We are not here" (5.1.114–15). *Delight* is one of the key words in Renaissance discussion of comic effects. It is the word that connects comedy to the overall didactic function of literature, the word that evokes extended explication and definition by both Sidney and Gosson, and that appears regularly in contemporary discussions of comedy. The "sweet Comedy," the "tragical mirth" of "Pyramus and Thisbe" does not fit the discussions of delight offered by the literary critics; it cannot be translated into the "teaching delightfulness" that Sidney sees as the achievement of comedy. As the Prologue teeters between offense and defense, it creates a new "space," erasing the easy connection between genre, effect, and final purpose pursued by Elizabethan literary criticism. The Prologue's announcement, in its garbling of its sense, heralds a garbling of genres and effects in "Pyramus and Thisbe."

"Pyramus and Thisbe" has been thought to carry out a number of functions within the context of *A Midsummer Night's Dream*. It evokes, to transform and banish, the tragic potential of desire, provides a festive celebration for marriage, burlesques amateur theatricals and earlier drama, parodies constricting dramatic conventions, and effects a social unity.[26] The very plurality of interpretation that the scene seems to offer suggests the futility of categorizing and labelling the dramatic experience, the futility of the Thesean project. Lest it be noted that the interpretations cited above are twentieth-century readings of the episode, the very "topical relevance" (Marcus 1988, 48) of the "Pyramus and Thisbe" plot to the lovers' travails in *A Midsummer Night's Dream* offers an abundance of meanings.

Indeed, the effect of "Pyramus and Thisbe" is difficult to circumscribe. Though one may argue the vagaries of *A Midsummer Night's Dream*'s stage history, which includes some distinctly unfunny versions, those productions can be contested by Philostrate's assertion of boisterous laughter as the response to the play. The Renaissance traditions of clowning that Bottom and company have in their repertory also evoke just such laughter. Bottom matches all the qualities Sidney identifies as evoking "scornful laughter." He is a "deformed creature," experiences "mischaunces," is a "clowne," and "speake[s] not English so well as we do" (I2^{r-v}; see p. 90 above). The laughter, furthermore, is intemperate, which Gosson feared would create an audience of fools, an audience who mirrors the players. Yet laughter, this particular point of anxiety for Sidney the courtier and Gosson the moralist, constitutes a serious response to much Renaissance literature, having "a deep philosophical meaning" and "posing universal problems" (Bakhtin 1984, 66).

Indeed, the "Pyramus and Thisbe" episode is a contest of types of humor. Theseus leads Lysander and Demetrius in a witty assault on the troupe's playing. Bottom and company engage in burlesque and bawdiness, humor in the carnival tradition. Their effectiveness depends not upon their self-conscious contrivance of the effects but rather on their assertion of an order of experience—tied to the material, the everyday—that does not find the aristocratic conventions of performance to be "natural" (Bristol 1985, 178).

This contest does not remain inside the scene. Lines like Theseus's that the "dead" Pyramus "might yet recover, and prove an ass" (5.1.297–98) derive their humor less from Theseus' intellectual and social privilege to mock than from its reference to Bottom's transformation, a reference intelligible to the theater audience. As the audience interprets jokes based in its knowledge of the entire play, it signals the limitation of the aristocratic perspective and the theatrical triumph of the artisans and laughter. This laughter counters efforts to modulate the effects of stage comedy in favor of balance or reconciliation, the very project Sidney undertakes in his discussion of laughter in the *Defence*.

The perspective of Theseus, the social balance he creates in admitting the commoners to entertain at his wedding feast is not, finally, the drama. The dramatic and social balance the drama creates in its multiple plots, its groups of characters, and its alternations of scenes is not, finally, the theatrical experience, for the jig may follow. Bottom as the company clown may have concluded the entire afternoon's dramatic experience with his scurrilous jig on an amorous subject that would have constituted another parody, this time of the formally scripted *A Midsummer Night's Dream*.[27]

Shakespeare's creation of a play script that allows a socially marginal, politically threatening figure to create a powerful theatrical experience not sanctioned by any authoritative voice in Elizabethan England puts his theater squarely in the debate over the function of the stage. The broad comic laughter created by Bottom occupies the stage successfully. *A Midsummer Night's Dream* takes all the charges of scurrility, vice, sedition, lasciviousness, and social disorder, and all the strategies of stage type, comic representation, and audience response, producing through its metatheatricality a construction of theater that expands the theater's power to reproduce and revise the language and codes of its culture.

To give Bottom such a profound position in a play so reflective on the world and the stage is to make "symbolically central" what is "socially peripheral" (Babcock 1978, 32). Babcock's formulation for her anthropological study of inversion helps identify the way that the Elizabethan theater escapes service to a totalizing state ideology or an aristocratic aesthetic and creates new patterns or relationships among cultural codes. To conflate Bottom's theatrical power with his social status, as, for example, Kavanagh does in arguing for a "reconciliation effect" curbing all to "a rigid social hierarchy of aristocratic and patriarchal privilege" (Kavanagh

1985, 156), is to disregard the theater's power to produce its own space, which is precisely what it does in *A Midsummer Night's Dream*. Montrose's argument for the play's theatrical "*re*-present[ation]" of the "Elizabethan sex/gender system" to "enlarg[e] the dimensions of the cultural field . . . altering the lines of force within it" (Montrose 1988, 32) provides an analysis analogous to mine that identifies the theater's engagement with, rather than subservience to, a court or state ideology. The theater's ability to create its own representations, by transforming conventional modes of representation, character types, symbols, allowing them to accrue new meanings, is the theater's internal mechanism for establishing its place, while crown, council, polemicist, and critic jockey for control.

To see such a consequence for *A Midsummer Night's Dream*, we must return it to the public stage, indeed perhaps its only provenance. The notion of the play's performance at an aristocratic wedding has proven one sure way to validate Theseus' voice. However, as Harold Brooks reminds us, just before embarking upon a summary of the various wedding occasions proposed, "there is no proof" (Brooks 1979, liii). The quarto title page asserts that the play has been "sundry times publickely acted." Though such an assertion is not an unusual one, it does provide evidence for staging not paralleled by those who advocate an aristocratic wedding performance. On the public stage, where "[p]oetic language, rhetorical ornament and classical learning are compelled to share communicative space with vernacular speech and with vernacular misinterpretations of high culture" (Bristol 1985, 123), Bottom's voice gains strength and resonance; indeed, it is an essential language of the public stage. Situating the play on the public stage also gives us much more room to consider the validity of reading it as a text engaged with the heated contests over the theater.

The particular social, geographical, political, and cultural situation of the public stage in Elizabethan–Jacobean England allowed it to project otherwise marginal voices. Mullaney's description of the theater as a marginal institution itself, located in the "liberties" from which the "horizon of the community" was visible, shows how the stage could provide a strategic view of its culture: revealing the "vulnerability of the social structure itself," disclosing its contradictions and "bringing reigning ideologies and cultural climates into view" (Mullaney 1988, 31, 38, 57). As an institution bestriding its cultural boundaries, so to speak, the stage dramatized the very processes of inclusion and exclusion, of centrality and marginality, that allowed not merely a look within its institutional conditions, but a look without onto the stage of Elizabethan London.

That Elizabethan London was experienced as a stage is suggested not just by the self-fashioning tropes of its court to claim place and privilege, [28] but also by the fluidity in social relationships occasioned by the long transition from feudal to market economy. Agnew argues that a "crisis of representation" emerged as the use of a money exchange brought a new liquidity to economic relations. This "crisis of representation" was displayed most powerfully in the theater: "Separated, like the market, from its original ritual and hierarchical aegis, the Elizabethan and Jacobean theater furnished a laboratory for representational possibilities for a society perplexed by the cultural consequences of its own liquidity" (Agnew, 1986, 54). The hostility of the puritans to the theater was related most pointedly to this display of shape-shifting, to this assuming and discarding of roles that pictured the fluidity of social roles in the society at large (Agnew 1986, 129; Howard 1987, 166–67).

Thus, the theater's self-reflexivity is an element of its realism, not an internal preoccupation, but precisely the element that connected it to its world. By presenting a "dramatistic world picture," Montrose argues, the theater "articulates—and thereby helps its heterogeneous audience of social actors to adjust to and to control—the ambiguities and conflicts, the hardships and opportunities, arising from the ideologically anomalous realities of change" (Montrage 1980, 55, 64).

Bottom displays the theater as understood in these descriptions. He is a socially marginal figure in the mid-1590s, one regarded as disruptive and threatening to social order. He is also a role-changer, a role-player, moving through a variety of roles, denominated by a variety of terms in the script. As a mimetic figure, a mode of reflection, Bottom is something like a funhouse mirror that curves and stretches what it reflects. On the one hand, he and his cohorts display what the stage of the 1590s is not: literal, predictable in effects, fixed in strategies of representation. These are the very things the London aldermen think the stage should be, perhaps because, as the polemicists claim, these are what the social order is no longer. On the other hand, Bottom presents what the stage is: protean, unpredictable in its effects, ambiguous in its relation to authority. These are the very things the London council fears the stage is and what the polemicists fear the social order is. In a society fixated on theatricality and anxious about its own order, Bottom stands as a peculiarly apt representation of the intersection of these two concerns.

Bottom is a representation of these concerns, not an agenda. Thus, it may be easy to dismiss the political dimension of the play or to see its social relations as conservative and harmonious. After all, according to Harrison's *Description of England*, artisans "have neither voice nor authoritie in the common wealth, but are to be ruled; and not to rule other" (Harrison, 1587, 163). Though Bottom has no subversive program for his theatricality, his very ability to wield theatrical power, to create an intense, lived community experience for a heterogeneous audience in the public theater may be a signal to social power, especially in an age, as noted above, anxious about theatricality and anxious about social order. As Raymond Williams comments about English Renaissance drama, these plays "enacted elements of the preconditions of what could nevertheless, beyond the limits of these forms, be politically acted quite differently" (Williams 1981, 159).

A Midsummer Night's Dream is a play fluid in its generic bounds as well as in the figure of Bottom. It resists the standard literary definitions of comedy of its day, affirming laughter over delight, mongrel characters, as Sidney might say, over types. In presenting genre as yet another "theater," another concept whose edges are fluid, it complicates the effort to prescribe (or proscribe) a cultural project for the stage and/or for the literature of the stage. As Sidney's *Defence* and the other texts related to it show, "poesy's" place in culture is assured by the certainty of its effects. Teaching, virtuous action—these ends can be met if the effects created by poetry can be said to "move" audiences to these ends. When genres mingle and mangle their effects, it becomes impossible to sustain a cultural project for literature (or for the stage drama as part of that project) as Sidney describes. In allowing Theseus an agenda but not the ability to define or explain Bottom, and in denying Bottom an agenda though not his power to move an audience, Shakespeare defeats the effort to construct a specific cultural project for the stage, especially a project that would bring it into accord with aristocratic taste or puritan authority. *A Midsummer Night's Dream* is not neutral as a result; it is actually quite tendentious on the issues of representation and effect outlined in the discussion above. Its resistance to the formulations of a Sidney or the strictures of the authorities and polemicists becomes an advocacy for the theater's space. It is the theater, after all, that will "mend" and "amend" any indiscretions in this play, as Puck assures the audience in the Epilogue (5.1.415, 420, 424).

Bottom's funhouse mirror held up to his own mode of production, the theater, stretches it vastly beyond its physical size and geopolitical location.

Into this advocacy for a broad, unconstructed theatrical space has entered a variety of strategies for authorizing one voice or another, for creating hierachies of effect in stage productions as well as critical discussions over the years. The mechanicals, the fairies, the lovers, the poetry, the woods, the festive marriage ending, the ritual associations—all these elements and more have had their advocates for a framework around which to build a hierarchy of effects. Though I admit to erecting some hierarchies of my own—I hope corrective ones—I think *A Midsummer Night's Dream* invites us in the community of teachers and scholars to reflect upon our interpretive privileges. As teachers and scholars, we may feel a powerful need to authorize the voice of Theseus, the judge and interpreter, who can fathom meaning from the most tongue-tied of subjects. We face versions of Bottom each class day—students, especially first-time readers of Shakespeare, who meet a Shakespearean text with questions and assumptions analogous to those Bottom asks about "Pyramus and Thisbe"; students who may be quite literate in relation to their own culture, but who approach Shakespeare only marginally literate; students for whom Shakespeare has become impossibly "high culture," and who hope desperately to come up with an interpretation that willl allow them to escape hanging. *A Midsummer Night's Dream* contests the privilege to appropriate interpretation and to circumscribe the space of the stage. Instead, *A Midsummer Night's Dream* "celebrates hybridity, impurity, intermingling, the transformation that comes of new and unexpected combinations of human beings, cultures, ideas, politics, movies, songs. It rejoices in mongrelization and fears the absolutism of the Pure. Melange, hotchpotch, a bit of this and a bit of that is *how newness enters the world*" (Rushdie 1990, 52). This description, which sounds as if it might have been written of *A Midsummer Night's Dream,* is actually Salman Rushdie's own description of *The Satanic Verses,* a novel that will mark the politics of our own day. *A Midsummer Night's Dream,* a work that has often looked conventional, may have been for its day, and may actually still be, quite new.

Notes

1. For this suggestion in particular, and for a thoughtful and helpful review of this project as a whole, I am indebted to Annabel Patterson and to my col-

leagues in her 1990 NEH Summer Seminar on Shakespeare and Cultural History. In addition, I am grateful to Scott Colley, to Doug Bisson, and John Paine, and to Irene Dash and members of Frances Teague's 1990 Shakespeare Association of America seminar on Comic Theory and Practice for their generous and helpful comments on the various rehearsals of this project. Any failure to stand upon points remains my own. Citations, unless otherwise noted, are from Harold Brooks's Arden edition of *A Midsummer Night's Dream* (London: Methuen, 1979), cited in this essay as Brooks 1979.

2. See Philip Sidney, *The Defence of Poesie,* facs. 1595 edn. London: Noel Douglas, 1928. See also Stephen Gosson, *The Schoole of Abuse* and *Playes Confuted in Fiue Actions* in Arthur Kinney, *Markets of Bawdrie,* Salzburg Studies in English Literature: Elizabethan Studies 4 (1974).

3. See William Ringler, *Stephen Gosson* (Princeton: Princeton University Press, 1942), 36–37; see also Kinney 1974, 15.

4. See Kinney 1974, 65–67; see also Jean-Christophe Agnew, *Worlds Apart* (Cambridge: Cambridge University Press 1986), 125–135.

5. In quotations from Gosson and Sidney, I have normalized spelling by changing "u" to "v," long "s" to "s," and "i" to "j."

6. See S. P. Zitner, "Gosson, Ovid, and the Elizabethan Audience," *Shakespeare Quarterly* 9 (1958): 206–208.

7. See Michael D. Bristol, *Carnival and Theater* (New York: Methuen, 1985), 128–29.

8. See Geoffrey Shepherd, ed., *An Apology for Poetry or The Defence of Poesy by Sir Philip Sidney* (London: Thomas Nelson, 1965), 224, for a discussion of Sidney's formulation within the context of classical and sixteenth-century tradition.

9. See Christopher Martin, "Sidney's *Defence:* The Art of Slander and the Slander of Art," *Sidney Newsletter* 9 (1988): 3, 9; Bristol, 128–29.

10. See Daniel Javitch, *Poetry and Courtliness in Renaissance England* (Princeton: Princeton University Press, 1976), 38.

11. See Ferguson 1983, 161; Martin 1988, 9; Javitch 1976, 38–43; See also Edward Berry, "The Poet as Warrior in Sidney's *Defence of Poetry,*" *Studies in English Literature* 29 (1989).

12. See Margaret Ferguson, "Sidney's *A Defence of Poetry:* A Retrial," *boundary 2* 7 (1979): 64–65; Martin Raitiere, "The Unity of Sidney's *Apology for Poetry,*" *Studies in English Literature* 21 (1981): 44; and John Hunt, "Allusive Coherence in Sidney's *Apology for Poetry,*" *Studies in English Literature* 27 (1987): 7–11 for three versions of Sidney's "mediating" strategy. My version differs somewhat from these articles.

13. See Jonathan V. Crewe, "The Hegemonic Theater of George Puttenham," *English Literary Renaissance* 16 (1986): 72, 85.

14. See John Harington, A Preface or rather, a brief apologie of poetrie . . . . *Orlando Furioso,* ed. Robert McNulty (Oxford: Clarendon, 1972), 9.

15. Edmund Spenser, "The Teares of the Muses" in *The Works of Edmund Spenser: A Variorum Edition,* ed. Edwin Greenlaw, et al. (Baltimore: Johns Hopkins University Press, 1932–1949), 7.2: 57–79, lines 210–11, 212–13. Robin Headlam Wells, *Spenser's "Faerie Queene" and the Cult of Elizabeth* (London: Croom Helm, 1983) considers Spenser's topicality.

16. Roger Manning, *Village Revolts* (Oxford: Oxford University Press, 1988), 208–210; Steve Rappaport, *Worlds within Words* (Cambridge: Cambridge University Press, 1989), 11–13; Theodore B. Leinwand, "'I believe we must leave the

killing out': Deference and Accommodation in *A Midsummer Night's Dream*," *Renaissance Papers* (1986): 15–20; Annabel Patterson, *Shakespeare and the Popular Voice* (Oxford: Basil Blackwell,1989), 55–57.

17. See also Patterson, *Shakespeare and the Popular Voice*, 56–57.

18. This study shows the following: 49–62% illiterate, rural populations; 34–44% illiterate, London population (Cressy 1980, 132–35).

19. See J. W. Robinson, "'Palpable Hot Ice': Dramatic Burlesque in *A Midsummer Night's Dream*," *Studies in Philology* 61 (1964): 197.

20. For this point I am indebted to David Linton for sharing his work in progress on literacy in Shakespeare with me.

21. See Roy Strong, *The Cult of Elizabeth* (Berkeley: University of California Press, 1977), 48–49; and *Gloriana* (New York: Thames and Hudson, 1987), 125–28.

22. *Endimion* in *The Complete Works*, ed. R. Warwick Bond (Oxford: Clarendon Press, 1902) 3: 18–80.

23. In other references to the moon in *A Midsummer Night's Dream*, Shakespeare reworks the image to evoke its varying qualities. See 3.1.191–93 and William Carroll, *The Metamorphoses of Shakespearean Comedy* (Princeton: Princeton University Press, 1985), 152–53.

24. Quarto: "Enter the Clownes," s.d. D^r; "Clo" for Bottom, G1^v Folio as Quarto (151, 158), and "The Clownes all Exit," s.d., 152. In *Shakespeare's Plays in Quarto*, ed. Michael J. B. Allen and Kenneth Muir (Berkeley: University of California Press, 1981).

25. See Stephen Orgel, "The Authentic Shakespeare," *Representations* 21 (1988): 7.

26. Carroll 1985, 159–67; Ralph Berry, *Shakespeare's Comedies* (Princeton: Princeton University Press, 1972), 187, 194; Anne Righter, *Shakespeare and the Idea of the Play* (New York: Barnes and Noble, 1962), 109; J. Dennis Huston, *Shakespeare's Comedies of Play* (New York: Columbia University Press, 1981), 97; Paul A. Olson, "*A Midsummer Night's Dream* and the Meaning of Court Marriage," *English Literary History* 24 (1957): 119.

27. See David Wiles, *Shakespeare's Clown* (Cambridge: Cambridge University Press, 1987), 56.

28. See Frank Whigham, *Ambition and Privilege* (Berkeley: University of California Press, 1984), 32.

"Gallia and Gaul, French and Welsh": Comic Ethnic Slander in the Gallia Wars

ALAN POWERS

For all the implied horror in *Henry V*, such as Henry's threats of plunder, rape, and child murder to the Mayor of Harfleur, the offstage killing of prisoners of war, the again offstage hanging of Bardolph, and even the vividly narrated death of Falstaff, this reader of the text finds that its comedy predominates. True, Shakespeare defaults on the first part of his promise in the epilogue of *Henry IV, Part Two*, to "continue the story, with Sir John in it"; but the playwright does "make [us] merry with fair Katherine of France." After King Hal banishes Falstaff in *Part Two*, Shakespeare himself adds the coup de grace of killing him in his bed. Both the king and the author want him gone. The author's motive—besides Will Kemp's disappearance—may have been to prepare a different kind of comedy, a reconciliation of conflicting nationalities via a comic resolution, an harmony symbolized (however preposterously) by marriage. Largely, this spirit of comic reconciliation derives from the author's linguistic play within the play. (Anticipating my next sentence, I had almost said, "loinguistic play.")

Henry V may be called Shakespeare's *Finnegans Wake*, relying as it does on at least two distinct languages and three dialect accents to represent English, French, Scots, Irish, and Welsh. Additionally, this play, famous for national mythology and public rhetoric like "Once more unto the breach," burgeons with private quarrels that thrive on ethnic and linguistic divisions. In *Henry V*, English words of challenge and insult are more likely to be flung at members of the same army: the Dolphin and the Constable of France, Fluellen and Macmorris, Pistol and everybody. In real life after 1603, the next forty-five years of Stuart reign reads like *Henry V* backwards: the French wife of the English monarch, Henrietta Maria, will return to France, Macmorris and the Irish will be fighting against the King again, Ramy and the Scots will be supporting Parliament, and as for the Welsh Fluellen, we shall turn to the Welsh shortly.

However the historical Henry actually conquered France, on Shakespeare's stage he wins by courting and joking in two languages. In "*Henry V* as Heroic Comedy," Roy Battenhouse points out that Henry achieves France not through the red herring of the Salic Law, but through the title of "son" to France, "by marrying the *living* female Kate, not by reason of any dead great-grandmother's claim" (Battonhouse 1962, 175). Here Shakespeare graces a foregone, forced, patriarchally arranged marriage with all the qualities of intimate self-revelation. The culminating word-play of the courting scene charms us from the cares of history, the play's ostensible subject (and form), even as it releases the author from the constraints of writing history. This final banter was set up by bilingual scenes earlier. If this is a play laden with conflict, it is not primarily the swordplay of noble against noble as in *Henry VI, Part Three*, but the wordplay of mutual insult and ethnic division. The dialect humor and comedic structure, leading to marriage at the end of the play, resolve on stage those same ethnic and political divisions that threatened the Tudor establishment.

Take, for instance, the Scottish and Welsh. What was their place in Shakespeare's England? The mockery of the Scottish on the stage reached a point where King James felt it necessary to forbid it, perhaps partly because it so amused his queen, Anne of Denmark. A biographer of the queen, for instance, remarks of the coarseness of the Blackfriars productions not censored by the Master of the Revels: "In spite of their coarseness, Queen Anne enjoyed the boys' acting and laughed loudly at pointed jokes aimed at her husband" (Williams 1970, 94). Many of these jokes were simply Scottish allusions. Chambers records that the French ambassador was shocked in June 1604 because the queen attended "these performances in order to enjoy the laugh against her husband" (Chambers 1923 1: 325). Spevack's Shakespeare concordance lists seventeen uses of "Scot," eight more of the plural, a couple each of "Scotch" and "Scottish," with twenty-eight uses of the name "Scotland."[1] These references occur in the second tetralogy and of course *Macbeth*. Surprisingly, Welsh references are slightly higher. Shakespeare's works include thirty-four instances of "Wales," and twenty uses of "Welsh," all confined to the second tetralogy histories, *Henry IV, Part One, Part Two*, and *Henry V*, and a play of the same period, *The Merry Wives of Wind-*

sor. Additionally, there are six instances of "Welshman" and five more in the plural, "Welshmen," plus the one famous use of "Welshwomen" as perpetrators of war atrocities in *Henry IV, Part One,* Act One.

The word "Welsh" was used in Elizabethan mockery, almost the ethnic and linguistic equivalent of "Polish" in ethnic jokes in our era, as we can infer from canon court rewards in defamation suits. These court records give us a window—or at least a peephole—onto the oral culture of the Early Modern period. Although an Elizabethan could not sue for being called "Welsh," it was a common modifier in defamation. John Godolphin's discussion of defamation in *Reportorium Canonicum* includes cases like, "Suit being in the Ecclesiastical Court for calling a Man's *Welsh Jade* and *Welsh Rogue*" in the Court of Arches (Godolphin 1678). When the defendant appealed (to the Court of Audience), "and a *Welsh Thief*" was interlineated, but "that Action lies at Common Law," not in the Spiritual Court (Godolphin 1678, 522). Godolphin explains, "And the words *Welsh Jade* were shewn in the Libel to be expounded and so known to be a *Welsh Whore;* which being a Spiritual Cause and examinable there [in the Canon Courts]." On the other hand, *"pimperly Quean"* was judged not actionable, since "quean" was "not a word of certain sense, but an *individuum vagum;* however, an unrelated case on the previous page remarks an early use of this apparently French-derived word for a panderer: *"Thou art a Pimp,* averring that in London that word was known to be intended a *Bawd"* (Godolphin 1678, 521).[2] "Welsh" continued to carry insulting associations through the Restoration, when Congreve's Foible says, "He may have her for the asking, as they say of a Welsh maidenhead" (Congreve 1982, 3.6).

Name-calling is a common convention of comic conflict, as when Pistol challenges his wife's former admirer, Nym, with such sobriquets as: "Iceland dog! thou prick-ear'd cur of Iceland!" and "O hound of Crete" (2.1.42, 73). The paranoiac reciprocal to Pistol is a man who always feels his ethnic background attacked, the Irishman Macmorris, who misinterprets the gentlemanly Fluellen's polite inquiry:

> *Fluellen.* Captain Macmorris, I think, look you, under your correction, there is not many of your nation—
> *Macmorris.* Of my nation? What ish my nation? Ish a villain, a bastard, and a knave, and a rascal. What ish my nation? Who talks of my nation?

(3.2.120–124)

This is lively comic stereotyping, but if we should want to discomedy it, we may note that Macmorris may be reading Fluellen's "real" attitude, a subtext. Earlier in the scene, Fluellen had disagreed with Macmorris's military strategy, saying to Captain Gower, "By Cheshu, he is an ass. . . . He has no more directions in the true disciplines of the wars, look you, of the Roman disciplines, than is a puppy-dog" (3.2.70).

Such name-calling is one of the pervasive pastimes of the human mind. Every oral culture has a taunting game. Whether we call it "flyting" as in the English fifteenth century, or the "dozens" as in contemporary African American culture, quick wit at mutual insult appears to be an universal amusement. Flyting is of course a literary form (e.g., Skelton's "Tunning of Eleanor Rumming") as well as an oral form. Murray's *OED* defines it first as "contention, wrangling; scolding, rebuking" and then as a literary form: "Poetical invective: chiefly, a kind of contest practiced by the Scottish poets of the sixteenth century, in which two persons assailed each other alternately with tirades of abusive verse." Note that Murray marginalizes so raw a wit by classifying flyting as an ethnic Scottish practice.

Walter Ong considers our contemporary ethnic patter to be largely a male adolescent ritual, as in previous work he showed Latin instruction in the Renaissance to be. Here he writes of *Orality and Literacy:*

> Many, if not all, oral or residually oral cultures strike literates as extraordinarily agonistic in their verbal performance. . . . Standard in oral societies across the world, reciprocal name-calling has been fitted with a specific name in linguistics: flyting (or fliting). Growing up in a still dominantly oral culture, certain young black males in the United States, the Caribbean, and elsewhere, engage in what is known variously as the "dozens" or "joning" or "sounding" or by other names, in which one opponent tries to outdo the other in vilifying the other's mother. (Ong 1982, 44)

During my schooldays in Springfield, Massachusetts, this word-game (though it did not seem like a game at the time) was called, probably because of its prevalence in the army, "ranking out." The principal difference between this American street game and the insulting repartee in the Shakespearean text is that one's mother is seldom the subject of Shakespearean insult. It was, after all, quite a different oral culture. But literature editors and commentators should not be too quick to gloss puns and combative insult as peculiarities of Elizabethan taste; rather, they appear universal attributes of oral cultures.

If not one's mother, towards whom was Elizabethan insult addressed? What was the word thing an Elizabethan could call another? Besides "Welsh," "Hedge-Priest," "cuckold" and "wittal" (a knowing cuckold) were popular, as was earlier "priest's whore" in the archdiocese of Norwich from 1520 to 1555.[3] The conflation of both religious and sexual marginality appear in cases such as the Jesuit priest condemned for his part in the Gunpowder Plot. Garnet was "falsely accused of fornication with Mrs. Vaux, a slander he repudiated in a speech on the scaffold" (Muir 1973, xviii). Later, during the reign of Charles I, one Aylsworth and his wife sued in canon court a certain Gooday for saying of Aylsworth that "he was a Cuckhold and a Wittal, which is worse than a Cuckhold, and that Aylsworth had layen with Ayloff's wife" (Godolphin 1678, 514). When the case was reviewed by an higher ecclesiastical court, all the court agreed that "there ought not to have been any Suit for the first words, they being too general; yet being coupled with a particular, shewing that the wife committed such an Offense with such a particular person, that they be not now general words of spleen in common and usual discourse and parlance."

Incidentally, another case in Godolphin bears strong resemblance to one of the greatest comic scenes in the *Henriad*. Consider: D. had sued T. that "whereas she was of good Fame, and kept a Victualling House in good Order; that D. said T. had published that D. kept an house of Bawdry" (Godolphin 1678, 523).[4] We recall Falstaff's accusation, "This house is turned bawdyhouse, they pick pockets" (*Henry IV, Part One* 3.3.99), and Mistress Quickly's defense, "I am an honest man's wife." Falstaff's comic slanders in that scene turn on his tone, which we can hear across four centuries, "Go to, you are a woman, go." Clearly, to be called "woman" is not actionable; it is all in the tone of implication. We can hear Falstaff's tone because of Mistress Quickly's denial, "Who, I? No, I defy thee. I was never call'd so in mine own house before" (3.3.63). Falstaff even slanders her with grateful praise when he calls her "a thing" (perhaps the French *belle chose?*) and when challenged by the Hostess to say "what thing?" exudes, "Why, a thing to thank God on." Of course, the culminating joke is the Hostess's inadvertent self-slander, "Thou *or any man* knows where to have me, thou knave, thou!" [my emphasis]. Incidentally, to be called a "knave" was actionable in certain courts in this period.

Many comic scenes have such sources, if we may adapt the old scholarly term to the unwritten and nonwriting culture of the period. Perhaps court records add fuel to the critical common-place that comedy is somehow more realistic, closer to the world of cash and commerce. Then again, Shakespeare transforms the everyday fracas by a change of tone. His quotidian variations in *Henry V* involve linguistic play; for instance, the "Gallia" in my title. Pistol plans to use to his advantage the Welsh thrashing he receives from Fluellen, "And patches will I get unto these cud-gell'd scars, / And [swear] I got them in the Gallia wars" (5.1.89). Onions and Evans gloss "Gallia" as "French," although Onions notes that it means "Welsh" in the chiasmus of "Gallia and Gaul, French and Welsh" (*The Merry Wives of Windsor* 3.1.98). Reading Pistol's phrase as a multilingual pun typical of this play, clearly "the Gallia wars" are his private battle with a Welshman on French soil. Pistol's hometown boast about his wounds in the "Gallia wars" will be doubly true, since he got them in Gallia from a Celt!

In Elizabethan England, the French and the Welsh held the dubious affinity of mutual marginality. They were considered the natural recipients of insult, congenital butts of humor. Moreover, in a familiar corollary of scapegoating, they were themselves blamed. Both the French and the Welsh were considered unnatu-rally quarrelsome; and, it must be said, often unnaturally learned. In *The Merry Wives of Windsor*, for example, Shakespeare sets up comic strife between the Welsh Parson and the French Physician, i.e., the intelligentsia of Windsor! When Dr. Caius and Reverend Evans offer to duel, the Host steps in,

> Disarm them, and let them question. Let them keep their limbs whole and hack our English.
>
> (3.1.76)

Shakespeare's whole project in *Henry V* is exactly such a substitu-tion of ethnic and dialect stage conflict for stage wars of national-ity. The author "keeps the play whole" by "hacking our English" rather than through swaggering stage swordplay. In *The Merry Wives of Windsor*, the Host later urges the very kind of resolution that *Henry V* achieves, "Peace, I say, Gallia and Gaul, French and Welsh, soul-curer and body-curer!" (3.1.97–98). But in the world of *Henry V*, there are no bourgeois (or guild) distinctions between career choices like doctor and minister (those very distinctions upon which Chaucer's Canterburian comedy depends). In *Henry*

V, everybody is a soldier. Hence Falstaffian mockery of heroic virtues must die. Another kind of comedy takes its place, the comedy of ethnic difference seen through the lens of dialect and accent.

While plays like *The Taming of the Shrew, Love's Labor's Lost*, and *The Merry Wives of Windsor* include comic scenes of language instruction, exclusively in Latin, no other play actually culminates in a scene like Henry's wooing of Katherine, one of the most charming love scenes in the canon. Here Shakespeare graces a foregone, forced, patriarchally arranged marriage with all the qualities of intimate self-revelation. King Henry displays a captivating self-knowledge in confessing his lack of looks, as well as his lack of skills in dancing and in speaking French. Charmingly, Katherine does not follow the most Shakespearean of Henry's courting conceits: "And, Kate, when France is mine and I am yours, then yours is France and you are mine," to which she answers, "I cannot tell what is dat" (5.2.175–77). Any student in an introduction to literature course might say the same.

This linguistic hodgepodge, composed of multilingual puns and malapropisms caused by dialect variants, results in an overall comic effect that distances the grand historical questions with all their political and compositional constraints. For instance, right after King Henry's horrible speech threatening future atrocities, "Your fathers taken by the silver beards, / And their most reverend heads dash'd to the walls; / Your naked infants spitted upon pikes" (3.3.36–38), comes Princess Katherine's English lesson, which ends in multilingual bawdy. She is justifiably horrified at the English words for a bodily extremity and for "dress": "Le foot et le count! O Seigneur Dieu!" (3.4.52). In the Riverside edition, Evans glosses the joke here, "She mistakes them for indecent French words," but that is not strictly true. She pronounces them as words that the audience can conflate with indecent English, "le foot" probably the "F" word (whether it's the French high back vowel or the English middle one), and "le count" doubtless the word the Wife of Bath pronounces, "queynte." In fact, it is so clearly meant to be heard as an English obscenity that it takes imagination to guess what English word Katherine is learning, evidently "gown."

Such wordplay provides the freedom that the historical givens (both historical details and Elizabethan political necessities) constrain. To apply Freud's "Wit and the Various Forms of the Comic," Shakespeare overcomes the textual inhibitions of historical constraint and vexed ethnic relations with his multilingual wordplay. In another instance, when Pistol the swaggerer takes a prisoner, Monsieur le Fer, Pistol mistakes his despairing oath, "O Seigneur Dieu" for a military I.D.: "O Signieur Dew should be a gentleman" (4.4.7). Pistol goes on to intimidate the prisoner to compel a high ransom: "I'll fer him, and firk him, and ferret him. Discuss the same in French unto him" (4.4.30). His boy translator confesses, "I do not know the French for fer, and ferret, and firk." In fact, we modern readers may not know the English for them either, until Pistol says them. They are part of Pistol's stagey, alliterative braggadocio, in the manner of the player's Priam in *Hamlet*. A few lines later, Pistol repeats his boy's French in a pidgin reminiscent of the "Moscovite" capture of Parolles in *All's Well That Ends Well*; echoing the threat to cut his throat, "de couper votre gorge," Pistol parrots, "Owy, cuppele gorge, parmafoy." (Recall that Parolles was greeted with, "Throca mouvosus, cargo, cargo, cargo.")

Shakespeare appears to discover his comic emphasis as he writes further into the play. Fluellen's accent, for instance, grows more pronounced; or, his pronunciation grows more accented. In earlier scenes, Fluellen transposes an occasional unvoiced "f" for a "v"; but, by Act Four, scene seven, he always says "p" for "b," often "t" for "d," and occasionally "th" for "d" in words like "athversary." These result in "wear the leek upon Saint Tavy's Day [St. Davy's Day]" (4.7.101–102), "All the water in the Wye cannot wash your Majesty's Welsh plood out of your pody" (4.7.107), "Come, wherefore should you be so pashful? your shoes is not so good" (4.8.71).

Shakespeare's most daring and problematic distancing via dialect occurs earlier in the scene, where perhaps the greatest atrocity is aerated with comedy: "*Fluellen*. Kill the poys and the luggage! 'Tis expressly against the law of arms" (4.7.1–2). Then, to Gower's approval of the King's order, reciprocally, to kill the French prisoners, Fluellen claims kin: "Ay, he was porn at Monmouth, Captain Gower. What call you the town's name where Alexander the Pig was born?" (4.7.11–13). This is the line that all the "p's" for "b's" set up. Gower corrects him, "Alexander the Great," to which Fluellen, sensibly,

Why, I pray you, is not "pig" great? The pig, or the great, or the mighty, or the huge, or the magnanimous, are all one reckonings, save the phrase is a little variations. (4.7.15)

I wonder what a French genre critic like Rapin would do with a passage like this one. It is closest to modern absurdist drama, in which terrible events are submerged in a delightful language game.

Fluellen is not the only comic Welsh character. King Henry himself claims kin, "For I am Welsh, you know, good countryman" (4.7.105); moreover, he enacts the fellow comedian as well. After Agincourt, Henry becomes almost a *servus callidus*, setting up the Fluellen–Williams glove-token in the cap conflict. One would think an English Alexander had better things to do. But no, he must now lead the actors into the realms of comedy, as he first led his troops into France.

Comedy in the histories is often an agonistic strife of mutual insult à la the "dozens" of black culture. One of my favorite examples of such an insult contest in the *Henriad* occurs in *Henry IV, Part One*, just before the extempore play, when to Hal's fat insults, "this bed-presser, this horse-back breaker, this huge hill of flesh–" Falstaff responds with anorectic jogger jokes:

> 'Sblood, you starveling, you eelskin, you dried neat's tongue, you bull's pizzle, you stock-fish! O for breath to utter what is like thee! you tailer's yard, you sheath, you bowcase, you vile standing tuck—
> (2.4.244)

Falstaff has won the flyting. His brilliant plenitude of metaphors for thinness (*pace* Harbage's count favoring Hal) suggests the speed of the author's mind—and they ring out today in an era of scarecrow beauty.

In my other favorite case of Shakespearean "dozens," the sides are unequal, but the victim literally "asks for it." In the last act of *Love's Labor's Lost*, the professorial Holofernes keeps his aplomb upon stage until:

> *Holofernes.* I will not be put out of countenance.
> *Berowne.* Because thou hast no face.
> *Holofernes.* What is this?
> *Boyet.* A cittern-head.
> *Dumain.* The head of a bodkin.
> *Berowne.* A death's face in a ring.
> *Longaville.* The face of an old Roman coin, scarce seen.
> *Boyet.* The pommel of Caesar's falchion.
> *Dumain.* The carv'd-bone face on a flask.
> *Berowne.* Saint George's half-cheek in a brooch.
> *Dumain.* Ay, and in a brooch of lead.
> *Berowne.* Ay, and worn in the cap of a tooth-drawer.
> (5.2.607ff)

Holofernes admits defeat, partly because of the odds, four against
one; his mockers are not playing the oral culture game fairly.
Holofernes rightly says, "This is not generous, not gentle, not
humble." But it *is* funny. (Perhaps this game is never played fairly,
for certainly Falstaff is the equal of four, in both girth and wit.) Let
us return from the agon of insult to specifically ethnic differences.

The ethnic discord in *Henry IV, Part One,* between Northumbrian Hotspur and the Welsh Glendower, remains unresolved except "pro tem," during the battle. Hostpur mocks Glendower's
accent, as well as his magical beliefs. Glendower claims wondrous
events occurred at his nativity:

> Give me leave
> To tell you once again that at my birth
> The front of heaven was full of firey shapes,
> The goats ran from the mountains, and the herds
> Were strangely clamorous to the frighted fields.
> These signs have mark'd me extraordinary.

> (3.1.35–40)

Hotspur responds, of course, with a simple ethnic slur, "I think
there's no man speaks better Welsh." And later, in a direct contention of wills over their respective portions of the divided kingdom,
when Glendower says he will stand up to him, Hotspur sneers,
"Let me not understand you then, / Speak it in Welsh" (3.1.119–
20). Across the centuries, we can hear the taunt of that "Welsh."
It is so powerful that mighty Glendower sounds apologetic, de-
fensive,

> I can speak English, lord, as well as you,
> For I was train'd up in the English court,
> Where being but young I framed to the harp
> Many an English ditty lovely well.

Hotspur, like any American schoolboy jock, mocks these literary
and artistic accomplishments, especially writing poetry.

> I had rather hear a brazen canstick turn'd,
> Or a dry wheel grate on the axle-tree,
> And that would set my teeth nothing on edge,
> Nothing so much as mincing poetry.

In this scene, Glendower's speech is not perforated with dialect
spellings and humor, although I assume he has a Welsh lilt to his

pronunciation. Hotspur the Northumbrian philistine contrasts with the bookish but druidical Glendower. Ethnic differences reinforce character differences.

In *Henry V* the comic agon counterpoints the battles and even displaces them. Consider as a parallel the literacy jokes against Cade in *Henry VI, Part Two;* those suggest to me a comic displacement of real charges, ongoing grievances, that may have prevented that play from performance, as they did *The Book of Sir Thomas More.* Cade's charges parody the usual court procedure in cases of treason, profanity, blasphemy, and slander. Cade there seems a Woody Allen, charging that Lord Say has "traitorously corrupted the youth of the realm in erecting a grammar school . . . [and] that thou has men about thee that usually talk of a *noun* and a *verb,* and such abominable words as no Christian ear can endure" (my emphasis; 4.7.32). The revolutionary Cade accuses Lord Say,

> Thou has appointed justices of the peace, to call poor men before them about matters they were not able to answer. Moreover, thou hast put them in prison, and because they could not read, thou hast hang'd them, when, indeed, only for that cause they have been most worthy to live. (4.7.41)

A reader's sympathies throughout this lie with Lord Say—all the more so if one teaches, for Lord Say may be the first literary character to be fired or killed because of students' or rebels' evaluations based on ignorance.

Even if Cade's topsy-turvy accusations appear true from historical records (and they do), how are we to move from such hilarity to the bald fact that Lord Say is killed by the mob? It appears to me that Shakespeare, in a rare passage, does not fully control his material here. I do credit him with a wily use of the literary accusation, where literacy is substituted for other real political objections that would be treasonable if presented on stage. Tudor monarchs had no particular love of uprising scenes, so Shakespeare tries to get around the censors by distancing the rebellion with some comedy. It works. After all, *The Book of Sir Thomas More* was prevented from performance because of its rebellion scene, which Tilney interlineated, "leave out the insurrection wholely."

The comic dispacement in *Henry V* is much more successful than in the early history, although here too there is a modern, almost absurdist sense of violence and terror behind wordplay. The difference is that Shakespeare lets the verbal and comic take over; when the battle for France is over, the comic Franglais hodgepodge wins over negotiations or sealed proclamations. The stage has been less graced with the business of swordplay, and it is likely that some playgoers will be disappointed. In this context, all the unusual choral apologies ("this unworthy scaffold" "this cockpit," "this wooden O") make particular sense. Shakespeare has indeed been "mangling by starts the full course of their glory"; in fact, if my argument holds, he has not dispensed with that history. He has let another kind of play unfold, a comedy that is almost a romance, in that this comedy resolves those ethnic and political differences that would eventually pull the Stuart settlement apart—and, not incidentally, close all the unworthy scaffolds in England.

Sexual slander in *Othello* leads to tragic scapegoating. Interestingly, Iago slanders both the Moor's supposed lasciviousness and Desdemona's Venetian upper-class sexual mores. Ethnic and racial differences play into Iago's supposed jokes in that tragedy. In *Othello*, the ethnic differences grow; language that the Moor thought he understood he now doubts. I have shown that to be called "Welsh," or to be accused of being Catholic—and specifically, a Catholic official who breaks his vows, seduces in the hedges—these are terms of difference to which stigma also attaches in seventeenth-century England. However, the continuing human love of gossip (what Jane Austen calls "the accustomary intervention of kind friends") makes the sexual charges appear almost modern; for instance, recent news coverage of an evangelist's liaison essentially charged him with being an "Hedge-Priest," except that in Tudor England the word "priest" carried the added onus of an illegal minority religion—and an international political organization. "Hedge-Priest" may translate into 1950s American lingo, "[sexually] Dirty Commie"!

Shakespeare relies upon ethnic humor, namely dialect jokes, in his comic stereotyping in *Henry V*. As in his comedy composed in the same years, *The Merry Wives of Windsor*, the principal butts of humor are the French and Welsh accents; indeed, much of the *Henriad* can be seen as an elaborate Welsh joke. Defamation suits from canon court records, the closest we can come to Early Modern oral culture, show that to be Welsh was the Elizabethan ethnic and linguistic equivalent of being "Polish" in our era, with the one significant proviso that our greatest national hero be Polish. (In the year that Lech Walesa is movingly welcomed to our Congress as a teacher of democracy, this proviso may not be far-fetched.) For at the heart of *Henry V*, and its dialect humor, is

King Henry's nationality, confessed to Fluellen, "For I am Welsh, you know, good countryman" (4.7.105). Instead of Falstaff's imperious incredulity, "Have I liv'd to stand at the taunt of one that makes fritters of English?" (*The Merry Wives of Windsor* 5.5.143), the reader or playgoer is urged toward tolerance, first by King Henry himself, "Though it appear a little out of fashion, / There is much care and valor in this Welshman," and finally by Gower, "You thought, because he could not speak in the native garb, he could not therefore handle an English cudgel. You find it otherwise, and henceforth let a Welsh correction teach you a good English condition" (5.1.75). The charm of the final scene includes even the French in this toleration.

As I have said, this dream of multiethnic toleration was not to exist in the Renaissance, except on stage. At the very time of this play, the Irish were in continuing outbreaks, as too the Scots by midcentury. It is perhaps not jingoistic to argue that the ideals of multiethnic toleration have been most achieved, however moderately, in our own New World. Unfortunately, Branagh's recent film version cuts all the ethnic and comedic byplay that we have examined; linguistically, he keeps only the Franglais of Katherine's English lesson and the courting scene. If, as I have argued and Schlegel first observed, this play aspires to the structure of comedy, this director's cutting of the Welsh and Irish accents disassembles the text even more than his foregrounding of poor Bardolph's hanging for stealing the religious item (a "pax"), or his excision of the king's order to execute the hostages, or his general cinematic substitution of luscious pictorial representation (say, the battlefield at Agincourt) for Shakespeare's apologetic appeal to the theater audience's imagination: "Think when we talk of horses that you see them." In Branagh's film, Katherine first appears as if in a modern solarium, awash with light. Where did she come from—another planet? This almost works. Such discontinuities are commonplace in the modern cinema, possibly because of television's influence. But the final, courting scene fits even less. Some audiences around Boston, unfamiliar with the text, left after the resounding choral "Non nobis" and the spectacular camera pan across the beaten dead horses of Agincourt. This was The End, literally a Dead End, of a different story.

Notes

1. From Marvin Spevack, *The Harvard Concordance to Shakespeare* (Cambridge: Belknap Press of Harvard University, 1973).

2. Note that London slang was not used nationwide.

3. See Ralph Houlbrooke, *Church Courts and the People During the English Reformation, 1520–1570* (Oxford: Oxford University Press, 1979), 79–81.

4. The point in law is that keeping an "House of Bawdry" was determinable at Common Law upon indictment, whereas "Thou art a Bawd" was determinable in Spiritual Court (Godolphin 1678, 37.13).

Shakespearean Comic Character: Ethos and Epideictic in *Cymbeline*

CHRISTY DESMET

In *Of Grammatology*, Jacques Derrida pursued to its conclusion the lesson of Saussurian linguistics, the nonidentity of the signifier and signified: writing, says Derrida, is finally the "forgetting of the self" (Derrida 1974, 24).[1] Shakespearean studies has adopted this axiom as a critical imperative, and recent years have seen a spate of books dismantling the myth of essential selfhood in Shakespeare's plays. In *The Subject of Tragedy*, Catherine Belsey defines eloquently the subject's fate under writing's rigorous rule:

> To be a subject is to have access to signifying practice, to identify with the "I" of utterance and the "I" who speaks. The subject is held in place in a specific discourse, a specific knowledge, by the meanings available there. In so far as signifying practice always precedes the individual, is always learned, the subject is a subjected being, an effect of the meanings it seems to possess. (Belsey 1985, 5).

In at least one important way, however, the new attack on character resembles the old reverence for Shakespearean character, for both tend to privilege tragedy over comedy; the tacit assumption seems to be that while comedy can reflect cultural assumptions or dramatize the struggle between individual and ideology, tragedy addresses more directly the formation and deformation of the self. For this reason, Aristotle's four requirements for the tragic hero in chapter fifteen of the *Poetics* (goodness or badness, appropriateness or decorum, verisimilitude, and consistency) are still powerfully evocative for critics, whether they represent an authentic psychological model or a powerful myth to be debunked; in either case, we lack alternative paradigms for reading and evaluating Shakespearean character.

In this essay I would like to suggest a way of analyzing Shakespearean character through ethical rather than psychological categories, an approach that is traditionally associated with comedy rather than tragedy. For my exemplary text I have chosen Shakespeare's *Cymbeline*, which is poised generically between comedy and tragedy and therefore invites speculation about the relationship between psychology and ethical character. In a sense I am building on the work done by Karen Newman in *Shakespeare's Rhetoric of Comic Character*, but focusing more explicitly on ethical character has led me to concentrate on epideictic rhetoric and its relevance to dramatic characterization.

Criticism about *Cymbeline* often returns to the problem of its disjointed characterization. Posthumus Leonatus, a poor but worthy gentleman, secretly marries Imogen, the king's daughter. Banished by her angry father, he takes refuge in Italy, where Iachimo, a jealous Italian, goads him into a wager on his wife's virtue. Iachimo, by a trick, wins the bet; Posthumus, although his friends are skeptical, immediately accepts Iachimo's lurid account of Imogen's infidelity, flies into a rage, then plots the murder of his supposedly errant wife. In the brief moment it takes for him to exit, then reappear on stage, he is transformed from the most sanguine of husbands to the most bitter of misogynists. When Rome and England go to war, Posthumus fights on the side of his Italian hosts but then changes his mind, and, dressed as a peasant, fights for England against the intruders; the change of clothes, signifying his shifting loyalties, shows Posthumus to be as quixotic in affairs of honor as in affairs of the heart.

In *Cymbeline*, characters respond to events rather than shape their own destinies. Like Posthumus on the battlefield, they change their minds with their clothes, to fit altered circumstances. Critics have discussed the difficulty of distinguishing appearance from reality in this play, plus the use of verbal and presentational clothing imagery to emphasize discrepancies between externals and inner essence; they disagree, however, about the significance of *Cymbeline's* inconsistent characterization.[2] Responses to the play's characters fall roughly into two categories. Some readers consider them as by-products of *Cymbeline's* byzantine plot, rather than as individuals with unified personalities and moral natures. It has been argued, most extensively by R. A. Foakes, that in *Cymbeline* Shakespeare creates a dramatic world in which "human intentions, the will, the act of choice, play a very subdued role." By making his characters discontinuous, Shakespeare represents the human condition as a mutable and self-contradictory and asks spectators not to interpret events, but to "wonder at their strangeness" (Foakes 1971, 95, 115).[3] Other readers, particularly psychoanalytic critics of recent years, seek a deeper coherence beneath the chaotic surface of the characters' behavior. Posthumus, for instance, according to Murray Schwartz's extensive analysis of the play, behaves inconsistently for good reason: burdened with a cultural worship of women, he treads an uneasy path between "platonic sublimation" and "crude sexual expression" (Schwartz 1970, 231). Arthur Kirsch agrees that Posthumus believes Iachimo's slander against Imogen so easily because "he is unconsciously disposed to do so": he begins "at once to over-idealize her chastity and to resent and doubt it" (Kirsch 1981, 147).[4]

In this schematic account of critical responses to *Cymbeline*, both groups assume—wrongly, I will argue—that "character" is intrinsically coherent, even if its logic is difficult to discern. The argument that *Cymbeline's* sketchy characterization indicates Shakespeare's lack of interest in "character" is undermined by the fact that individuals within the play obsessively rationalize the inscrutable behavior of those around them. Jupiter appears near the end of *Cymbeline* to claim credit for its neat resolution, explaining that he has afflicted Posthumus with the trials of Job to increase his happiness: "Whom best I love I cross; to make my gift, / the more delay'd, delighted" (5.4.101–102). Jupiter's control over events, however, is open to question; he contributes only a riddling prophecy to the play's resolution, leaving sharp-witted Imogen to spot Posthumus's ring on Iachimo's finger and start the chain of revelations that ends the play happily.[5] Furthermore, the characters respond to their trials less with "wonder" than with a driving desire to understand the strange events controlling them. Posthumus, disillusioned by Imogen's "infidelity," surmises that his own mother must have cuckolded his father; his rage and grief find an immediate outlet in explanations. Imogen, certain that she can read Posthumus's inner self as she reads the characters of his writing, cannot tolerate Iachimo's innuendo about his behavior abroad: she asks to be given bad news plainly, "for certainties / Either are past remedies, or, timely knowing, / The remedy then born" (1.6.96–98). Even when she awakes to discover Cloten's headless corpse dressed in Posthumus's clothes, within a few lines Imogen surmises that Pisanio (Posthumus's servant) must have murdered him; her enthusiasm for certainty has not been dampened by experience.

On the other hand, while psychoanalytic criticism has done much to fill in the play's sketchy characterization, *Cymbeline's* action turns on questions about *ethos* or ethical character rather than about psychology. Both the urge to evaluate moral character and the difficulties attendant on moral judgment are evident even in *Cymbeline*'s opening lines. The First Gentleman, explaining the chaos at Cymbeline's court, struggles to define Posthumus Leonatus, who

> is a creature such
> As, to seek through the regions of the earth
> For one his like, there would be something failing
> In him that should compare. I do not think
> So fair an outward and such stuff within
> Endows a man but he.
>
> (1.1.19–24)

"You speak him far," the Second Gentleman remarks, with perhaps a trace of skepticism. Critics, as well as the Second Gentleman, have responded warily to the First Gentleman's hyperbole. Murray Schwartz hears doubt in the First Gentleman's hesitation, a questioning of Posthumus's exemplary virtue when he says that "I do not think / So fair an outward and such stuff within / Endows a man but he" (Schwartz 1970, 232). G. Wilson Knight, who locates the problem in the First Gentleman's style rather than in Posthumus's character, argues that the speaker's style becomes "periphrastically involved in the attempt to define an extreme worth without committing itself to the high-sounding phrase" (Knight 1947, 141). Others see in the stylistic distortions of this set piece a more general reflection on rhetoric's shortcomings, a failure of language as an empirical tool that results in what Maurice Hunt has called "inadvertent slander" (Hunt 1980, 324).[6] The First Gentleman's rhetoric may ring falsely in modern ears, but a Renaissance audience would recognize his speech as a perfectly conventional if truncated *encomium*, or speech praising Posthumus's moral character. When challenged, the First Gentleman stands his ground but apologizes for his own shortcomings as orator: "I do extend him, sir, within himself, / Crush him together rather than unfold / His measure duly" (1.1.25–27). An inchoate metaphor conflates Posthumus with his character portrait: rather than stretch the "stuff" or fabric of Posthumus's nature beyond the limits of credibility, the First Gentleman insists, he "crushes" it together.[7] His contention that Posthumus is too noble to be compared with other men ("outdoing topos"), and his apology for "crushing" such a superlative subject ("inexpressibility topos") are both part of the encomiast's standard repertoire.[8]

I would like to reexamine *Cymbeline*'s concern with ethical character and with the rhetoric used to represent character. Madeleine Doran, in her thorough study of form in the Elizabethan drama, has noted the influence of Renaissance ethical theory on dramatic characterization and has identified the presence of rhetorical forms such as the encomium in the drama.[9] But the importance of rhetoric to understanding both moral character and characterization has not been explored sufficiently. The First Gentleman's encomium, as a formal speech of praise, belongs to epideictic rhetoric, the category used by classical rhetoricians to designate all kinds of ceremonial oratory, speeches designed for "display" rather than for the courtroom or the political arena. Epideictic is associated with the ornamented middle style in classical rhetoric; that connection is solidified as poetry gradually comes to be subsumed under epideictic. Defined more specifically in the Renaissance as the rhetoric of praise and blame, epideictic also comes to be associated more strongly with ethics, particularly in Renaissance defenses of poetry, which shield poetry from charges of indecency by classifying it under epideictic rhetoric. By praising good behavior and vituperating bad, poetry nudges audiences toward virtue.[10] Thus, in the Renaissance, decorative style and explorations of ethical character can be linked.

At three crucial points in the play's action—Iachimo's rhapsody over the sleeping Imogen (2.2.10–51), Posthumus's rant against womankind (2.5.1–35), and the masque of the Leonati (5.4.1–150)—*Cymbeline* dramatizes the tensions that characterize epideictic rhetoric, examining self-consciously the relationship between *ethos* and the decorative rhetoric used for its representation. Iachimo's fanciful picture of Imogen as a seductive Venus, a showpiece of characterization that wins the wager for him, begins as an *effictio* or blazon, an enthusiastic head-to-toe catalogue of her physical charms. To enact his fantasy of a blissful night spent with Posthumus's wife, Iachimo relies on the decorative figures and tropes—hyperbole, metaphor, and other figures of amplification—that characterize epideictic rhetoric.[11] Imogen's skin is white as a lily, her lips like "rubies unparagon'd"; even the candle is attracted to her heavenly eyes, and tries to peep under Imogen's eyelids, to see her blue eyes "now canopied / Under these windows, white and azure lac'd / With blue of heaven's own tinct" (2.2.21–23).

Iachimo's stylistic excesses are frequently linked to his role as rapist or as artist.[12] Both possibilities are suggested by his verse, which marks Shakespeare's return to an earlier style in his late plays, what Harley Granville-Barker calls his "new Euphuism of imagination" (Granville-Barker 1958, 1: 498). Yet as Granville-Barker also observes, this new euphuism is strained, since thoughts or emotions behind the poetry often seem too farfetched for the occasion or speaker; in this case, especially, Iachimo's extravagant poetry seems doomed to self-parody. Just as he reaches a climax, Iachimo abruptly changes tone:

> But my design!
> To note the chamber, I will write all down:
> Such and such pictures; there the window; such
> Th' adornment of her bed; the arras, figures,
> Why, such and such; and the contents o' th' story.
> (2.2.23–27)

Suddenly he reverts to business: no longer a passionate Tarquin gloating over his Lucrece, Iachimo has become an accountant.[13] Iachimo's sudden change from lover to scribe (he exchanges the penis for the pen, one is tempted to say) typifies Shakespeare's deflationary dramatic technique in this play, what Leonard Powlick has labeled his "comedy of anticlimax" (Powlick 1974, 131–41). For this reason, although the first half of this scene may be susceptible to psychological analysis, the surprising twists in Iachimo's performance encourage self-consciousness about his rhetoric and about Shakespeare's dramaturgy. As a cunningly manipulative Petrarchan poet, Iachimo remakes Imogen's nature at will, transforming the chaste wife who retires to bed early with a book into an overblown love goddess. Iachimo, as rhetorician, successfully gives his verbal picture *enargeia*, defined by Erasmus in this way: "we use [*enargeia*] whenever, for the sake of amplifying, adorning, or pleasing, we do not state a thing simply, but set it forth to be viewed as though portrayed in color on a tablet, so that it may seem that we have painted, not narrated, and that the reader has seen, not read" (Erasmus 1963, 47). With metaphor, then, he gives Imogen life and motion.

At the turning point in his staged "seduction," however, Iachimo's style flattens out. Gone are the enthusiastic metaphors, the urge to kiss and touch: as he bustles about, taking notes and stealing Imogen's bracelet, Iachimo's poetry degenerates into noise, grunts, and exclamations to accompany his frantic gestures. His loss of eloquence calls attention to the uneasy relationship between his hyperbolic praise and its subject and questions rhetoric's metamorphic power. Iachimo leaps back into his trunk, crying out "one, two, three: time, time!" (2.2.51). The tolling bell, a signal that the speech has spanned three hours, testifies also to Iachimo's impotence as orator. Tarquin made good his rape; in Iachimo's proleptic speech, however, rhetoric must substitute for experience—the event is over before the speechifying has ended. The reminder of stage time reinforces another detail of staging, the belated revelation that Imogen has left her copy of Ovid's *Metamorphoses* open at the rape of Philomel. Thus Iachimo finds that instead of directing the action, he follows a script by Ovid.[14]

Speculation about rhetoric's relation to character, aroused by the metadramatic touches in the bedroom scene, is complicated further when Posthumus, having accepted Iachimo's fictional account, reworks the story of Imogen's sexual infidelity. In his speech, however, the speaker's relationship to his subject matter becomes the focus of interest. Wolfgang Clemen cautions that many Renaissance soliloquies are not spontaneous outbursts revealing a character's inner self; Posthumus's soliloquy, although marked by Philario's alarm as a speech of passion, nevertheless reveals little of its speaker's psychology.[15] Posthumus's rhetorical method, which progressively distances both speaker and stage audience from his subject—Imogen's supposed adultery—works against his highly charged emotion. He opens with a sweeping question followed by an enthymeme, a probable rather than necessary syllogism that lacks one term:

> Is there no way for men to be, but women
> Must be half-workers? We are all bastards,
> And that most venerable man which I
> Did call my father, was I know not where
> When I was stamp'd.
>
> (2.5.1–5)

From the general premise that "we are all bastards", Posthumus concludes that his own mother must have cuckolded his father; this belief in turn prompts the ugly image of Iachimo making love to Imogen: "Perchance he spoke not, but / Like a full-acorn'd boar, a German one, / Cried "O!" and mounted" (2.5.15–17). Posthumus's soliloquy frustrates attempts to follow the progress of his passion because his theme is developed deductively rather than inductively, deriving a galling image from an unspoken cultural cliché: "women are all inconstant."

Imagery also becomes disruptive. Freer writes that the imagery "that tumbles out now is radically mixed and only barely under rational control. Coining and tools, sun and snow, the 'yellow Iachimo' and the 'full-acorn'd boar'—it is as if Posthumus's belief in Imogen's infidelity had released a flood of images, the sheer quantity of which he could not have managed before" (Freer 1981, 114). The central boar image, in particular, fails to resonate elsewhere in the play. Several possible puns exist: on "boar" and "boor," on "German" as cousin, and on "full-acorn'd" as a reference to Iachimo's sexuality (his testicles) or his uncivilized nature (as one who eats acorns). But because these puns give the comparison an aural and intellectual rather than a visual emphasis, they undermine the picture of animal copulation. The fantasy, in other words, lack enargeia. Posthumus quickly abandons logic for imagination, so that his change of heart seems a fait accompli. Posthumus himself appears on stage as two radically different stereotypes—fond lover and raging cuckold—but shifts identities instantaneously and offstage, since Philario and his companions leave the stage in search of Posthumus. Thus he rehearses, more than he develops, a profound disgust for Imogen's "adultery."

While the first half of his rant casts an unreal light on Posthumus's motives, the second offers an alternative picture of Imogen's ethical nature. The soliloquy ends with a compact list of women's faults:

> There's no motion
> That tends to vice in man, but I affirm
> It is the woman's part: be it lying, note it,
> The woman's: flattering, hers; deceiving, hers;
> Lust, and rank thoughts, hers, hers; revenges, hers;
> Ambitions, covetings, change of prides, disdain,
> Nice longing, slanders, mutability,
> All faults that name, nay, that hell knows,
> Why, hers, in part, or all; but rather, all.

> (2.5.20–28)

A set piece within the already heavily framed soliloquy, this *ethopoeia* lacks the concreteness that often characterizes the Renaissance moral "character" as a genre. Posthumus's diction remains resolutely abstract, his style curt. The portrait anatomizes rather than describes woman, unfolding the general concept of inconstancy into its parts by the standard method of *distributio,* or more specifically, by enumeration. Posthumus's *enumeratio* is a list built on nouns. Asyndeton (lack of connectives) and isocolon (repetitive clausal structure) give the enumeration an impersonal authority alien to Posthumus's passion. The speech also exploits the advantages of amplification, ticking off vices in rapid succession until it seems that woman must possess "all faults that name, nay, that hell knows."

Posthumus's excessive style, like Iachimo's, eventually becomes comic. After the angular symmetry of the portrait, which builds in pitch and speech, his rambling, paratactic coda—"hers, in part, or all: *but rather all*" (my emphases) follows lamely. With this belated qualification, Posthumus disrupts his rhythm, and moves toward bathos. As his rhetoric fails, so apparently does Posthumus's rage. No longer set on committing mayhem, he decides instead to write satires against women, to "detest them, curse them," and finally to do nothing at all: "yet 'tis greater skill / In a true hate, to pray they have their will: / The very devils cannot plague them better" (2.5.33–35). In the last line, Posthumus makes the satirist's gesture of disinvolvement; he will let women be their own worst punishment. Adopting a literary stance, he makes ludicrous his righteous indignation: Posthumus as satirist follows a traditional script, reworking the topics covered in popular classical satires such as Juvenal's sixth satire, which incidentally warns another Posthumus against marriage. If Shakespeare does allude to Juvenal's satire, the comparison emphasizes Posthumus's subservience to literary precedent.[16] Just as Iachimo discovers too late that Imogen's *Metamorphoses* foretells his attempted seduction, the advice against marriage ironically comes too late for Posthumus.

The complementary assessments of Imogen's *ethos* work together to confound distinctions between fact and fiction. Iachimo's portrait literally provides the "ground" for Posthumus's—Iachimo may even speak from the back of the stage, while Posthumus moves down front to deliver his soliloquy. Thus, Iachimo's carefully-wrought fiction (in the etymological sense as something "made" or "invented") gives rise to Posthumus's dry ethopoeia; a half-truth, constructed with some degree of self-consciousness, yields a two-dimensional improbability. Ironically, Iachimo's hyperbolic vision has greater verisimilitude than Posthumus's passionate and straightforward analysis of female character; the play's most fictionalized representation of character is therefore the most credible.[17]

The relationship between fact and fiction never stabilizes. As Harley Granville-Barker noticed, Imogen's furniture—not to mention miniature details such as the bracelet and crimson-spotted mole—are fully realized only through Iachimo's retelling of his alleged seduction (Granville-Barker 1958, 1: 473). A practical necessity for the acting company, Shakespeare's reliance on verbal imagery for this emblematic moment also calls attention to the fact that Iachimo's damning evidence against Imogen (like Desdemona's handkerchief in Cassio's hands) is a reconstruction rather than a visible presence. Iachimo's rhetoric, although supplementing the dramatic scene centered around Iachimo's trunk and Imogen's bed, becomes central to any attempt to weigh the merits of competing versions of the "seduction."

Discussions of epideictic rhetoric recognize that hyperbolic praise and verifiable fact coexist uneasily in speeches of praise and blame. In Aristotle's *Rhetoric,* for instance, fact is subordinated to rhetorical purpose; praise and blame are based on deeds, but those deeds may be real or imaginary, and unsuitable material may be excised.[18] Tradition and common knowledge constrain the orator, since his encomium must be probable, but he need not stick to recorded "truth," even if he could learn all the facts of his case. The Renaissance rhetorician Leonard Cox also reminds readers that the encomiast may enlarge deeds to show virtue and vice.[19] Within the rhetorical tradition, then, the speaker selects facts and shapes his subject's life to pass a final judgment on him: he both describes and creates his subject's character, chronicles a life and fabricates a fiction. Coherence, then, is the result of character analysis rather than its starting point.

Cymbeline's conflation of fact and fiction has tragic potential, since Imogen, like Posthumus, is nearly "crushed" by attempts to unfold or remake her nature. But if rhetoric helps to push *Cymbeline's* plot toward tragedy, it also plays a role in the comic conclusion; epideictic histrionics help to redeem Posthumus when the Leonati court Jupiter with their encomium from beyond the grave. The family's challenge and Jupiter's masque follow hard on Posthumus's martial valor and his repentance while awaiting execution. The repentance speech and the challenge from the Leonati form a second diptych, one that also reverses the relationship between figure and ground.[20] In preparation for death, Posthumus offers a prayer to the gods that for many readers confirms his inner regeneration.[21] Welcoming his imprisonment, Posthumus analyzes the paradox that bondage provides a way to liberty. Most of the speech is organized around comparisons and similitudes. Posthumus resembles a man sick with gout, while Death acts simultaneously as his physician and as a key to unlock his fetters. Having banished death's terrors, Posthumus applies the lesson to himself and offers his life in exchange for Imogen's, since he still thinks her dead: "If you will take this audit, take this life, / And cancel these cold bonds" (5.4.27–28). Showing a Christian stoic's cheerfulness in the face of death, Posthumus appears to be sincerely repentant. Although his prayer contains a number of standard *topoi* from the classical consolation—including the ideas that "the great misery of this world makes life wearisome" and that "life is a debt that must be paid"—the absence of comic framing in this scene deflects attention from its literary qualities.[22]

Posthumus's redemption is not confirmed and completed, however, until the Leonati restore his good name with their own rhetorical effort. Shakespeare toys with cause and effect relationships here, since Jupiter's providence, Posthumus's contrition, and the Leonati's persistence all contribute to the play's peripateia. The Leonati, however, wield a good deal of power at this point. Posthumus, immobilized by his chains, lies asleep on the floor; and Jupiter does respond to the demands of his rebellious subjects, no matter how gruffly he dismisses them.[23] The Leonati call down the god in the machine. Their speech may be read as a prayer (following G. Wilson Knight) or as a challenge, since the Leonati refer to Jupiter's own marital infidelities and threaten to take their case to the "shining synod" of the gods. More important, by reciting formally the facts of Posthumus's biography, the Leonati provide a rhetorical equivalent to Jupiter's divine grace.

A crucial Renaissance topos used not only for lyric poetry and elegy, but also for biography and history writing, the encomium is so common and so conventional in its structure that it would be recognizable to Shakespeare's audience, even in a foreshortened version. The Leonati organize their praise according to the three standard topics: they refer to Posthumus's gifts of fortune, such as his worthy ancestry and noble wife (5.4.37–47, 52–57); to gifts of the body, his "stuff so fair" molded by nature (5.4.48–51); and finally to his spiritual gifts, a noble heart and brain (5.4.63–68). The encomium's three-part structure, arranging information chronologically, emphasizes the individual's ancestry, national background, and family. Public information—details such as the subject's native city, fellow citizens, parents, and family—and personal details such as his education, friends, fame, public service, wealth, and children, take up a good part of the encomium. Thus the Leonati, by their very appearance and their recitation of their bravery and suffering, provide the historical frame required in an encomium.

Meredith Skura, focusing on the psychology of Posthumus's dream, writes that the masque of Leonati represents either a "revelation of the divine forces in human affairs" or "a revelation of the familial matrix that underlies all human experience" (Skura 1980). Skura interprets the masque as a psychological metaphor dramatizing a human truth: Posthumus cannot "find himself as husband until he finds himself as son, as part of the family he was torn from long ago" (Skura 1980, 211, 204). Shakespeare, however, refuses to valorize the biological family's influence on individuals in this play. Posthumus, Cymbeline's lost sons, and even Cymbeline himself, spend their formative years with substitute families and surrogate parents. The nature-nuture debate becomes particularly knotty when Belarius claims that Cymbeline's sons show sparks of royal nature because they yearn to fight against the Romans; yet these same boys have acquired their taste for heroics by listening to old Belarius's war stories (3.3.86–95). The masque also provides a reminder that Posthumus did not know his family, since his father died before his birth, his mother in childbirth; his identifying traits, both his nobility and his poverty, are defined by the father's deeds before Posthumus's birth, by Posthumus's position in Cymbeline's household, and by his "election" as Imogen's husband.

Posthumus does not merely recover his family; rhetorically and dramatically, they create him anew. Because Posthumus's repentance is given a public context by the epideictic biography, finding his place in the family is a rhetorical more than a spiritual or psychological event. The Leonati accomplish what the First Gentleman in the opening scene could not: they "delve" Posthumus "to the root" (1.1.28). But their panegyric biography, foregrounding some details from his life and suppressing others, is transparently a fiction.

The epideictic theory and practice that lies behind this encomium recognizes that human biographies are socially-constructed fictions. Public judgment—rhetorical effect—ratifies man's moral nature. Aristotle's *Rhetoric* acknowledges that the encomiast must sometimes shape contradictory evidence. In practice, he must assert that "coincidents and accidents" reflect choice: "produce a number of good actions, all of the same kind, and people will think they are signs of excellence and choice." Detailing the subject's noble birth, education, and friends thus makes the praise more plausible, since "good fathers are likely to have good sons, and good training is likely to produce good character" (Aristotle 1984, I.ix.1367b). Because virtue lies both in man's nature and in society's judgment, Aristotle arrives at a circular definition of the noble man (Aristotle 1984, I.ix.1366b). We can recognize the virtuous man by his good deeds, since man tends to become what he does. On the other hand, the virtuous man's behavior will be virtuous because he is. Character produces action while action molds character. Nobility therefore depends on a probable congruence between a man's past and his behavior. The Leonati exploit this paradox inherent in epideictic tradition with their "proof" of Posthumus's virtue. They begin with the highly debatable question, "Hath my poor boy done aught but good?", and conclude "Since Jupiter, our son is good, take off his miseries." Focusing on Posthumus's ancestry, they establish a causal relationship between noble background and moral virtue. The rhetoric of characterization, by submitting the chaos of an individual's life to extreme categories of virtue and vice, necessarily falsifies character. But because the structures are public and traditional, they reflect the truth of social judgment.

Herein lies the paradox of Shakespearean character: in representations of character, traditional structures such as the encomium, by organizing praise or blame, permit judgment; on the other hand, the reliance of all epideictic rhetoric on tropes works against the stability offered by these larger forms. Central to any act of praise or blame are simile, metaphor, and especially hyperbole, which George Puttenham calls the "overreacher" or "loud liar." Characterized by "immoderate excesse" and "dissimulation," hyperbole lurks on the fringes of an upright and polite society. Put to proper use, it helps to "advaunce or greatly abase the reputation of any thing or person." But its power to influence reputation also makes hyperbole potentially dangerous, and so we must use it "very discreetly, or else it will seeme odious, for although a prayse . . . may be allowed beyond credit, it may not be beyond all measure" (Puttenham 1936, 191–92).[24] Hyperbole therefore works well as a tool for praise and dispraise, providing that the hyperbolist uses it discreetly and providing that the subject's worth is well-established. In other words, hyperbole should put itself at the service of existing hierarchies. Puttenham's call for caution in using hyperbole reveals a common fear of figurative language's ability to subvert established truths. While the encomium, effictio, and ethopoeia—the larger forms of epideictic discourse—attempt to fix character, the tropes that transform description into evaluation undermine rhetoric's pretensions to finality by calling attention to its tendency to "overreach."[25]

Because the rhetoric of characterization is by nature volatile, *Cymbeline*'s judgments about character can never be final. Since the Leonati's encomium involves a struggle for power—they threaten Jupiter as they praise Posthumus—the political origins of their ceremonial rhetoric are apparent. Further, in the extended final scene, as secrets are unraveled and enemies are reconciled, other orators claim the floor, seeking to control the past with their own characterizations. While most of the characters seek to exonerate themselves, Posthumus and Iachimo, former rivals in love, now compete as villains. Iachimo, retelling the story of their wager, praises Posthumus as a "true knight," (5.5.186), one "too good to be where ill men were" (5.5.158–59). Posthumus, in response, denounces himself as a "credulous fool / Egregious murtherer, thief, any thing / That's due to all the villains past, in being, / To come!" (5.5.210–13). He ends melodramatically, with a desire that "every villain / Be call'd Posthumus Leonatus," just as every go-between has become known as a pander (5.5.223–24). This oratorical competition between Posthumus and Iachimo highlights the epideictic rhetorician's paradoxical position as a "loud liar" who nevertheless courts an audience's assent to his fiction. The orator's vulnerability to social opinion is aggravated by every retelling of events behind the praise or blame. Posthumus, by emphasizing his intent to murder Imogen, a facet of his ethos suppressed by the Leonati, challenges the portrait of himself as a "noble knight" and "true lover"; he counters Iachimo's praise of his innocent virtue with an equally hyperbolic gesture, calling for every villain to be called "Posthumus Leonatus." The rhetoric of characterization is therefore threatened both from within and without, by the instability of its tropes and by the unruliness of its underlying narratives.

Cymbeline's fascination with problems of ethos may be symptomatic of a general Renaissance preoccupation with problems of character. The paradoxes marking the rhetoric of characterization extend also to its subject matter, since in the Aristotelian definition a noble man becomes noble by behaving properly, while he behaves properly because of a disposition to act nobly. Richard Lanham, in The Motives of Eloquence, argues that Renaissance man, as rhetorical man, does not enter this world equipped with a unified "central self." He is "an actor, his reality public, dramatic. His sense of identity, his self, depends on the reassurance of daily histrionic reenactment" (Lanham 1976, 4).[26] Renaissance man gains an identity by constant role-playing, imagining himself as a series of historical or literary characters.

The encomium, effictio, and ethopoeia—epideictic structures important to Cymbeline—were typical of the rhetorical exercises used in school curricula, part of the Renaissance fashioning of character. Trained at school in fictional verse epistles and in the *progymnasmata*, preliminary exercises anticipating the full-scale oration, boys learned early to personate classical and mythological figures. In this way, according to Lanham, a rhetorical education encourages the boy to try on many identities; the Renaissance self is therefore a loose collection of public and private roles, not an organically unified whole. Such role-playing has an ethical purpose, since fledgling orators learned not only that others could think differently from them, but that they could *be* different. Educators, notably Erasmus, agree that fictional exercises shape character by schooling the judgment through imaginative projection. Although in *Modus Conscribendis Epistolis*, he prudently dismisses Ovid's *Amores* as unfit for the very young, Erasmus lists a series of fictional letters, based loosely on the *Heroides*, to guide boys along virtue's path. The epistles exploit a youthful potential for histrionics. An imaginary letter addressed to Achilles, for instance, counsels him to bear the seizing of Briseis nobly, "showing that even a wicked king must be obeyed, that the common good must take precedence over private grief, and finally, that it is utterly unbecoming of Achilles' high birth, noble spirit, and brilliant career that he should forget his valour for the love of a foreign slave girl" (Erasmus 1985, 25: 24). But even such a highly-charged and adult topic can train a child's moral faculties; this topic, according to Erasmus, attacks "disreputable pleasure" and praises "exceptional heroism." The schoolmaster's effort to shape his charges' judgment extends to their sense of self; even so circumscribed an activity as translation from Greek, for instance, demonstrates not only the particular nature of the Greek language, but also the "points of similarity and variance between ourselves and the Greeks" (Erasmus 1978, 24: 679). Rhetorical exercises therefore work, to use Kenneth Burke's terms from *The Rhetoric of Motives*, by encouraging identification, which in turn implies division: "Identification is proclaimed with earnestness precisely because there is division. Identification is compensatory to division. If men were not apart from one another, there would be no need for the rhetorician to proclaim their unity. If men were wholly and truly of one substance, absolute communication would be of man's very essence" (Burke 1967, 22).

The play of similarity and difference, at the heart of rhetorical education, may also characterize Renaissance perceptions of dramatic experience. Marion Trousdale argues that both Shakespeare and his Renaissance audience interpreted characters through the frame of rhetorical structures. Character portraits are therefore *exempla,* invitations to analysis rather than artifacts, or the products of interpretation. Like rhetorical exercises from the schoolroom, drama encourages identification, an act that by nature entails a recognition of division.[27]

The aim of such an exercise, according to Trousdale, is didactic: drama cultivates ethical knowledge, which is acquired only through experience, by providing occasions for the kind of analysis that leads to practical understanding. The educators concur: a rhetorical education ultimately exists, as Erasmus says in *De Ratione Studii,* to cultivate "what is, in everything, of paramount importance—judgment" (Erasmus 1978, 24: 689). *Cymbeline* is notable more for its irony than its didactic value; indeed, when Imogen mistakenly identifies Cloten's headless corpse as that of Posthumus, dramatizing the difficulties facing the student of character, the play suggests that reading character correctly is impossible. While Imogen has confidently valued Posthumus's "meanest garment" beyond any virtues of Cloten, she is fooled by accidental marks of character, a mere change of clothing. Acts of characterization, such as Imogen's inverted effictio—she moves up rather than down Cloten's disguised body—necessarily involve omissions that prevent any intuitive recognition of virtue and vice. The absence of Cloten's head, rather than any individuating features, tricks her into misidentifying the corpse. While omissions are necessary to epideictic rhetoric, since praise and blame depends on smoothing out the rough edges in a character portrait, they make possible the substitution of a "thing too bad for report" for the noble Posthumus, and by extension, an endless substitution of individuals as signs for one another.

But because plays, like other rhetorical constructions, are *exempla* rather than applications of precept, they resist theorizing, as Victoria Kahn points out (Kahn 198[6] 386–90). Thus Cloten's headless corpse testifies less to the undecidability of meaning than to an urgent need for continued attempts to read character.

During the long recognition scene that concludes *Cymbeline,* Cornelius the physician reports the wicked queen's dying confession that she had always hated her royal spouse and had planned to poison him. Cymbeline responds to this information with amazement: "O most delicate fiend! / Who is't can read a woman?" (5.5.47–48). Nevertheless, he denies any responsibility for his deception:

> Mine eyes
> Were not in fault, for she was beautiful;

Mine ears, that heard her flattery, nor my heart,
That thought her like her seeming. It had been vicious
To have mistrusted her.

                                                        (5.5.62–66)

Cymbeline complains not only about deceptive exteriors, but also about a failure of method, the inability of the senses to report moral character accurately. Perception alone will not reveal ethos because moral character is a construct, a fiction created from an individual's background and actions and ratified by society's judgment. Without the formal structures of rhetoric, moral character is not only inaccessible—it does not exist. Cymbeline's recognition of character's opacity nevertheless also reveals a rhetorical imperative. Only through repeated attempts to read the unreadable, through the play of identification and differentiation created by the conflict between tropes and larger rhetorical forms, does practical knowledge of human nature become possible. Rhetoric, although a barrier to reading character, is necessary to that act of reading, because as Imogen herself laments, "our very eyes are sometimes like our judgments, blind" (4.2.301–302).

Notes

1. All references to Shakespeare's works are from the Riverside edition.
2. Among recent articles, the fullest discussion of "seeming" and problems of appearance and reality is in Nancy K. Hayles, "Sexual Disguise in *Cymbeline*," *Modern Language Quarterly* 41 (1980): 231–47; the most extended treatment of clothing imagery in *Cymbeline* is John Scott Colley, "Disguise and New Guise in *Cymbeline*," *Shakespeare Studies* 7 (1974): 233–52.
3. See also R. A. Foakes, "Character and Dramatic Technique in *Cymbeline* and *The Winter's Tale*," in Francis Warner, *Studies in the Arts* (Oxford: Basil Blackwell, 1968), 116–30.
4. For a critique of Schwartz's argument, see David M. Bergeron, "Sexuality in *Cymbeline*," *Essays in Literature* 10 (1983): 159–68.
5. Bertrand Evans calls Jupiter's masque an "artistic fraud." *Shakespeare's Comedies* (Oxford): Clarendon Press, 1960), 286.
6. Hunt and I discuss many of the same issues, particularly the problem of how language and experience relate within the play, but come to very different conclusions.
7. Shakespeare uses the verb *extend* sometimes as "to stretch," suggesting physical extension in space; sometimes the word has an emotional meaning, as "to magnify or extol." In this particular instance, *extend* may refer also to rhetorical amplification, translating as "to magnify or extol." Cf. Alexander Schmidt, *Shakespeare-Lexicon*, rev. Gregor Sarrazin, 2 vols. (Berlin and New York: Walter de Gruyter, 1971).
8. For the topics and structure of the *encomium*, see Aphthonius, *Progymnas-*

mata, trans. Ray Nadeau, *Speech Monographs* 19 (1952); 272–75; for the topics of epideictic in general, see Cicero's *Rhetorica Ad Herennium,* trans. Harry Caplan, Loeb Classical Library (Cambridge: Harvard University Press, 1954), III.vi.–viii; for "outdoing" and the "inexpressibility topos," see Marjorie Donker and George M. Muldrow, *Dictionary of Literary-Rhetorical Conventions of the Renaissance* (Westport, Conn.: Greenwood, 1982), 91–92.

9. See Madeleine Doran, *Endeavors of Art* (Madison: University of Wisconsin Press, 1954), 232–41.

10. A succinct summary of how epideictic's scope and purpose change as it comes to be associated with poetry and with ethics can be found in Brian Vickers, "Epideictic and Epic in the Renaissance," *New Literary History* 14 (1983): 497–537. For the influence of epideictic theory and practice on Renaissance literature, see O. B. Hardison, *The Enduring Monument* (Chapel Hill: University of North Carolina Press, 1962); and Barbara Kiefer Lewalski, *Donne's "Anniversaries" and the Poetry of Praise* (Princeton: Princeton University Press, 1973).

11. O. B. Hardison, in his discussion of style in epideictic rhetoric, lists not only broader strategies such as periphrasis, negation, expressions of doubt, digressions, and apostrophe, but also figures of ornamentation such as hyperbole, simile and metaphor (Hardison 1962, 31).

12. Murray Schwartz, for instance, argues that Iachimo activates, then distances his sexual fantasies, substituting a visual rape for "taboo touch"; images such as the amorous candle flame therefore personify Iachimo's urge to violate Imogen visually, if not physically (Schwartz 1970 238–39). Harley Granville-Barker, on the other hand, feels that although Iachimo's "sensuality is dominant again in the soliloquy in her bedchamber," the "night's lonely silence brings it to an aesthetic fineness" (Granville-Barker 1958, 1:519).

13. My sense of the scene's pacing parallels the analysis of Hallett Smith, *Shakespeare's Romances* (San Marino, Calif.: Huntington Library, 1972), 183–85.

14. For the connections between Ovid's version of the Philomela story and *Cymbeline,* see Ann Thompson, "Philomel in *Titus Andronicus* and *Cymbeline,*" *Shakespeare Survey* 31 (1978): 23–32, and R. J. Schork, "Allusion, Theme, and Characterization in *Cymbeline,*" *Studies in Philology* 69 (1972): 210–16. For *Cymbeline* and the Lucrece story, see Robert Miola, *Shakespeare's Rome* (Cambridge: Cambridge University Press, 1983), 212–14.

Jonathan Goldberg, in a discussion of Shakespearean character based on postmodern theory, also analyzes *Cymbeline's* bedroom scene. I share a number of assumptions with him, including the idea that "inner being is a text," but am less exclusively concerned with figuration; because I concentrate also on larger epideictic forms, such as the encomium and ethopoeia, I stress the potentially stabilizing effect of larger rhetorical forms. See Jonathan Goldberg, "Shakespearean Characters: The Generation of Silvia," chap. 4 in *Voice Terminal Echo* (London: Methuen, 1986), 68–100.

15. See Wolfgang Clemen, *Shakespeare's Dramatic Art* (London: Methuen, 1972), 147–62.

16. Juvenal's "Satire Six" provides the basis for misogynistic rants in a number of plays, including Beaumont and Fletcher's *Philaster* (IV.iii.13), which Arthur Kirsch compares to *Cymbeline.* See Robert Y. Turner, "Slander in *Cymbeline* and Other Jacobean Tragicomedies," *English Literary Renaissance* 13 (1983), 182–202; Arthur C. Kirsch, "*Cymbeline* and Coterie Dramaturgy," *English Literary History* 34 (1967): 285–306.

17. Francis Berry, *The Shakespearean Inset,* (New York: Theater Arts Books,

1965), 68–74, provides a useful analysis of these two companion "insets," even though he assumes the presence of an inner stage. Berry points out that the narrative scene (Iachimo in Imogen's bedroom) seems more dramatic than the truly dramatic scene (Iachimo's rehearsal for Posthumus).

18. See Aristotle, *Rhetoric*, trans. W. Rhys Roberts, in *The Complete Works of Aristotle*, ed. Jonathan Barnes (Princeton: Princeton University Press, 1984), II.xxii.1396a.

19. See Leonard Cox, *The Arte or Crafte of Rhetorike*, ed. Frederic Ives Carpenter (Chicago: Chicago University Press, 1899), 17.

20. See Judiana Lawrence, "Natural Bonds and Artistic Coherence in the Ending of *Cymbeline*," *Shakespeare Quarterly* 35 (1984): 452. I followed G. Wilson Knight and J. A. Nosworthy, the New Arden editor (London: Methuen, 1955), in accepting the masque's authenticity.

21. See, for instance, Robert Grams Hunter, *Shakespeare and the Comedy of Forgiveness* (New York: Columbia University Press, 1965), 142–84.

22. A list of topics for the consolation appears in A. L. Bennett, "The Principal Rhetorical Conventions in the Renaissance Personal Elegy," *Studies in Philology* 51 (1954): 107–26; see also Thomas Wilson's example of "comfort" in the *Arte of Rhetorique*, 147–84.

23. For the argument that Shakespeare would have used chains to represent a prison, see Alan Dessen, *Elizabethan Stage Conventions and Modern Interpreters* (Cambridge: Cambridge University Press, 1984), 99.

24. I will not attempt to survey here the definitions of hyperbole from classical and Renaissance rhetoricians, but virtually all writers from Quintilian on stress that hyperbole violates norms of "literal" or "ordinary" language, except in those rare cases in which hyperbole is applied to an exceptional subject.

25. For these observations, I am generally indebted to Victoria Kahn's discussions of the relationship between Renaissance rhetoric and postmodern theory, suggested in *Rhetoric, Prudence, and Skepticism in the Renaissance* (Ithaca: Cornell University Press, 1985), but explicated more fully in "Humanism and the Resistance to Theory," in *Literary Theory / Renaissance Texts*, ed. Patricia Parker and David Quint (Baltimore: Johns Hopkins, University Press, 1986), 373–96. Kahn points out that while in humanist rhetoric the *sensus communis*, a search for agreement, is rhetoric's goal, the rise of "method" under Ramism and its concomitant distrust of figurative language as a deviation from "ordinary" language sets up a conflict between cultural forms and figurative language.

26. Also relevant to my argument are Joel B. Altman, *The Tudor Play of Mind* (Berkeley: University of California Press, 1978) and Stephen Greenblatt, *Renaissance Self-Fashioning* (Chicago: University of Chicago Press 1980).

27. Trousdale discusses the relation between rhetoric and drama in *Shakespeare and the Rhetoricians* (Chapel Hill: University of North Carolina Press, 1982). An earlier article, "A Possible Renaissance View of Form," *English Literary History* 40 (1973): 179–204, addresses more directly the idea of form as *exemplum* for analysis.

Falstaff: Shakespeare's Cosmic (Comic) Representation

THELMA N. GREENFIELD

The "comicity" of Falstaff becomes undeniably a part of the "cosmicity" of . . . history (Farnham 1971, 50)

The comic figure, outrageous, larger-than-life, riding for a fall, is a familiar stage presence in our time, as it was in Shakespeare's. A powerful foe to moral and social restraint, such a figure, usually male, commandeers the stage world to his own purposes, imposing his own rules, exploiting the vulnerable, or wallowing in pleasure. He may undertake all of these at once. The comedy built around him vigorously dramatizes both his going beyond the bounds and also whatever conspires to bring this disturber of social regularity under control. It finally provides a resolution that includes a comeuppance, surprising but satisfyingly commensurate with the comic suffering he inflicts. In general outline, Shakespeare's most imposing comic creation, the Falstaff of the history plays, seems to fit such a traditional comic scheme. The temptation has sometimes been to put him there and leave it at that.

Yet to do so is to place Falstaff in a brotherhood where he is hardly at home, one that coincides nicely (and much better than he does) with the contemporary theories of comedy that spoke to exemplary picturings of vices to be shunned, a kind of drama that Puttenham gave the name "the poem reprehensive." Today in an attempt to be historically accurate, or perhaps because Falstaff loses the game, he has rather often been reduced to such a bad example and the Prince, who destroys him, by contrast validated.

Charlton, in an early twentieth-century instance of what has been a surprisingly persistent interpretation, referred to Falstaff's "failure," his "incompleteness" (assumed to be a weakness), and described his world "not worth the conquest" (Charlton n.d., 206). In such a view, Falstaff becomes a companion who must be scorned, a tempter to be rejected, an educator not to be tenured (Siegel among others on this last.)[1] Writing so well on Falstaff's saturnalian triumphs, C. L. Barber, also taking what is for what must be, assumed that Shakespeare dramatized a necessity to curtail holiday (Barber 1959, 192). Barber's Falstaff must be tried and "sacrificed" in what Barber called an impersonalized ritual, the word *impersonalized* removing the new King Henry from the hook. In such judgments, Falstaff must, however difficult it is to do, be "brought to book" (Barber 1959, 213).

We need to exercise some caution in treating Falstaff, funny as he is, as if he were an overreaching character in a comedy. The Falstaff I am talking about appears in history plays. Nor can I agree with Steven Mullaney that *Henry IV, Part One* is a mixed genre "throughout" (Mullaney 1988b, 85). Shakespeare's *Henry IV* plays keep front and center concerns of the body politic, and that Falstaff makes his appearance in this context—that is, in history plays instead of comedies—constitutes a large difference. His comic behavior necessarily and obviously by design resonates against a political sounding board to give what he says and does an import quite distinct from meanings that accrue in a comic world. His ultimate defeat occurs in an environment where (as Sidney pointed out in discussing the problem of history) whatever is is not necessarily right. A comedy by definition becomes more or less bound to an assumed propriety of its conclusion, but history, even a history play, however much tied to its selected eventualities, implies consideration of alternatives.

There may be, as I was once taught, no if's in history, and yet—history can be viewed as being as much a study of choices as of events. The choices are those of the historians and those of the enactors of what they record. For the historians, E. H. Carr in *What Is History* uses the metaphor of a blank check with its formal printed apparatus of lofty words, though "the cheque is valueless until we fill [it] in . . . ," stating "how much liberty we purpose to allocate to whom, whom we recognize as our equals and up to what amount. The way we fill in the cheque from time to time is a matter of history" (Carr 1962, 76). The history play is likely to become even more explicitly a blank check, epecially if it introduces a notable fictional element standing at odds with the orthodox and purportedly literal presentation of an historical movement. Either to read Falstaff as moving on a defined comic trajectory or to see him as a part of a historical necessity becomes I think a doubtful course.

The problem of Falstaff as a strongly funny fictional figure in a dramatized history and a figure offering a discernible alternative in itself, in its very physical presence, is the matter this paper will go on to explore.

The beginning of Falstaff's end, at the conclusion of *Henry IV, Part Two*, points up the two widely held interpretations of his being brought to book that I have been discussing. Though to many the scene brings little of the validating sense of relief that a comic conclusion achieves, Dover Wilson, determined to be unembarrassed by Falstaff's brutal banishment, writes "There can be no question of the rightness of Shakespeare's finale" (Wilson 1964, 123)[2] and attributes our unease to modern muddleheadedness. Readers like Mullaney shift the ground to a cultural "inevitability" that *we* cannot comprehend (Mullaney 1988b, 85), and many, like Traversi, are happy to move it to a "growing necessity" of political expediency (Traversi 1957, 156). Palmer puts things rather more nostalgically: if Henry V must "dwindle" into a hero, Falstaff must die (Palmer 1961, 218).

Asserting the "rightness" of Falstaff's fate puts him into a traditional progression of comedy as a figure who pursues the path of a number of characters on the English Renaissance stage—the spectacular and disreputable path headed for defeat, a point the audience impatiently waits for. Yet most of the others who might be seen as comparable illuminate his case more by contrast than similarity. Among such figures only a select few—Volpone, say, or Zeal-of-the-land Busy or Sir Epicure Mammon, or other similarly powerful characters among the Ben Jonson confraternity—generate the tremendous comic force of Shakespeare's Falstaff; but though Shakespeare's knight can conjure up at will the range that they achieve together of self-indulgence, mendacity, hypocrisy, and general exploitive inventiveness, the sources of their power and attraction lie far from his. Driven, unlike Falstaff, by peculiarly self-destructive impulses, the towering Jonsonian figures, also unlike him, gain much of their definition and energy through circumscriptions of social place, and they frenetically utilize their social fixing (or pretended social fixing) to exploit their gullible fellows. Risk is their lifeblood; disguises stand high among their useful weapons; speed and timing become in their hands finely-honed skills. (Middleton's comic figures can easily be fitted to the same mold.) However unpredictable their egregious progresses, each thing they do—each risk they take—reiterates the social fabric and retraces the outlines of manifestly dangerous limits.

Falstaff, who prefers to avoid risk, remains socially slippery. His first affirmed place is Companion to the prince, the last he should logically occupy. That position is, in fact, invalidated from the beginning by the prince's soliloquy, though our definition of Falstaff continues to be the "Prince's friend." Falstaff also quickly demonstrates his vocation of highway robber—he is actually shown in action—though again he slips out of position by becoming the victim of the robbery and then, in his own words, its hero. He is at the same time left more than once a knight without a horse; he is a soldier whose first priority is his own safety. His verbal dexterity and mimicry also shift him from one definition to another. The Jonsonian comic figures, though deviant, are much more fixed socially and much better suit moral theories of comedy of the time in their emphasis on social structures. Their alienation comes from conforming too much to certain characteristics of their class. The social placement of the Jonson figure— added to his headlong self-destructiveness—separates him from the audience and permits it to assume a judgmental stance that can take pleasure in his defeat. We are not so removed from Falstaff. His powerful impulse to self-preservation, his social fluidity, his gift for socializing do not generate distancing. They take us to the thought of alternatives. We want Volpone stopped; not Falstaff.

We should not allow comment based on the punitive development that is often found in comedy to color Falstaff for us. Nor, because Falstaff is defeated, should we rest easy in some "inevitable" historical process at work. "Historians," writes Carr drily, "do not assume that events are inevitable before they have taken place." We might do well to apply Carr's dicta to our consideration of the history play when he goes on to avow his perfect willingness to "do without 'inevitable,' 'unavoidable,' 'inescapable' and even 'ineluctable'" (Carr 1962, 90). Neither view should rationalize away the permanence of Falstaff as an alternative or the unshakable values attaching to the fat knight, sinful as he is.

Harold Bloom says something to the point in his *Ruin the Sacred Truths*, as he imperiously dismisses punitive views of Falstaff, as well as the relevance of Marxists' and deconstructionists' pronouncements. Bloom finally abandons even Freud to get at our interaction with Shakespeare's most powerful comic figure: "With Falstaff," he writes, ". . . Shakespearean representation is so self-begotten and so influential that we can apprehend it only by seeing that it originates us." He later adds, "Falstaff is not how meaning is renewed, but rather how meaning gets started" (Bloom 1989, 85, 86). Finally, he sees Falstaff's approach to us as a challenge "not to bore him" (Bloom 1989, 87). As usual Bloom goes far. He sees Falstaff not as of us but "beyond us." "We cannot judge a mode of representation that has overdetermined our ideas of representation" (Bloom 1989, 85).

Falstaff may be beyond our theories of literary representation, but it seems to me that we can find one way of approaching his representation and our responses to it by allowing scope to the comic grotesque aspect that he and some of his comic kinsmen share. Bakhtin, who focused on positive values in the grotesque, found what he believed to be "truth" in its comedy. It is a truth that lives through adjusting what Bakhtin calls the "conception of the completed atomized being" (a conception Bakhtin terms "bourgeois"), meeting it with the uncompleted, contradictory and "open" body. "It is cosmic, it represents the entire material bodily world in all its elements" (Bakhtin 1984, 27). He explains that the laughter he writes of is not corrective but nonoppressive and nonrestrictive; unlike its primitive origins, it is also nonofficial. It defeats power; it defeats fear.

One might argue that Volpone contains features of the grotesque, but that character assumes grotesqueness as a disguise. He closes off his body. Officialdom in his play is too weak to offer substantial opposition: Volpone must in effect destroy himself.

Bakhtin was writing of Gargantua and Pantagruel, but Falstaff (to whom he alludes in passing) also emerges through Bakhtin's kind of grotesquery, and it is this quality that the Henry IV plays emphasize as sitting at odds with officialdom. I should add that Falstaff provides us both embarrassment and release—showing what should not be shown while we look at what should not be looked at. Falstaff violates the secrets of our existence and the inhibitions of our looking. He is, furthermore, at odds with officialdom both within the eventualities of the plays and externally, to the plays' generic formulation. While suggesting alternatives, history also shows us what we should see. History, even fictionalized, is official, and thus history and Falstaff make problems for each other. But to help alleviate some of the rationalized diminishing and negations of Falstaff—negations that so much offend Bloom—we can employ the validity of the grotesque to underscore a validity in Falstaff that makes him so potent, valuable, and threatening a comic representation.

On stage, history, without losing its identity as history, may readily manifest some features of the more traditionally defined genres—tragedy, comedy, or satire—and find an especially happy congeniality in those essential theatrical components, rhetoric and spectacle. In the comic parts of the Henry IV plays, it is Prince

Hal, in fact, who adopts the conventional comedic devices of disguise, eavesdropping, badinage and trickery, yet he offers no threat to the integrity of his plays as history plays. He is always the prince of the realm, always on the attack against subversion. For these plays must, as Hal helps to do, keep the body politic on track for whatever destination.[3] Falstaff, however, threatens a derailment, not only by encouraging parody of official persons, events, and values and hierarchical structures sacrosanct to history, but by posing his own notably dimensioned body against the body politic.

Barbara Everett, writing to another purpose in "The Fatness of Falstaff," calls his fatness more than incidental: "Certainly we may say that the groundlings fell silent because of his superlative free-wheeling play of wit, enthrallingly dangerous in a political milieu. But perhaps they also fell silent when he first walked onto the stage: entranced to find the simple individual body (and so much of it!) given a star part in the drama of History" (Everett 1990, 18). She speaks later of a "king of metaphysical witty status to Falstaff's fatness" (Everett 1990, 19).

Falstaff is a sometimes funny, sometimes painful, representation of the antithetical. For the demands the body politic makes in the *Henry IV* plays are not merely for a Jonsonian posture of moral respectability and balance (one uses the word *posture* advisedly here), but for something much more basic, that is, for an allegiance the end of which is nothing less than a willing death. Long before things reach that point Falstaff draws the line.

Participant in illicit and licit pursuits that ask for risk of life and limb, Falstaff manages largely to evade the risks, even contriving in their place a few unauthorized benefits; rather than allowing history to invade him, he invades it. In that undertaking he rewrites the history of Hotspur's death as he rewrites the history of his own heroism. He rewrites his own death as well, managing against heavy odds to die in bed. Falstaff reminds us constantly that it is a physical body that is ultimately at stake when history imposes its requirements.

The prince shows himself as alert to the dangers inherent in Falstaff's assertive and self-protective physicality. Most of his attacks on Falstaff aim at Falstaff's grotesquely large body. He insults its size and age. He also unhorses it to make Falstaff run, pant, sweat, march, and fight. His premature eulogy for the not-yet-deceased knight interposes Falstaff's fat flesh between himself and grieving. His gesture of kindness to the presumed corpse is a promise to bring it down to size by disembowelment. The final rough farewell in *Henry IV, Part Two*, with its evoking of white hairs and girth and its command for physical distancing to the very mile, gives as advice "Make less thy body" and remember the grave, an enormous grave, "For thee thrice wider than for other men" (5.5.52–54). Falstaff is to shrink and to die three times over, for the new King Henry knows his first enemy. Actually, devoted as he is to life, these history plays and the officialdom they represent make sure that the death of that great body hangs in the air from the start, death by the gallows, by old age, or by sickness if the death it "owes God" and country cannot apprehend its owner on the battlefield.

Falstaff's monumental flesh does link him to at least one Jonsonian creation in whose kind of comedy he shares. To cite Ursula the Pig-Woman as exemplary, as a social deviant bent on self-destruction would be ludicrous. Ursula endures simply as Ursula, dwelling, as her misfortunes illustrate, in the flesh rather than in social placement. At worst, her sweating body may become wedged in her chair or suffer scalding or thirst, but these mishaps have nothing to do with social place. We cannot find her grotesque physicality essentially alien, for it speaks to a large and unshakable part of recognized existence. Her intensity receives reinforcement from the heat of her quarters and her holiday pigs, oozing above the fire, a memorable reminder of a perceived human predicament as well as of the gross human satisfactions of the feast. Whatever dubious business goes forward on her premises, she provides the appropriate feasting and that necessary earthy aftermath, a comfort station. My point is that with all her outrageous enormities in business and invective, her bid is not to denial but to acknowledgment.

Traub presents in psychoanalytic terms a threatening, sow-related Falstaff, who can join Ursula the Pig-Woman in gender implications as well as in figuring forth (or, rather, *therefore* figuring forth) the grotesque (Traub 1989, 463). Traub's approach, however, depends on distancing the grotesque, and this, I feel, denies its insistence on our recognizing its validity by waving before us large reminders of what we normally suppress.

What Bakhtin says about the Rabelaisian grotesque can be usefully seen to apply to Falstaff, too: concern with life and death, for example, with wine and food, with carnal love, with time. Like the two giants, Falstaff appears at the center of a gathering of laughter-providing drinkers and like them, he has connections with laughter-providing folk traditions—his kind of mummer's death and revival on the battlefield, his giving and receiving barrages of billingsgate, his playing at being king. Other items in Bakhtin's vivid catalogue are recognizable in Falstaff, from associations with sweat and urine to linkages with diseases of overindulgence, especially gout and venereal sickness. And of course he has the traditional comic grotesquery of exaggerated body size, of existing much in the area of the gut. He, too, the whoreson round man, bolting-hutch of beastliness and parcel of dropsies, he the muddy rascal and honeysuckle villain receives praises as physically abusive as the blame—the fat stricken deer, poor ape, the whoreson little tidy Barthelomew boar-pig.

Bakhtin's views on the value of the grotesque are, according to Stallybrass and Wright, too utopian (Stallybrass and White 1986, 9–14). But I would argue that Bakhtin speaks well through its agency to remind us that codes operating in their unlaughing "isolation" need not—should not—be mistaken for truth; even, I should add, for the "truth" of the *Henry IV* plays. The closed systems are not the whole story. Though they more or less triumph, their requirements are not exclusively the necessities to be considered. Through the bodily grotesque, Falstaff compellingly asserts his own necessity.

There is, of course, a question of the falling off physically and in attractiveness in the second *Henry* play. It is as if the playwright gives us still other alternatives to the alternatives. What if Falstaff dwindles into semirespectability? What if he is no longer so attractive? In fact, much of the second play is so constructed in relation to its predecessor as even things ostensibly honored in the first play here take on a disreputable shading. What if Hotspur's value must only be respected through further dishonor? What if there is no heroism in warfare? What if Henry Bolingbroke admits that he is a crook and the prince himself reenacts a kind of usurpation? What if Hal as Henry V no longer considers that losing Falstaff might even possibly be a sore miss? The second play is not simply a linear continuation, but a darkened recapitulation questioning the official even more intensely. This latter picturing does not cause us to forget the brightness of *Henry IV, Part One*, however; it does not vitiate our sense of Falstaff's comic value.

Other writers than Bakhtin have remarked on Falstaff's kinship with greatly comic characters invented by Rabelais and Cervantes. Walter Kaiser some years ago devoted a book to the subject, including Erasmus's *The Praise of Folly*, as well. Kaiser, too— though in the end he feels "obliged to concur" in the condemnation of Falstaff (Kaiser 1963, 251)—sees the similarity among these

figures as a wisdom derived from inversions of conventional formulations and as a resulting freedom.

But Falstaff presents a special difficulty. Dramatic theorists do
not habitually anticipate for us an established role for comic elements in history plays. Renaissance writers saw the comic as appropriate to comedy, which, to begin with, must present private
affairs, but never "meddle" with "any Princes matters nor such
high personages." Comedy was to offer fictional characters of
given trades, classes, ages, "evil professions," etc., behaving always consistently with the expectations accorded their type and
functioning always to the "good amendment of man by discipline
and example" (Puttenham 1936, 33). Falstaff cannot be so classi-
fied and is also too various to appear "the same at all times"
(Robortellus in Herrick 1984, 235). In his history plays, however
rich the laughter he provides, he is too integrated with public
affairs and high personages to have a separate comic role apart
from them.

Even if we could pry loose from comedy-as-genre the remarks
on the comic offered by Renaissance writers and their guides from
antiquity, we would find little in Falstaff to fit their observations.
Laughter, according to Aristotle, is provoked by ugliness and de-
formity. Conceivably, Falstaff provides laughter in that way, perhaps even when it becomes clear that by these terms Aristotle is
referring to faults, but when Aristotle further refines his explanation by remarking that laughable faults do not serve to cause pain,
Falstaff no longer qualifies, any more than Rabelais's Gargantua
or Friar John or Cervantes's Don Quixote. Without departing from
the realm of the comic, all of these adventurers leave a shocking
trail of havoc behind them.

As for the contempt and scorn the audience was supposed to
feel for the comic figure, so as to make it "impossible that any
beholder can be content with such a one" (Castelvetro in Herrick
1984, 87; also Sidney 1928, 117), once again Falstaff fails to qualify.
It is in an occasional Renaissance defense of the wholesomeness
of mirth that we find a liberation that might permit Falstaff in
his rascality his place as irrelevant to moralizing and expediency
(whether of the sixteenth or the twentieth century) except as their
opponent, an opponent to be reckoned with as offering the larger
perspective that can be attained through laughter. The liberation
he brings, nevertheless, cannot be disengaged from his rattling
the cages of codes of law and soldiership and official history. That
he makes the impact he does, being but a measured part of several history plays named for their royal personae, and not *about*

him, is a tribute to his comic energies, to the undeniable gifts he offers along with his disreputable behavior and codes.

In examining these gifts, we see an oddity in their being subversive. Like his Rabelaisian siblings, Falstaff belongs to a brotherhood of drinkers and he and they bring first and foremost the offering of companionship. Pantagruel and Gargantua are nearly always seen "socializing"; Don Quixote is only completed by his companion, Sancho Panza; while Erasmus's orating Folly superintends the very possibility of fellowship. Here, however, Falstaff also presents another difference. His gift of companionship rests at the heart of the problem he represents, for to quote Bloom one more time, "future monarchs have no friends, only followers, and Falstaff . . . is no one's follower" (Bloom 1989, 86).

With companionship comes talk. Falstaff and his comic kin are all great talkers and here, again, Falstaff might be said to fit the prescriptions of the comic in its allowed place for rhetoric. He performs brilliantly whether it be rhetoric deliberative (offering counsel), forensic (dealing with proofs), or demonstrative (offering praise or blame). Through Falstaff's talk comes the distinct voice of pointed protests of flesh and blood against the unquestioning sacrifices that the body politic would exact of it. Falstaff's persuasive rhetoric certainly does not persuade the prince, and their companionable verbal battles are not just good fun. They are part of a struggle to the death.

Falstaff also gives us the excitement of seeing life as a quest, a journey of ardent pursuit. He journeys out from his home base at the Boarshead Tavern to appear at four in the morning at the infamous Gad's Hill Highway. He leads his tattered prodigals to Shrewsbury. He collects men and money in Gloucestershire and a prisoner in Yorkshire. He marches about the London streets, making his presence universally felt. From the beginning we watch him seek a paradise of plenty and disregard for the law, where "squires of the night's body" will be called "Diana's foresters . . . minions of the moon." Though on each of his journeys the old soldier-highwayman labors assiduously for it, the paradise he yearns for does not exist. At the end of the *Henry IV, Part Two,* the taste is in his mouth but what he finds instead is a closing of the ranks. The new king will allow only followers. If, as Bloom says, Falstaff lacks a superego, the fifth Henry will invent one for him.

I have said enough about Falstaff's gift of the flesh that so much implicates us, but it brings up his final offering, the gift of dying. For that, we should not shed too many tears. Bakhtin cheerfully includes dying among his colorful categories of laughter-imbued grotesqueries because to be warm flesh and blood is to be vulnerable; and they do die, Falstaff and his type. They die because they exist in time. They exist in nature. Falstaff's instinct is for self-preservation and if he is to die, he must be killed—by age, by sickness, by the king who kills his heart. In fact he has been dying all along in his connections with time and age, with disease and wasting away. When his death is made complete, it is a significant gesture of self-defense by the official aspect of the genre he has surged into.

If Falstaffian alternatives make problems in the history play, how much less do they fit into a dramatic comedy. "Comedy," writes one commentator, "evades, circumvents or defers death . . . or represents mock death, or symbolic or illusory deaths which are triumphantly overcome" (Nevo 1987, 5). But in the Falstaffian fellowship, natural processes prevail. Pantagruel can be born only through his mother's death, a condition that leads Gargantua to his famously funny debate on whether to grieve or celebrate.

As Falstaff lives in the flesh, he dies in the flesh, from the feet up, a fitting death, as the Hostess describes how she felt upward and upward and found all (she says it twice), "Cold as any stone." Her indelicate innuendo softly mantles both the natural and the monumental aspects of the image. Here Shakespeare pays a handsome tribute to the energies he was able to pour into this comic prodigy who is not in a comedy, this subversive prodigy who flourishes and fades among the quarrels, bloodshed, pieties, and betrayals that are sanctioned—indeed honored—in the orthodox progress of dramatized history.

Notes

1. The critic who comments on tenure is Paul Siegal, "Falstaff and His Social Milieu," in Norman Rudich, *Weapons of Criticism* (Palo Alto, Calif.: Ramparts Press, 1976).

2. At the same time Wilson argues the disappearance of Will Kempe from the company to account for Falstaff's nonappearance in the play which follows. The Epilogue of *Henry IV, Part Two* tentatively promises both his reappearance and his death (in France).

3. See Herbert Blau, *The Audience* (Baltimore: Johns Hopkins University Press, 1990), 207.

Shakespeare's Treatment of Comic Sentiment *(Hasya Rasa):* An Indian Perspective

M. AROGYASAMI

In a perceptive comment on Shakespeare's mode of composition, Samuel Johnson notes that "through all denominations of the drama, Shakespeare's mode of composition is the same; an interchange of seriousness and merriment, by which the mind is softened at one time, and exhilarated at another" (Johnson 1962, 138).[1] In his tragedies, lower-class characters often provide the comic spirit. Ironically, these minor characters, the marginal or socially insignificant ones, change the tragic spirit of the plays, entertaining us more than some clowns in his comedies. These comic moments, so often peopled by lower-class characters, have already been analyzed by scholars as various as Samuel Johnson, Thomas DeQuincy, George Bernard Shaw, A. C. Bradley, Harley Granville-Barker, Ralph Berry, and R. A. Foakes. Yet no one has analyzed the flow of comic sentiment associated with low-class society in Shakespearean tragedies from an Indian perspective. Such an analysis may help account for Shakespeare's association of comic sentiment with lower-class society in tragedies. It can also defamiliarize the topic, permitting critics to see it afresh and to discover new implications. Hence I intend to use the perspective of Indian dramatic convention in a discussion of Shakespeare's treatment of comic sentiment (Bharata uses the term *hasya rasa* for comic sentiment and its mood, *hasya,* for laughter) as it is associated with lower-class society in *Hamlet, Macbeth,* and *Antony and Cleopatra.'*

Bharata Muni's *Natyasastra* (400 A.D.), the source of Indian dramatic convention, is a treatise on Indian dramaturgy that was totally unknown to Shakespeare (1564–1616). But Bharata and Shakespeare share a "common stage," crossing the barriers of time, place, and culture. In *Natyasastra,* comic sentiment is attributed to lower-class society because comic sentiment is "mostly to be seen in women and men of the inferior type" (Bharata, 1961, 111). Analogously, Shakespeare's lower-class characters in the tragedies provide comic moments.[2] In their scenes the lower-class characters draw on an association that Bharata makes between the lower-class comic sentiment and the erotic.

In order to apply Bharata's theories to Shakespeare's treatment of lower-class society, I must describe some of Bharata's aesthetic concepts: the determinants, consequences, and kinds of comic sentiment according to the social status; I shall then turn to the techniques of juxtaposition and of mimicry with reference to three tragedies. Before I describe the origin, determinants, consequences, and kinds of comic sentiments according to social status, I should explain what Bharata means by sentiment (rasa) and mood (bhava) and how they are related. Sentiment is a combination of feelings that are practically perceived from certain happenings, ideally conceived from those perceptions, and emotionally feigned on the stage. Sentiment is not firsthand emotion or raw passion; sentiment is not a quixotic sensation or sudden emotional outburst. Its feigning is neither artificial nor awkward. According to Bharata, "the sentiment [rasa] is produced from a combination of determinants (vibhava, happenings), consequents (anubhava, experiences), and complementary psychological states (vyabhicari-bhava, feigning of perceived knowledge from those happenings and experiences)" (Bharata 1961, 105).

To make Bharata's formulae easily understandable, he uses an analogy from culinary arts in keeping with the etymological sense of sentiment (sentiment, rasa, literally means capable of being tasted). Bharata explains the meaning of being tasted and the combination of sentiment by a parallel instance:

> it is said, as taste [here rasa takes the etymological sense] results from a combination of various spices, vegetables and other articles, and as six tastes are produced by articles such as raw sugar or spices or vegetables, so Durable Psychological States (sthayibhava), when they come together with various other Psychological States, attain the quality of a Sentiment (i.e., become Sentiment). (Bharata 1961 105; emphasis added)

The food products of sweet (American pie) or hot spices (Madras curry) are a mixture of different condiments with sugar and apple or meat. When the product is served to well-disposed persons, they enjoy the taste of the combination with satisfaction. Similarly, spectators or scholars derive pleasure and satisfaction by looking at a play's manifestation of sentiments and moods on the stage in keeping with the dialogues, gestures imitated, and the credibility of the incidents feigned. The mood is the psychological state related to the sentiments of a character that an actor feigns to manifest on the stage.

Sentiment attains its quality when the emotions and moods in an actor *interact* in such a way as to be mutually appropriate and smoothly related when juxtaposed.[3] The quality of a sentiment increases when an actor presents one sentiment in juxtaposition with other sentiments and moods. To put it in other words, sugar is sweet, but it becomes sweeter when a person takes it after tasting sour pickles or hot spices. Analogously, an anxious lover, a helpless daughter, and an irate father become objects of laughter in a bedroom farce. A duchess slipping on a banana peel is an apt instance of conflicting sentiments and moods. Thus, the relationship is synergistic: sentiments, as they are manifested, are revealed as the root of all the moods, and moods the source of all sentiments.

Bharata specifically defines the comic sentiment of lower-class society when he discusses sentiments and moods. He observes that there are four basic sentiments.[4] Comic sentiment arises from the erotic—the happiness or pleasure that is "connected with desired objects, enjoyment of seasons, garlands, and similar things, and it relates to the union of man and woman"—and "includes conditions available in all other sentiments" (Bharata 1961, 110). Comic sentiment creates determinants, such as the use of irrelevant words, uncouth behavior, showing unseemly dress or ornament, mentioning different faults, and quarrels; and their consequences, such as throbbing of the lips, nose, and cheek, opening the eyes wide, perspiration, impudence, greediness, and defective limbs. The complementary moods are dreaming, dissimulation, indolence, and insomnia. Bharata illustrates all these incongruous feelings or incompatible actions by juxtaposition, the functional technique or comic sentiment and its determinant, consequent, and psychological state.

The mood of comic sentiment is laughter. "Laughter *(hasya)* is caused by determinants such as mimicry of others' actions, incoherent talk, obstrusiveness, foolishness" and it is represented on the stage by a smile (Bharata 1961, 122). In *Natyasastra*, laughter is differentiated according to social status. Bharata identifies six varieties, and the last two kinds belong to lower-class society: vulgar laughter *(apahasita)*, "the laughter on occasions not suitable to it . . . or with the shoulder and head violently shaking"; and excessive laughter *(atihasita)* in which "the eyes are expanded and tearful sound is loud and excessive, and the sides are covered by hands" (Bharata 1961, 111–12). Comic sentiment is of two kinds: self-centered, when the character laughs at himself; and centered in others, when the character laughs at others. Bharata's two sorts of clowns are, more or less, similar to Shakespeare's rustic fools, such as Costard, Dogberry, and Verges, and his jesters, such as Falstaff, Feste, and Touchstone.

Bharata's vital techniques to manifest comic sentiment are juxta- position and mimicry. Although Bharata does not use the term *juxtaposition,* I have not arbitrarily chosen that term. It gives the quintessence of Bharata's terms *com*[*ing*] *together* and *interaction,* illustrating the determinants, consequents, and moods of comic sentiment that reveal the technique of juxtaposition either ver- bally or by action (Bharata 1961, 105, 107). Juxtaposition com- pares, contrasts, complements, splits, parallels, reiterates, and symbolizes the four basic sentiments. The fluidity of basic emo- tions helps them attract each other and come together or interact when comic sentiment and its mood are illustrated through in- congruous feelings and actions. The technique is a "centripetal tendency" or "other seekingness" between sentiments and moods when they are juxtaposed.[5] Juxtaposition is a technique of placing sentiments and moods side by side, or one thing with or beside another; the condition of being so placed lets them merge with each other. It is similar to the fusion of bodies in the process of orgasm: one spirit in two bodies, united but split, symbolized but paralleled and juxtaposed, complemented but compared or contrasted and reiterated. The second technique Bharata presents is the art of mimicry, which needs no expla- nation.

Shakespeare effectively illustrates Bharata's vital techniques of comic sentiment in his treatment of lower-class characters in *Ham- let, Macbeth,* and *Antony and Cleopatra.* To demonstrate or awaken predominant sentiments is the aim of an Indian drama. Arguably, *Hamlet* deals with a pair of dominant sentiments: joy and grief; certainly the graveyard scene does this. In the juxtaposed theme of "mirth in funeral," Shakespeare presents class distinctions and erotic elements interpenetrating as the gravediggers analyze the pros and cons of Ophelia's death. In *Hamlet,* Shakespeare's juxta- position of the clowns with brooding Hamlet brightens the stage and reflects contemporary class consciousness on two issues. First, the gravedigger, outwitting his companion, questions the hierarchy of contemporary society; second, the clown excells Hamlet in equivocation.

Shakespeare lets the gravedigger outwit his companion about Ophelia's death and present a classless society in the argument on social hierarchy. Shakespeare's presentation of the coroner's verdict of Christian burial for Ophelia—an implicit reference to Sir James Hales's suicide—is not a new issue to the Elizabethan audience.[6] With this rhetorical and comic background, Shakespeare lets the second clown cynically refer to the class distinction involved in the burial: "If this had not been a gentlewoman, she should have been buried out a' Christian burial" (5.1.23–25). The word *gentle* implies a large sense of social mobility and it explains why Shakespeare put the skulls of a contemporary lawyer, farmer, politician, and Yorick—the royal jester—in Ophelia's graveyard. The first clown outwits his companion, saying that "there is no ancient gentlemen but gard'ners, ditchers, and gravemakers; they hold up Adam's profession (5.1.29–31). He mirthfully establishes that gallows and graveyards are more useful than churches.

As for the second issue—the rhetorical triumph of a lower-class character over an upper-class one—the gravedigger continues in the same vein of comic spirit when Hamlet appears with Horatio and asks the first clown for whom he digs the grave. The gravedigger neither answers Hamlet's questions about the graveyard directly nor reveals the name of the dead woman. His argument about Ophelia's death proves to be a mockery of Hamlet's investigating skills and social rank. Hamlet observes the underlying crosscurrents of the class-consciousness:

> How absolute the knave is! We must speak by the card, or equivocation will undo us . . . the age is grown so pick'd that the toe of the peasant comes so near the heel of the courtier. (5.1.136–40)

Hamlet finds that class differences have been chaotic and social manners have changed during his absence. W. R. Elton speaks of how "upper-class social mobility had led, in the Elizabethan scramble for 'honour,' to a confusion in social hierarchy" (Muir and Schoenbaum 1971, 191). Shakespeare presents the decadence of the nobility in Rosencrantz, Guilderstern, Osric, Polonius, and Claudius, juxtaposed with the refined sentiments of lower-class society such as the merciless pirates and vigilant soldiers—a remarkable Shakespearean sociocomic awareness.

Comic sentiment, according to Bharata, arises from erotic senti-

ment, and can be found in the evasive replies and roles of the
clown and the clown-prince. Bharata's principle is illustrated by
involving Claudius, Gertrude, Ophelia, and Hamlet in the com-
plication. Hamlet's discourse with Ophelia about "country matters," prior to the actors' presentation of "The Mouse-Trap,"
demonstrates how comic sentiment flows from erotic elements.
Just before the play, as part of Hamlet's scheme to "catch the
conscience of the king"—the climax—he plays a "spicy" role with
Ophelia by hiding and evading his true love for her:

> *Hamlet.* Lady, shall I lie in your lap?
> *Ophelia.* No, my lord.
> *Hamlet.* I mean, my head upon your lap?
> *Ophelia.* Ay, my lord.
> *Hamlet.* Do you think I meant country matters?
> *Ophelia.* I think nothing, my lord.
> *Hamlet.* That's a fair thought to lie between maid's legs.
>
> (3.2.112–19)

Here Hamlet closely fulfills the literal definition of Bharata's com-
plication (i.e., *garbhasandhi,* which means the "juncture of forming
fetus"). He meticulously enacts a scene of a cheap, lower-class,
and lascivious relationship before Claudius, and it reflects the
incongruity between Hamlet's love and Claudius's lust. To match
Hamlet's enactment, the clown, ironically, plays an evasive and
subtle part with Hamlet and hides the death of his beloved
Ophelia.

In *Macbeth,* the impudent lower-class porter magnifies the
comic sentiment when he lectures on lechery in lower-class terms.
In his lecture on lechery the porter stands as the source and sum
of all comedy, illustrating Bharata's two kinds of comic sentiment:
self-centered, and centered in others: (both of which may be seen
in the porters at Madras Victoria Terminus lecturing on global
issues):

> Lechery, sir, it provokes, and unprovokes: it provokes the desire, but
> it takes away the performance. Therefore, much drink may be said to
> be an equivocator with lechery: it makes him, and it mars him; it sets
> him on, and it takes him off; it persuades him, and disheartens him;
> makes him stand to, and not stand to; in conclusion, equivocates him
> in a sleep, and giving him the lie, leaves him. (2.3.29–36)

It is a coitionless performance: minds distracted, bodies disjointed, desires unfulfilled, sentiments juxtaposed, and moods

disoriented. It is a quick and short act similar to the lascivious and cheap "country matters," that Hamlet mentions. George L. Kittredge observes that the porter's style is "low comedy" as he "evokes" laughter "full-throated" (*atihasita*) (Rosenberg 1978, 353). As a pure clown figure, the porter raises laughter of ridicule (*uphastia*), and as an Elizabethan, he may create laughter (*vihasita*) at the plight of Macbeth and his un-sexed wife.

Antony and Cleopatra is a tale of passions: love and lust—the very complex of erotic sentiment within which Shakespeare weaves innumerable episodes of comic sentiment using lower-class idiom. As a result, Cleopatra becomes a harlot of the 1920s, as Shaw observes, because of her lower-class desires and her adulterous life with Antony. Howard Felperin observes how "the play's dominant ambiguity of effect arises from the juxtaposition of older and newer . . . levels of action" between Egyptian and Roman traditions (Felperin 1988, 87).

In *Antony and Cleopatra* (5.2), Shakespeare suddenly opens the lower-class phenomenon and lets it flash back from the beginning to the conclusion, juxtaposing Egyptian and Roman epic traditions. In Egypt, Cleopatra loves Antony, and she desires to be one of those women who are "but [e'en] a woman, and commanded / by such poor passion as the maid that milks / And does the meanest chares" (4.15.73–75). She grows jealous of the Roman horse that bears the weight of Antony. Her determination to entertain Antony knows no bounds.

Cleopatra becomes comically obtrusive and violent when the messenger delivers the message of Antony's "better turn" in Octavia's bed. Cleopatra beats him and curses,

> I'll spurn thine eyes
> Like balls before me; I'll unhair thy head,
> Thou shall be whipt with wire, and skew'd in brine,
> Smarting in ling'ring pickle
>
> (2.5.63–65).

Cleopatra, the queen, acts like a jealous market-maid in a fish stall in Tamil Nadu. The audience enjoys Cleopatra's envy when she inquires about Octavia's height, body, color of hair, et cetera. She is delighted when the messenger mentions Octavia's cold features. This lower-class comic background justifies Shaw's comment on how Shakespeare "transfigured" her from a "harlot" to an "immortal lover (Shaw 1934, 748).

The clown in Act Five aptly describes an illicit sexual relation-

ship from lower-class society as a precedent for the queen to follow, if she wants to avoid the sweaty Roman laborers and
plebians. The clown dissects Cleopatra's adulterous life in terms
of a lower-class phenomenon. The clown is an honest fellow, like
the traditional Indian fool (vidusaka),[7] but he is not as simple as
one would think. His seemingly innocent and irrelevant words
bring Cleopatra's past back to our memory as if she were a lower-
class woman. Her royal love assumes a dynamic sense of the lust
of a street whore when his utterances gain double meanings. He
tells a story of a lower-class woman who resolved her conflict and
found happiness in the worms as follows:

> I heard one of them no longer than yesterday, a very honest woman—
> but something given to lie, as a woman should not do, but in way of
> honesty—how she died of biting of it, what pain she felt. (5.2.250–54)

The honest woman neither sacrifices her honor nor renounces
her pleasures. He suggests that the pain she felt may not be true,
for she has lived at least in those moments of sexual relationship
instead of being a hopeless spinster. Her desires brought happiness, but ended her life as well with an ineffable and ambiguous
sensation. The clown warns Cleopatra to be cautious for "the
worm is not to be trusted but in the keeping of wise people; for
indeed, there is no goodness in the worm" (5.2.265–67). Shakespeare thus brings out Cleopatra's resolution through the rustic,
for she too finds goodness (marriage and death) in the worm.

The protagonists in Hamlet, Macbeth, and Antony and Cleopatra
are implicated in low comedy, for the clowns mimic the protagonists. When the protagonists "act funny," the rhythms of comic
sentiment route the transition from juxtaposition to mimicry.
C. L. Barber states that the clowns serve as "foils" and that their
mocking or imitation serves as an "aberration made relevant to
the main action" (Barber 1959, 13). Shakespeare brings out the
element of mimicry with sleep and death, and sows the weeds
of equivocation through lower-class characters. Death is a mime
to Hamlet, a parodist to Macbeth, and a dissembler to Cleopatra.
Shakespeare's touch of mimicry, connecting exceptional, monstrous reality with the ordinary reality of low-class society has
been transformed into a universal mimicker, namely death.
Analogous to this Shakespearean technique of mimicry, Bharata
aptly suggests that laughter arises out of mimicry, particularly
out of mimicking other people's actions.

In Hamlet, the mimicry of death is introduced when the

gravedigger elevates Hamlet from his temporal concerns and shows him the macabre dance of the sergeant death. Though the gravedigger does not recognize Hamlet, he knows of Hamlet's birth, education, and his visit to England. The gravedigger is a personification of death, and as such, he parodies the ambitions of the overreachers and laughs at the Elizabethan politician, farmer, and lawyer. All of these dissimulating climbers turned to dust in eight years, while the tanner survived nine years. Following the clown's path, Hamlet develops the comic phenomenon into cosmic phenomenon, addressing Horatio:

> Dost thou think Alexander look'd a' this fashion i' th' earth? . . . And smelt so. . . . To what base uses we may return, Horatio! Why may not imagination trace the noble dust of Alexander, till 'a find it stopping a bunghole? Alexander died, Alexander was buried, Alexander returneth to dust, the dust is earth, of earth we make loam, and why of that loam whereto he was converted might they not stop a beer-barrel? (5.1.197–212).

Alexander's dust makes the beer-barrel bungholes in a country inn and Caesar's plugs the holes in a poor woman's hut. The illusion imitates reality, and reality, illusion: the comic is converted into a universal phenomenon on the stage.

In *Macbeth*, Shakespeare lets the porter consciously usurp the stage from the usurpers of the royal throne and establishes equivocation as an instrument for Macbeth to attain his resolution. Shakespeare implements the Machiavellian concept that "the ends justify the means" by resurrecting the porter's Elizabethan guests: a farmer, an equivocator, and an English tailor parade in the minds of his audience. They are not only impersonators of the Macbeths' unfulfilled desires and untimely performances but also patrons of equivocation. The porter says that "an equivocator is one that could swear in both scales against either scale, who committed treason enough for God's sake, yet could not equivocate to heaven" (2.3.8–11). Unrighteous actions of the Elizabethan counterfeiters are parodied when the porter mimics Macbeth. Marvin Rosenberg appropriately observes that "the Porter scene reflects . . . the motif of equivocation weaving through the play: the doubling of voices, attitudes, images in [juxta]opposition, or . . . in contradiction" (Rosenberg 1978, 357). And so the porter mimics Macbeth, the king of mimes.

In *Antony and Cleopatra*, Shakespeare's treatment of mimicry between Cleopatra and death begins when Enorbarbus comments on Cleopatra's "celerity in dying" (1.2.144). The clown comes with the figs (the basket of figs, *phala*, assume the literal sense of fruits [as in *phala-yoga*]), and he plays with her, as he impersonates death. Cleopatra finds the worm her means to attain Antony. Moreover, she hears Antony, mocking at the empty victory of Caesar, calling her. She addresses Antony: "Husband, I come! / Now to that name my courage prove my title" (5.2.287–88). She gives up Nile and Egypt at the call and pinch of her lover and for the ambiguous sensations of an ordinary woman. Death does not become Antony, but mimics Antony. Antony does not come to redeem Cleopatra but the clown comes, and Cleopatra dies in orgasmic bliss. As H. C. Goddard says, "The spirit of tragedy masquerading as farce, the chariot of comedy driven by death. It is anything you please that is consummate" (Goddard 1960, 2: 188).

When we use Bharata's non-Western perspective to view comic elements, we see a defamiliarized Shakespeare. The canon joins comic sentiment and lower-class society in the tragedies in an important association. That association offers a new dimension for comedic acting and it enlarges the compositional criterion of Shakespeare, demonstrating the way that his plays move toward the paradigm of metadrama.

Notes

1. All quotations from Shakespeare are from the Riverside edition.
2. In addition to using lower-class characters to furnish comic relief, Shakespeare sometimes disguises his kings and nobles and lets them indulge themselves like inferior men and women, further demonstrating Bharata's principle on comic sentiment.
3. I would recommend Sivaji Ganesan's acting in *Navaratri* (1963), a Tamil movie, to anyone who wishes to see the histrionic representation and juxtaposition of all sentiments and moods.

In brief, sentiment takes the shades of meaning in the *OED*'s definition as follows:

1. a mental feeling which involves intellectual and physical elements;
2. a reflection colored by or proceeding from emotion;
3. a refined and tender emotion;
4. exercise or manifestation of sensibility;
5. emotional reflection or meditation.

These definitions implicitly include the elements of histrionics *(bhava)* in terms such as "colored by," "proceeding from," "refined," "exercise," and "manifestation."

4. "The Comic (sentiment) arises from the Erotic, the Pathetic from the Furious, the Marvellous from the Heroic and the Terrible from the Odious" (Bharata 1961, 107).

5. Berry illustrates how this organic principle "centripetal tendency" works in his analysis of *The Comedy of Errors* (Berry 1972, 27).

6. The issue of class consciousness in Sir Hales's Christian burial provided Elizabethans with a wide range of gossip and fictitious arguments about whether the "subject is agent or patient; or in the words of the clown whether man went to the water or the water came to him," H. H. Furness, *Variorum Shakespeare: Hamlet* (Philadelphia: J. B. Lippincott, 1877), 382.

7. Characteristics of a Jester: "one who looks to people's pleasure, can imitate manners of all people, resorts to various [means] and mixes with women, is ready-witted in disclosures made through Pleasantry, or Covert Pleasure and is clever, and can give censure through his words, is known as a Jester *(vidusaka)*" (Bharata 1961 226).

Comic Material: "Shakespeare" in the Classic Detective Story

SUSAN BAKER

The longest running play in the history of the London theater is *The Mousetrap:* story and dialogue by Agatha Christie, title by Hamlet. Although (in this instance) Christie borrows little from Shakespeare beyond her title, this collaboration of sorts between two of the best-selling and most widely translated authors in the English language is highly appropriate and not at all surprising. In titles and plots, in epigraphs and characters' names, in frequent bardic clues and in a sometimes irritating propensity for quotation, classic detective stories constantly allude to "Shakespeare."[1] Despite these multitudinous allusions, however, I would argue that Shakespeare's literary works themselves are not engaged intertextually by classic detective stories, at least not in ways we usually think of intertextuality. That is, although classic detective stories repeatedly invoke Shakespeare, they engage only superficially the plays and poems for which he is supposedly famous. The *idea* of Shakespeare, however, Shakespeare as cultural token or totem, runs through classic detective stories with such frequency as to be all but a generic requisite.[2] As a first move, we might say that the idea of Shakespeare serves as part of the classic detective story's decor, but a decor that exceeds mere window-dressing. Like potted plants and tasteful bibelots, the appearances of "Shakespeare" in classic detective stories betoken the aspirations and anxieties, the demons and desires, of those who read and write in this genre.

Some clarification may be in order. First, "Shakespeare" here refers less to the man from Stratford and the plays included in the First Folio than to what we can call the *idea* of Shakespeare or the Shakespeare myth.[3] This is the Shakespeare whose plays can be parodied in *Ducktales* and *Moonlighting,* whose face appears in advertisements for rugs and sunglasses, whose words are quoted in *Hagar the Horrible* and *Frank and Ernest*. The town of his birth has become virtually a theme park in his honor, and he often appears as a category on *Jeopardy*. There were at least fifteen "Summer Shakespeare Festivals" across the U.S. in 1991— each no doubt with its own souvenir mugs and sweatshirts. News commentators have referred to both Margaret Thatcher and Mikhail Gorbachev as Shakespearean tragic heroes. United Airlines is currently advertising its flights to Heathrow with excerpts from John of Gaunt's deathbed speech in *Richard II*. In other words, far more than any other great writer, Shakespeare haunts the popular culture of our everyday lives. (There is certainly no other great writer in whose name so much money changes hands.) It is true that Shakespeare wrote wonderful plays, but this excellence alone hardly seems adequate to account for the pervasive presence of assorted Shakespearean images and allusions in our society. Every mass-media reference to Shakespeare attests to someone's belief that such allusions evoke responses in a mass audience—despite the obvious fact that only a tiny fraction of that audience knows the plays well and only a somewhat larger fraction has the leisure, cash, and inclination to attend theatrical performances with any frequency. Clearly, the practitioners of mass media both assume and perpetuate a popular perception of Shakespeare.[4] It is to understand something of this popular perception—how it is reproduced and what it may mean—that I am investigating appearances of Shakespeare in the classic detective story.

By "classic detective story" I refer specifically to the sort of murder mystery associated with Agatha Christie—as opposed to thrillers, tough-guy detective novels, spy stories, police procedurals, and so on. The Christie genre is sometimes called "cozy," or "country house," or "clue-puzzle," and as these labels perhaps suggest, critics generally agree that it is a *comic* form. George Grella has outlined several characteristics that qualify the classic detective story as "one of the last outposts of the comedy of manners in fiction" (Grella 1980, 88),[5] and subsequent scholarship has ratified his description. According to Grella,

> The central puzzle provides the usual complication, which the detective hero must remove; and its difficulty insures a typically comic engagement of the intellect. The whodunit's plot, full of deceptions, red herrings, clues real and fabricated, parallels the usually intricate plots of comedy, which often depend upon mistaken motives, confusion, and dissembling; it also supports the familiar romantic subplot.

And the upper class setting of the detective story places it even more precisely in the tradition of the comedy of manners. (Grella 1980, 88)

Earl Bargainnier offers as further evidence for the comic form of most detective stories "the renewal of harmony in society . . . signified by engagements, marriages, births or the announcements of forthcoming ones, dinners (the traditional feast of thanks), and other such symbolic acts" (Bargainner 1987, 1). Grella goes so far as to assert of classic detective stories that "There is more of Shakespeare, Congreve, and Sheridan than Poe, Conan Doyle, and Chesterton in their creation" (Grella 1980, 89). The reference to Shakespeare is particularly apt. Like classic detective stories, Shakespeare's comedies at once confront *and* distance such persistent conditions as the fact of death, the presence of social misfits, and the dangers of misplaced or illegitimate desires. (Don John's survival doesn't make *Much Ado About Nothing* a tragedy, any more than Horatio's survival makes *Hamlet* a comedy; Marcade's announcement of death doesn't turn *Love's Labor's Lost* into a tragedy, any more than the drunken porter turns *Macbeth* into a comedy.) This is not the place to argue against the critical puritanism that sees Shakespearean comedy as "undercut" or "subverted" by the absence of absolute or perfect harmony, but I will insist here that such absence in the resolutions of recent classic detective stories, as compared to those of the thirties, does not at all vitiate their formal status as comedies. As John G. Cawelti observes, the "comic universe" of classic detective stories "in which characters and action are so constructed as to continually reassure us that things will ultimately work out happily can encompass a considerable degree of disorder and danger" (Cawelti 1976, 108).

Although the golden age of classic detective stories is generally taken to have occurred between World Wars I and II, the best-known of mystery writers have continued to sell over the years. Further, the classic detective story is currently enjoying a surge in popularity. As even a quick glance at the shelves in any local bookstore indicates, older mysteries are being reprinted and new ones written in increasing numbers.[6] Significantly, new entries in the genre maintain the Shakespearean citation so characteristic of golden age mysteries. (The major change over time I've observed is that the more recent the mystery, the more likely it is to *identify* the source of its Shakespearean citations.)

Critics who attend to such things generally agree about the audience for and ideological thrust of classic detective stories. For example, writing of Agatha Christie, Stephen Knight concludes that "Christie's central audience was leisured, relatively unskilled but also competitive and self-conscious—the classic anxious bourgeois class. For them, she fashioned a form that ratified conservatism, the duty others owe the self, and ultimately the ability of very ordinary powers to cope with the disorder such people faced, in the world and within themselves" (Knight 1980, 133). Similarly, in his discussion of "drawing room" mysteries, Ernest Mandel observes that "Conventionalized and formalized 'trivial' literature, like conventionalized and formalized forms of art in general, are not supposed to reflect reality at all. They are intended to satisfy subjective needs, thus performing an objective function: to reconcile the upset, bored and anxious individual member of the middle class with the inevitability and permanence of bourgeois society" (Mandel 1984, 29).[7] Both Knight and Mandel locate various mystery subgenres within the particular historical circumstances of their emergence, but neither attends much to the persistent sales of many golden age writers and both wrote before the recent boom in publishing classic detective stories, old and new.

Given the continued and increasing popularity of this quintessentially bourgeois genre, a double question seems well worth asking: How is Shakespeare represented *in* classic detective stories, and what does Shakespeare represent *for* readers and writers of this comic genre? Before any further theorizing, it may be useful to consider an exemplary instance: P. D. James's recent *A Taste for Death* (1986). The novel's protagonist, Kate Miskin, is a young, ambitious, female C.I.D. Inspector assigned to Commander Adam Dalgliesh's newly formed elite squad charged with investigating "serious crimes which, for political or other reasons, needed particularly sensitive handling" (James 1986, 15). (Dalgliesh is James's series detective.) This assignment gives Kate her chance to succeed, to ensure her career in the C.I.D. An illegitimate child, Kate was reared by her grandmother in a "dirty, noisy flat on the seventh floor of a post-war tower block" (James 1986, 167). By moving to a flat off Holland Park Avenue, Kate has made the first step on her "planned upward progress"; she has escaped from "the shouting, the graffiti, the broken lifts, the stinking urine" (James 1986, 167). Unfortunately for Kate, her grandmother would like to escape these discomforts as well, and a subplot tracks the struggle between Kate's determination to escape her background and her sense of obligation to the woman who reared her. Although she does provide food and such for her grandmother, Kate resists the old woman's pleas to move in with her: "[Kate] couldn't give up her freedom . . . her privacy and peace at the end of the day for an old woman's impedimenta, the ceaseless noise of her television, the mess, the smell of old age, of failure, the smell of Ellison Fairweather House, of childhood, of the past" (James 1986, 175). As this quotation makes clear, Kate resists taking her grandmother in not simply because she fears inconvenience; rather, she cannot bear daily reminders of the past and place her grandmother signifies.

Shakespeare is crucial to Kate's upward mobility: just how crucial becomes clear only at the novel's end. Still, we are told early that

> Two half-remembered lines of Shakespeare which had met her eyes when she had casually opened the book in the school library had become for her the philosophy by which she intended to live.

> *What matters it what went before or after,*
> *Now with myself I will begin and end*

(James 1986, 168).

Despite this muddled commitment to independence, Kate does have a middle-class boyfriend, Alan Scully, who works in a theological library and collects old books. Notably, for their first date he had asked her "to go with him to see a Shakespearean production at the National Theatre" (James 1986, 172).

As the novel proceeds, Dalgliesh's special squad is called upon to investigate the violent death of Sir Paul Berowne. In life Berowne has been a baronet, once a barrister, more recently a minor minister in Her Majesty's Government until he resigned (only days before his death) because of a sudden religious fervor. Enter the usual suspects: Berowne's parvenu wife; her parasite brother; her lover; an unbalanced housekeeper; Berowne's estranged daughter; her Marxist boyfriend; Berowne's mother; even a troubled priest, who confesses to Dalgliesh that while serving mass he saw the stigmata on Paul Berowne's wrists. I won't dwell here on the mystery plot but would briefly note that with the crime's solution upstarts are chastened, Berowne's daughter is cured of radical politics, and Kate Miskin's improved social status is assured. Writing in the eighties, James does allow her heroine some upward mobility, but I would stress that the distribution of rewards and punishments at the novel's end perpetuates the classic detective story's traditional preference for people who know and accept their inherited place in the social order.

On beginning *A Taste For Death*, I couldn't help wondering—why Berowne? There may be—at a stretch—a slight echo of *Love's Labor's Lost* in Sir Paul's decision to withdraw from a world of corrupt politics, but something more is going on. The novel's first explicit reference to Shakespeare's play comes apparently as a bit of characterization. Kate and Alan are discussing the case, and he tells her that "Berowne is the name of an attendant lord in Shakespeare" (James 1986, 170). The ambitious girl from Ellison Fairweather House doesn't *really* know her bard. She's a quick study, however, with a good memory for useful facts, and her knowing the provenance of Berowne's name will save the day.

As the novel approaches its end, Kate and her ailing grand-mother are held hostage by the crazed villain. Cleverly, Kate persuades the murderer that she must cancel a dinner date with her boyfriend. She does so over the telephone, adding "And Alan, remember to bring me that book you promised. The Shakespeare *Love's Labour's Lost*, for Christ's sake. See you tomorrow. And remember the Shakespeare" (James 1986, 475). Alan, a clever fellow himself, decodes her allusion to Berowne and calls Dalgliesh. At the appropriate moment, Kate tackles the murderer, who can then be captured by the waiting police. Alas, Kate's grandmother is killed during the fracas, and Dalgliesh observes that "with murder there was never a final victim" (James 1986, 484).

Some have argued that this sort of commentary distinguishes James and her contemporaries from their golden age predecessors; James herself has said, "in the modern detective story, although we discover who did it and why and how and when and so forth, the effects of the crime are a great deal more disruptive than they were in the older mystery. . . . The modern detective story shows exactly how disruptive and contaminating murder can be and how no life in that society surrounding it is untouched by it."[8] I would argue, however, that such darkening of vision has not significantly altered the ideological force of the classic detective story. It certainly hasn't altered Shakespeare's role in that ideology. Shakespeare provides the secret that saves Kate's life and makes her a heroine, doubly ensured of her place in the middle class: she has proved her worthiness for her job in the upper police, and Alan discovers he's in love with her. That she loses her grandmother in the process may be sad, but this loss indeed frees her from the ties that bound her to her despised origins. And it is a piece of Shakespearean trivia, an oddment of Shakespearean knowledge, that captures the criminal, secures our detective's step up in class, and separates her—irrevocably—

from Ellison Fairweather House. Here, "Shakespeare" is less a playwright than a source of instrumental knowledge, a ticket to upward mobility, and a badge of middle-class membership.

It is Shakespeare, then, who provides Kate Miskin with credentials for the middle-class life she desires. This sort of certification may well appeal to the classic detective story's ever-anxious bourgeois audience. Knight's description of the genre may be worth reiterating: "a form that ratified . . . the ability of very ordinary powers to cope with the disorder such people faced, in the world and in themselves." Certainly a merely "very ordinary" knowledge of Shakespeare works for Kate Miskin, whose situation can stand for that of the classic detective story itself. In this genre, a little "Shakespeare" goes a long way toward supplying a perceived respectability.

The classic detective story is a popular genre, and I intend *popular* in both senses: "money-maker" and "not-high-art" (whatever that might mean). Unlike many popular genres, however, classic detective stories seem determined to avoid the taint of *popular* in the word's root sense. Apparently, obeisance to "Shakespeare" helps allay the classic detective story's uneasiness about its vaguely vulgar origins,[9] and just about any reference to Shakespeare, however trivial, will do. For the genre as a whole, then, as well as for the people it portrays, "Shakespeare" signals identification with a particular class.[10] Dorothy Sayers, looking back on the publication of E. C. Bentley's *Trent's Last Case* in 1913, is relevant: "In the years just before the War, the literature of crime was in rather a bad way. The grand old native school of Wilkie Collins, Dickens and Latham had sunk into vulgarity and absurdity in the pages of the cheap magazines. . . . The detective story had become a byword for dull illiteracy, and no writer of any distinction would turn his hand to a form of literature that was fast abandoning all claim to be considered literature at all" (Sayers 1978, x–xiii).[11] *Trent's Last Case* changed all that, according to Sayers, in part because "it was the work of an educated man, with the whole tradition of European letters behind him" (Sayers 1978, xi). Sayers praises Bentley's plotting and characterization, but she clearly values above all his *writing*: "the style ranges from a vividly coloured rhetoric to a delicate and ironical literary fancy" (Sayers 1978, xii). And, I would argue, part of that "literary fancy" is quotation from the "tradition of European letters," including (of course) Shakespeare. Indeed, I am persuaded that the multiple uses of Shakespeare in classic detective stories are, above all, gestures of self-declaration, affirmations of respectability for the genre, its writers, and its readers.

Such gestures, however, take on a certain life of their own, and numerous writers of classic detective stories have found Shakespeare handy as well for meeting assorted formal requirements of the genre. Of the several possibilities, I shall focus here on one way Shakespeare *materializes* in such books: as a token or fetish or relic. I will continue to use the term *token*, which does signify both nostalgia and exchange, both badge or emblem and metonymic substitution, rather than becoming embroiled in a Polonial effort to disentangle the commodified fetish from the fetishized commodity or the fetishized relic as commodity from the reliquated commodity as fetish, and so on. Whatever the taxonomy, however, I am certain that Shakespeare tokens in classic detective stories play economic, sexual, and quasi-religious roles, ones that perhaps cannot or should not always be disentangled. (My debts to Marjorie Garber's essay on "Shakespeare As Fetish" will be obvious.)[12] As objects of multiple desires, such tokens motivate mystery plots, and their disposition becomes crucial to comic resolutions.

Two novels must stand for many in this discussion: *The Long Farewell* (1958) by Michael Innes, and *Killer Dolphin* (1966) by Ngaio Marsh. In both cases, the impetus for murder is a Shakespeare token: in *Farewell*, a copy of Cinthio's *Hecatommithi* complete with Shakespeare's own marginalia; in *Dolphin* a child's glove embroidered with the initials "HS." (It is worth noting that both mysteries refer to these tokens as relics—without apology or quotation marks.)

In *The Long Farewell*, after the violent death of Lewis Packford (a scholar of the Leslie Hotson sort), detective Sir John Appleby speculates on what would be "the most valuable book in the world" (Innes 1958, 122), one prized enough to make someone murderous, whether an impoverished brother, a wife, a fanatic collector, or one of several scholars. Most of the novel's contempt is reserved for the collector, he of so little soul as to covet Packford's find for its (admittedly considerable) monetary value. The collector in *The Long Farewell* is an American, according to one character "a meat king, no doubt" (Innes 1958, 122), surfeited with money but notably lacking in taste and auxiliary verbs. In a classic detective story, overt commodification of a Shakespeare token is a sure symptom of vulgarity, even as dignified reverence is a sign of both refinement and moral worth. The contradiction here is telling. On the one hand, the classic detective story is compelled to stress the cash value of Shakespearean tokens. Partly, to be sure, this valuation is necessary in order to represent such tokens as objects of mimetic desire sufficient to motivate any of multiple suspects to murder; equally, I suspect, in this discourse "high-priced" is high praise, the best available name for something valorized. At the same time, however, to desire a Shakespeare token for its exchange value is to be marked as common, vulgar, "not our sort." It seems reasonable enough to assume that this ambivalence toward wealth (toward money-as-criterion) characterizes readers of this genre as well as its representations.

To be fair, Innes's scholars are hardly more attractive than the loutish collector; after all, "Michael Innes" is the pseudonym of J. I. M. Stewart, author of the classic study *Character and Motive in Shakespeare,* and academics portrayed in his mysteries are often absurd if rarely vulgar. Too, Innes (and other of the most entertaining classic detective story writers) is always at least skirting parody, even self-parody. Still, effective parodies depend upon much the same assumptions and arouse much the same responses as would be expected for that which they spoof. For instance, Innes is surely having fun when he mentions only two of Moody the meatpacker's prized collector's items: General Gordon's Bible and the prayer book Mary Queen of Scots carried to the scaffold—in their conflation of religion, patriotism, and romantic doom, these possessions are appropriate company indeed for Shakespeare's very own volume of Cinthio. But even in jest such items can be prized only for their sentimental associations, which—unlike the texts themselves—cannot be mechanically reproduced.

The American collector and his motives clearly mark this novel's Shakespearean token as both commodity and relic. Its role as sexual fetish is more oblique, but also more surprising. Early on, we are told that Packford, a middle-aged man, has appeared to all as a confirmed bachelor—nothing untoward, Innes reassures his audience, simply uninterested. At roughly the time that he was on the trail of Shakespearean treasure, however, Packford discovered sex. Implicitly at least, Shakespeare's handwriting serves here as fetish in the most clinical sense—as the token that enables erotic desire. In fact, just prior to Packford's untimely demise, his wives had appeared on the doorstep of his dilapidated ancestral home. Yes, both his wives: the newly lustful Packford had been leading not one but two secret lives. But then, we might expect a Shakespeare token to be an especially powerful aphrodisiac.

The twist in Innes's book is that murder occurs not because a Shakespearean relic exists, but because it doesn't—it's a forgery, or more precisely, its putatively Shakespearean annotations are forged. Genuine Cinthio is overwritten by fake Shakespeare. Forgery, of course, is a good Shakespearean (and poststructuralist) topic; certainly, the very act of forging Shakespeare's marginalia implies a shared belief in the value such jottings would have if authentic.[13] Forgery is also a perfect emblem for the classic detective story: the murderer's task is to make the crime appear the work of another hand, the original hand exposed only at the last minute (or chapter). The solution of such a crime is the discovery of a hidden—or lost—original. Innes's early assessment of the victim is relevant here: "All Packford's real traffic had been with the memorials and signs and traces of things, and not with things in themselves" (Innes 1958, 69). The large number of professors who read and write detective stories may be accounted for in part by the fact that both scholars (since the eighteenth century) and classic detectives are agents of a desire to recover lost originals.

In Ngaio Marsh's *Killer Dolphin,* this desire for a lost, originating hand is made dazzlingly explicit.[14] Some plot summary is necessary at this point. Our hero—his name is Peregrine Jay—visits The Dolphin, an abandoned and bomb-damaged theater on London's South Bank. (This book was published in 1966, eleven years before Queen Elizabeth II opened the National Theatre building and sixteen years before the RSC moved its London base to the Barbican.) In a peculiar twist on forger William Ireland's fantasies, poor Jay falls through rotting boards into "icy, stagnant water . . . unspeakable muck" (Marsh 1966, 14) and is rescued by the theater's mysterious owner, Vassily Conducis, a fabulously wealthy recluse of vaguely Levantine origins. Conducis takes the sodden Jay (in a chauffeured Daimler) to his exquisitely appointed townhouse. In the glow of recent shock and a restorative rum with lemon, Jay waxes exuberant on his dream: to restore The Dolphin to the glory it had known under renowned nineteenth-century manager Adolphus Ruby. (How far are we here from The Shakespeare Globe Trust?)[15] Jay describes the sort of theater he envisions: "Not twee. God, no! Not a pastiche either. Just a good theatre doing the job it was meant to do. And doing the stuff that doesn't belong to any bloody Method or Movement or Trend or Period or what-have-you" (Marsh 1966, 27). We might well ask where Jay will find this pure drama, untainted by its time or space. Mr. Conducis, however, assumes immediately that Jay is describing Shakespeare, as of course he is; these are, after all, characters in a classic detective story, a genre that regularly scorns theatrical productions that aspire to contemporary relevance. As a general rule, classic detective stories prefer and promote a timeless Shakespeare.

Peregrine having proved himself worthy, Conducis lays before him a shabby Victorian hand desk; beneath its false bottom is a silk-wrapped package in which Jay discovers a child's cheveril glove—"flaccid," Jay notes, "uncannily so, as if it had only just died" (Marsh 1966, 30). Beneath the glove lie two handwritten notes: the first reads, "This little glove and accompanying note were given to my Great-Great-Grandmother by her Beft Friend: a Mifs or Mrs. J. Hart. My dear Grandmother always infifted that it had belonged to the Poet. N. B. mark infide gauntlet. / M.E. 23 April [when else?] 1830"; the second, "Mayᵈ by my father for my sonne on his XI birtheᵈʸ and never worne butte yⁿᶜ" (Marsh 1966, 31). Note the succession of revelations here: a casket, a package, a glove, a first note that hints at "sacred" origins, the second note in *the hand* itself. Still, the focus throughout the novel is on the glove—the hand covering handed down first from father to son to son and then deflected to a female line. Obviously, from its first appearance in the novel, the glove is saturated with sexual and sacred significance. But as we shall see, this unveiling is just the beginning.

A few days later, Jay's guardian angel turns out to be an angel in the theatrical sense as well; that is, Conducis offers Jay the job of restoring the theatre and becoming its director-manager. Duly authenticated by the British Museum, the glove Shakespeare's father made for Shakespeare's son is exhibited in the refurbished Dolphin, and Jay writes a play in its honor: *The Glove*. Here, the glove functions as a fetish in the anthropological sense, as the object where, in Freud's words, "the savage sees the embodiment of his god." That is, the play Jay writes puts Will Shakespeare at its center, brings the bard back to life, as it were, responds to a desire to speak with the dead. Indeed, when Superintendent Alleyn (a gentleman descended from the actor) first sees the glove, he finds "himself wishing very heartily that Peregrine's play would perform the miracle of awareness which would take the sense of death away from Shakespeare's note and young Hamnet's glove" (Marsh 1966, 119–20). (Make what you will of the fact that the actress who plays Joan Hart becomes Jay's fiancée.)

Before returning to the novel's plot, some comment on Jay's play may be in order. Two details beyond a cast list are provided: a woman named Rosaline appears hopping toward Will's door— Jay quotes the relevant lines about Cleopatra as he coaches a rather dim actress through the Dark Lady's lines; the play ends with Shakespeare's revulsion as Rosaline dons dead Hamnet's glove—here, Sonnet 129 is invoked. Readers may well take pleasure in recognizing these allusions, but I would argue that such citations work primarily to reproduce naive assumptions about literature as straightforwardly autobiographical, both its general attitudes and circumstantial details utterly dependent upon and revelatory of a writer's personal experience.[16] Repeatedly, the construction of a fanciful Shakespeare biography within a classic detective story projects the playwright as an autonomous subject, the sovereign origin of his art.

At any rate, disaster strikes The Dolphin when the glove is stolen. An elderly caretaker is murdered and a "beastly" boy actor (Marsh 1966, 185) concussed in the process. Interestingly, Jobbins the caretaker and Trevor the ill-bred boy are the novel's only important characters indigenous to The Dolphin's seedy neighborhood. Uncannily, Marsh's novel adumbrates a conflict of interest between theatrical restoration and neighborhood continuity, between reverence for a cultural past and the needs of people in the present. As we have seen recently in Southwark, when sacred theatrical ground is at stake, the Jobbinses and Trevors of the world must go.[17]

Significantly, murder is not the only crime committed at The Dolphin, and thus merely a fake glove has been stolen. Jobbins has died for a forgery, a fortunate forgery, Marsh seems to suggest: for the duration of the novel, the substitution of a replica prevents the sale of Hamnet's glove to a (predictably) American collector. This Shakespearean forgery is a patriotic crime, perpetrated in order to prevent England's losing a national treasure.[18] It may seem a bit excessive to equate a tatty old glove with, say, the Elgin Marbles or Goya's Wellington, but Marsh explicitly does so and, further, seems to expect her audience to do so as well. Indeed, the theft of Hamnet's glove is made to seem noble, if foolishly so, and the well-bred forger (Jeremy Jones) isn't punished at all for his theft—unless one counts the fact that Alleyn gives this "young booby" (Marsh 1966, 224) "a blackguarding that would scour the hide off an alligator" (Marsh 1966, 257). The philistine murderer, who stole the (fake) glove in order to sell it to yet another American collector, will of course be prosecuted. This villain's identity is worth some consideration.

Although I believe the notion of "fair play" is generally over-weighted in discussions of classic detective stories,[19] readers of *Killer Dolphin* might well identify the *who* if not the *how* of Jobbins's death simply by attending to "Shakespeare." The murderer, Harry Grove, is the novel's only character to express doubts about the extraordinary value placed on Hamnet's glove (Marsh 1966, 255); this Shakespearean token serves throughout as touchstone, and Harry flunks the sensibility test. Not at all coincidentally, I believe, he is also the only character whose social status is dubious. When questioned by the C.I.D. Inspector, Harry insists upon his "lower-middle-class" background and acknowledges that he resents the influence of old school ties in his profession (Marsh 1966, 202)—indeed, he has been known to twit his public school colleagues with claims to be an "old Borstalian" (Marsh 1966, 227). Jay, however, believes that Grove is "an inverted snob" and that he "began in the RAF" (Marsh 1966, 227). The subtleties of this latter point are beyond my American grasp (Does flying with the RAF erase all previous class markers? Does life begin anew with enlistment in the RAF?),[20] but it seems clear enough that Harry's liminal place in the class structure makes him dangerous, deadly even. As Grella observes of the typical murderer in classical detective stories, "His crime is not the true cause of his defeat, only a symptom of it: like his victim, the murderer has guaranteed his doom by committing some earlier comic, social, or ethical mistake" (Marsh 1966, 98). Harry's "mistake" is, of course, his insufficient reverence for a Shakespearean relic.

As *Killer Dolphin* makes amply clear, in the social hierarchy of the classic detective story, "Shakespeare" plays a double role. First, *knowledge* of Shakespeare serves (persuasively enough) as a class marker, suggesting a particular sort of background, reinforced by a particular sort of education, and sustained by comfortable circumstances that allow for theatergoing and leisurely rereading. The genre, however, represents "Shakespeare" not simply as a domain of knowledge and pleasure, but equally as a moral touchstone, as a geiger counter for registering delicate sensibilities, which themselves signal integrity and virtue. (In *Killer Dolphin* Jeremy's theft of the glove cannot be a crime because his reverence for Shakespeare proves he is not a criminal.) In other words, these two roles of "Shakespeare" in classic detective stories combine to represent a consequence *of* privilege as a validation of or justification *for* privilege.

In its accumulation of Shakespearean detail, then, this popular genre operates to reproduce reverence for the idea of Shakespeare and, by metonymic extension, for ideas of "serious literature" and "high culture" more generally.[21] Further, the appearances of "Shakespeare" in classic detective stories also work to reproduce naive assumptions about reading, about authors, and about literature as universal and timeless. Finally, the genre's typical attitudes toward Shakespearean tokens work (hegemonically) to endorse and reproduce a social order. Even as such fictions seek through allusion to dignify themselves, they become both barometers and producers of a popular perception of "Shakespeare."

Notes

1. *The Armchair Detective* 14 (Spring 1981) includes two relevant essays: Jane Gottschalk, "Detective Fiction and Things Shakespearean," 100–107, and Jane S. Bakerman, "Advice Unheeded: Shakespeare in Some Modern Mystery Novels," 134–39. Both are primarily descriptive and concerned to evaluate the success of various mysteries as entertainment. An adequate sense of general directions in literary criticism of classic detective stories can be gleaned from three anthologies: Howard Haycraft, ed., *The Art of the Mystery Story: A Collection of Critical Essays* (New York: Simon and Schuster, 1946); Robin W. Winks, ed., *Detective Fiction: A Collection of Critical Essays* (Englewood Cliffs, N.J.: Prentice-Hall, 1980); Glenn W. Most and William W. Stone, eds., *The Poetics of Murder: Detective Fiction & Literary Theory* (New York: Harcourt Brace Jovanovich, 1983). Also useful is Peter Wolfe, "The Critics Did It: An Essay-Review," *Modern Fiction Studies* 29 (Autumn 1983): 389–433.

2. Indeed, when L. A. Morse, writing as "Runa Fairliegh," parodies the classic detective story in *An Old-Fashioned Mystery* (New York: Avon, 1983), he begins with a pair of twins—Violet and Sebastian. In this case, however, it is Sebastian who, cross-dressed and wearing a wig, is mistaken for Violet.

3. See Graham Holderness, ed., *The Shakespeare Myth* (New York: St. Martin's, 1988).

4. Strictly speaking, *perception* here probably should be *perceptions*. That is, without extended analysis of various popular forms and their intended audiences, I am wary of generalizing about any singular perception of "Shakespeare." Still, the classic detective story seems a good place to pursue such investigations.

5. "The Formal Detective Novel" first appeared as "Murder and Manners: The Formal Detective Novel," *Novel* 4 (1970): 30–48. For further development and updating of Grella's thesis, see Hanna Charney, *The Detective Novel of Manners* (Rutherford, N.J.: Farleigh Dickinson University Press, 1981). Also helpful are several of the essays in Earl Bargainnier, ed., *Comic Crime* (Bowling Green, Ohio: Bowling Green State University Popular Press, 1987).

6. On continuing popularity, see for example, the sales figures cited for various books in Dennis Sanders and Len Lovallo, *The Agatha Christie Companion*, rev. ed. (New York: Berkeley Books, 1989). Also useful in assessing the sustained popularity of detective fiction is Michael L. Cook, *Murder by Mail* (Bowling

Green, Ohio: Bowling Green University Popular Press, 1983). The recent boom no doubt has multiple causes, but among them is surely improved marketing and mall bookstores; for the effects of such developments on another pop genre, see Janice A. Radway, *Reading the Romance* (Chapel Hill: University of North Carolina Press, 1984), 19–45.

7. See as well the preface to John M. Reilly, ed., *Twentieth-Century Crime and Mystery Writers*, 2nd. ed. (New York: St. Martin's Press, 1985), vii–xi.

8. Quoted in "A Mind to Write: An Interview with P. D. James," *The Armchair Detective* 19 (Fall 1986): 343.

9. Tough-guy readers and writers share this anxiety, but the usual defenses mounted for the two subgenres are revealing. Classic detectives stories are most often defended on the grounds of who *reads* them (presidents, scholars, success-ful businessmen, and so on), and the form tends to be thus exonerated as a whole. Tough-guy defenses, on the other hand, tend to claim for *particular* instances of the form that they are "real novels," rather than mere detective fictions.

10. I am reasonably certain that *identification* is a more appropriate term here than *membership* would be. The readership for classic detective stories must be wider than the class it primarily portrays (the distinctly upper end of the middle class), and *identification* allows as well for the transatlantic, indeed international, phenomenon of the genre's popularity. I would also note that the classic detective story hardly encourages a rigorous analysis of class as economically deter-mined, as its stress on sensibility indicates.

11. The verso of the title page of this edition notes, "The new Introduction by Dorothy Sayers is from a draft of a talk intended for broadcasting found in the Marion Wade Collection at Wheaton College, Illinois. It bears no date nor any evidence of ever having been delivered" (Sayers 1978, vi). Internal evidence suggests this talk was written in the early twenties.

12. *Shakespeare Quarterly* 41 (1990): 242–50. The Innes and Marsh novels I discuss lend persuasive support to Garber's argument.

13. See, for example, Margreta de Grazia, *Shakespeare Verbatim* (Oxford: Clarendon Press, 1991): "It appears, then, that at the same time as the authentic texts, documents, and paintings were established, inauthentic items and coun-terfeits began to emerge. The real proliferation of forgeries did not begin until the early nineteenth century, after the standard of authenticity was firmly in place" (86).

14. For an exhaustive discussion of the resonance in the term *hand*, see Jona-than Goldberg, *Writing Matter* (Stanford, Calif.: Stanford University Press, 1990). In light of Goldberg's discussion, a particularly interesting detective story is Robert Richardson, *The Latimer Mercy* (New York: Signet, 1985)—in which what begins as a search for a stolen Bible inscribed with Bishop Latimer's handwriting becomes a search for a missing actress when her severed hands are returned to her friends.

15. Wanamaker gives "about 1970" as the date for early moves toward the Shakespeare Globe Trust. Interview in G. Holderness, Rd., *The Shakespeare Myth* (New York: St. Martin's Press, 1988), 16–23.

16. This assumption certainly governs the few murder mysteries that present Shakespeare as a character. A recent example is Faye Kellerman's *The Quality of Mercy* (New York: Ballantine, 1989) in which Shakespeare falls in love with Dr. Lopez's daughter and pens the title speech for her to deliver to Queen Elizabeth.

17. See John Drakakis, "Ideology and institution: Shakespeare and the road-sweepers," *The Shakespeare Myth*, 24–41.

18. In a more recent mystery—David Williams, *Unholy Writ* (New York: St. Martin's 1976)—most of the characters simply assume that Parliament would not allow a Shakespearean manuscript to leave England.

19. See my essay, "Interpretation of Fair Play Mysteries: The Rules of the Game," *Halcyon* 7 (1985): 119–28.

20. Marsh's *Death of a Fool* (1956) also includes an ex-RAF murderer. In this case, his wartime heroics have left him dissatisfied with his origins.

21. Here is a remarkable instance of Shakespeare as synecdoche for not only great literature but, indeed, the whole of Western civilization. The 1 April 1991, issue of *Forbes* tempts its business-minded readers with this blurb on its cover: "Was Shakespeare a male chauvinist racist?" The so-touted article (81–86) is entitled "The Visgoths in Tweed," and is excerpted from Dinesh D'Souza's *Illiberal Education: The Politics of Race and Sex on Campus* (cited as forthcoming from The Free Press). D'Souza's attack on the professoriat for "exalt[ing] a neo-Marxist ideology promoted in the name of multiculturism" (81) is thoroughly predictable except for one tiny detail: he never in this excerpt mentions Shakespeare, although the bard is indeed included in the illustrations representing the toppled and broken busts of great white men. Much as one would like to sue *Forbes* for false advertising, the cover blurb is indeed no such thing: "Shakespeare" is here simply a shorthand for everything D'Souza and his ilk feel compelled to defend. (You may be interested to note that his final paragraph urges "Don't just write a check to your alma mater; that's an abrogation of responsibility. Keep abreast of what is going on and don't be afraid to raise your voice and even to close your wallet in protest. Our Western, free-market culture need not provide the rope to hang itself" [86].)

Works Cited

Agnew, Jean-Christophe. 1986. *Worlds Apart: The Market and the Theater in Anglo-American Thought, 1550–1750*. Cambridge: Cambridge University Press.

Babcock, Barbara A., ed. 1978. *The Reversible World: Symbolic Inversion in Art and Society*. Ithaca: Cornell University Press.

Bakhtin, Mikhail. 1984. *Rabelais and his World*. Translated by Helene Iswolsky. Bloomington: Indiana University Press. Reprint of 1964 edition.

Barber, C. L. 1959. *Shakespeare's Festive Comedy*. Princeton: Princeton University Press.

Bargainnier, Earl, ed. 1987. *Comic Crime*. Bowling Green, Ohio: Bowling Green State University Popular Press.

Barker, Francis, et al. eds. 1981. *1642: Literature and Power in the Seventeenth Century*. Proceedings of the Essex Conference on Sociology of Literature. Colchester: University of Essex.

Barry, Jonathan. 1985. "Popular Culture in Seventeenth Century Bristol." In *Popular Culture in Seventeenth Century England*, edited by Barry Reay. New York: St. Martin's Press.

Berry, Ralph. 1972. *Shakespeare's Comedies*. Princeton: Princeton University Press.

Battenhouse, Roy. 1962. "*Henry V* as Heroic Comedy." In *Essays on Shakespeare and Elizabethan Drama*, edited by R. Hosley. Columbia: University of Missouri Press.

Begley, Sharon. 1989. "The Stuff that Dreams Are Made of." *Newsweek*, 14 August, 42.

Belsey, Catherine. 1985. *The Subject of Tragedy: Identity and Difference in Renaissance Drama*. London: Methuen.

Berry, Edward. 1989. "The Poet as Warrior in Sidney's *Defence of Poetry*." *Studies in English Literature* 29: 21–34.

———. 1984. *Shakespeare's Comic Rites*. Cambridge: Cambridge University Press.

Berry, Ralph. 1972. *Shakespeare's Comedies*. Princeton: Princeton University Press.

———. 1988. *Shakespeare and Social Class*. Atlantic Highlands, N.J.: Humanities Press International.

Bharata Muni. 1961. *Natyasastra*. Vol. 1. Translated and edited by Manomohan Ghosh. Calcutta: Granthalya.

———. 1967. *Natyasastra*. Vol. 2. Translated and edited by Manomohan Ghosh. Calcutta: Asiatic Society.

Bloom, Harold. 1989. *Ruin the Sacred Truths: Truth and Belief from the Bible to the Present*. Cambridge: Harvard University Press.

Bristol, Michael D. 1985. *Carnival and Theater: Plebian Culture and the Structure of Authority in Renaissance England*. New York: Methuen.

Brown, Paul. 1985. "'This Thing of Darkness I Acknowledge Mine': *The Tempest* and the Discourse of Colonialism." *Political Shakespeare*. See Dollimore and Sinfield, 1985.

Bullough, Geoffrey. 1975. *Narrative and Dramatic Sources of Shakespeare*. 8 vols. New York: Columbia University Press.

Burke, Kenneth. 1967. *The Rhetoric of Motives*. Berkeley: University of California Press.

Carr, Edward Hallett. 1962. *What Is History?* London: Macmillan, 1962.

Carr, Helen. 1985. "Woman/Indian: 'The American' and His Others." In *Europe and Its Others*, edited by Francis Barker and Peter Hulme. Proceedings of the Essex Conference on Sociology of Literature. Colchester: University of Essex.

Cawelti, John G. 1976. *Adventure, Mystery, and Romance: Formula Stories as Art and Popular Culture*. Chicago: University of Chicago Press.

Certeau, Michel de. 1986. *Heterologies: Discourse of the Other*. Translated by Brian Massumi. Minneapolis: University of Minnesota Press.

Chambers, E. K. 1923. *The Elizabethan Stage*. 4 vols. Oxford: Clarendon Press.

Charlton, H. B. N.d. *Shakespearian Comedy*. New York: Barnes and Noble Press. New York.

Charney, Maurice. 1980. *Shakespearean Comedy*. New York: New York Literary Forum 5–6.

Congreve, William. 1982. *The Way of the World*. In *Comedies of William Congreve*. Edited by Anthony Henderson. Cambridge: Cambridge University Press.

Cressy, David. 1980. *Literacy and the Social Order*. Cambridge: Cambridge University Press.

Danson, Lawrence. 1986. In *Cambridge Companion*. See Wells 1986.

Dash, Irene G. 1981. *Wooing, Wedding, and Power: Women in Shakespeare's Plays*. New York: Columbia University Press.

Dent, R. W. 1980. *Shakespeare's Proverbial Language: An Index*. Berkeley: University of California Press.

Dequincy, Thomas. 1902. *Selections from DeQuincy*. Edited by Milton Haight Turk. New York: Ginn and Co.

Derrida, Jacques. 1974. *Of Grammatology*. Translated by Gayatri Spivak. Baltimore: Johns Hopkins University Press.

Dollimore, Jonathan and Alan Sinfield, eds. 1985. *Political Shakespeare: New Essays in Cultural Materialism*. Ithaca: Cornell University Press.

Donahue, Charles, Jr. 1983. "The Canon Law on the Formation of Marriage and Social Practise in the Later Middle Ages." *Journal of Family History* 8: 130–58.

Drakakis, John, ed. 1985. *Alternative Shakespeares*. London: Methuen.

Duckworth, George E. 1952. *The Nature of Roman Comedy*. Princeton: Princeton University Press.

Duvignnaud, Jean. 1965. *Sociologie du Theatre*. Paris: Presses Universitaire de France.

Eco, Umberto. 1983. *The Name of the Rose*. Translated by William Weaver. New York: Harcourt, Brace, Jovanovich.

Erasmus, Desiderius. 1963. *On the Copia of Words and Ideas*. Translated by Donald B. King and H. David Rix. Milwaukee, Wisc.: Marquette University Press.

———. 1978. "On the Method of Study." Translated by Brian McGregor. *Collected*

Works of Erasmus, Literary and Educational Writings, 2. Edited by Craig R. Thompson. Toronto and London: University of Toronto Press.

———. 1985. "On the Writing of Letters." Translated by Charles Fantazzi. *Collected Works of Erasmus, Literary and Educational Writings*, 3. Edited by J. K. Sowards. Toronto and London: University of Toronto Press.

Evans-Pritchard, E. E. 1951. *Social Anthropology*. London: Oxford University Press.

Everett, Barbara. 1990. "The Fatness of Falstaff." *London Review of Books* 16 August.

Farnham, Willard. 1971. *The Shakespearean Grotesque: Its Genesis and Transformation*. Oxford: Clarendon Press.

Felperin, Howard. 1988. "Mimesis and Modernity in *Antony and Cleopatra*." In *William Shakespeare's "Antony and Cleopatra,"* edited by Harold Bloom. New York: Chelsea House Publishers.

Ferguson, Margaret W. 1979. "Sidney's *A Defence of Poetry*: A Retrial." *boundary 2*, 7: 61–95.

———. Maureen Quilligan and Nancy J. Vickers, eds. 1986. *Rewriting the Renaissance: The Discourses of Sexual Difference in Early Modern Europe*. Chicago: University of Chicago Press.

———. 1983. *Trials of Desire: Renaissance Defenses of Poetry*. New Haven: Yale University Press.

Foakes, R. A. 1971. *Shakespeare, The Dark Comedies to the Last Plays: From Satire to Celebration*. London: Routledge and Kegan Paul.

Freer, Colborn. 1981. *The Poetics of Jacobean Drama*. Baltimore: Johns Hopkins University Press.

Frye, Northrop. 1957. *Anatomy of Criticism: Four Essays*. Princeton: Princeton University Press.

Goddard, Harold C. 1960. *The Meaning of Shakespeare*. Vol. 2. Chicago: University of Chicago Press.

Godolphin, John. 1673. *Reportorium Canonicum; or an Abridgement of the Ecclesiastical Laws of the Realm consistent with the Temporal*. London: Wilkinson.

Godzich, Wlad. 1986. "Introduction" to Michel de Certeau, *Heterologies*. Translated by Brian Massumi. Minneapolis: University of Minnesota Press.

Granville-Barker, Harley. 1958. *Prefaces to Shakespeare*. 2 vols. London: B. T. Batsford.

Greenblatt, Stephen. 1988. *Representing the English Renaissance*. Berkeley: University of California Press.

Gregor, Thomas. 1985. *Anxious Pleasures: The Sexual Amazonian People* Chicago: University of Chicago Press.

———. 1977. *Mehinaku: The Drama of Daily Life in a Brazilian Indian Village*. Chicago: University of Chicago Press.

Grella, George. 1980. "The Formal Detective Novel." In *Detective Fiction*. See Winks 1980.

Grene, David. 1982. *The Actor in History*. University Park and London: Pennsylvania State University Press.

Gurr, Andrew. 1987. *Playgoing in Shakespeare's London*. New York: Cambridge University Press.

Hanson, John Arthur. 1965. "The Glorious Military." In *Roman Drama,* edited by T. A. Dorey and Donald R. Dudley. New York: Basic Books.

Harington, John. 1972. "A Preface or rather, a brief apologie of poetrie. . . ." *Orlando Furioso.* Edited by Robert McNulty. Oxford: Clarendon Press.

Hardison, O. B. 1962. *The Enduring Monument: A Study of Praise in Renaissance Literary Theory and Practice.* Chapel Hill: University of North Carolina Press.

Harrison, William. 1587. "An Historicall description of the Iland of Britaine. . . . " *The First and second volumes of Chronicles . . . by Raphaell Holinshed.* London.

Havelock, Eric. 1982. "The Oral Composition of Greek Drama." In *The Literate Revolution in Greece and its Cultural Consequences.* Princeton: Princeton University Press.

Heffner, Ray. 1977. "Hunting for Clues in *Much Ado About Nothing.*" In *Teaching Shakespeare,* edited by Walter Edens et al. Princeton: Princeton University Press.

Herrick, Marvin. 1984. *Comic Theory in the Sixteenth Century.* Urbana: Illinois University Press.

Heywood, Thomas. 1962. *An Apologie for Actors.* London, 1612. In *English Literary Criticism: The Renaissance,* edited by O. B. Hardison. New York: Goldentree Books.

Houlbrooke, Ralph. 1979. *Church Courts and the People During the English Reformation, 1520–1570.* Oxford: Oxford University Press.

Howard, Jean E. 1987. "Renaissance Antitheatricality and the Politics of Gender and Rank in *Much Ado about Nothing.*" In *Shakespeare Reproduced.* See Howard and O'Connor 1987.

Howard, Jean and Marian O'Connor, eds. 1987. *Shakespeare Reproduced: The Text in History and Ideology.* New York: Methuen.

Huizinga, Johan. 1955. *Homo Ludens: A Study of the Play Element in Culture.* Boston: Beacon.

Hunt, John. 1987. "Allusive Coherence in Sidney's *Apology for Poetry.*" *Studies in English Literature* 27: 1–16.

Hunt, Maurice. 1980. "Shakespeare's Empirical Romance: *Cymbeline* and Modern Knowledge." *Texas Studies in Literature and Language* 22: 322–42.

Huston, J. Dennis. 1981. *Shakespeare's Comedies of Play.* New York: Columbia University Press.

Innes, Michael. 1949. See Stewart 1949.

James I. 1597. *Daemonology: Elizabethan and Jacobean Quartos.* Edited by G. B. Harrison. Reprint. New York: Barnes and Noble.

James, P. D. 1986. *A Taste for Death.* New York: Warner Books.

Javitch, Daniel. 1976. *Poetry and Courtliness in Renaissance England.* Princeton: Princeton University Press.

Johnson, Samuel. 1962. "Preface to Shakespeare." *English Critical Texts.* Edited by D. J. Enright and Ernst de Chickera. London: Oxford University Press.

Jonson, Ben. *The Alchemist.* 1967. Revels edition. Edited by F. H. Mares. Cambridge: Harvard University Press.

———. 1969. *The Complete Masques.* Edited by Stephen Orgel. New Haven: Yale University Press.

————. 1970. *Timber, or Discoveries.* In *Ben Jonson's Literary Criticism,* edited by James D. Redwine, Jr. Lincoln: University of Nebraska Press.

Kahn, Victoria. 1985. *Rhetoric, Prudence, and Skepticism in the Renaissance.* Ithaca: Cornell University Press.

Kaiser, Walter. 1963. *Praisers of Folly: Erasmus, Rabelais, Shakespeare.* Cambridge: Harvard University Press.

Kavanagh, James. 1985. "Shakespeare in Ideology." In *Alternative Shakespeares,* 144–65. See Drakakis 1985.

Kinney, Arthur F. 1974. *Markets of Bawdrie: The Dramatic Criticism of Stephen Gosson.* Salzburg Studies in English Literature: Elizabethan Studies 4. Salzburg: Institut für Englische Sprache und Literatur.

Kirsch, Arthur. 1981. *Shakespeare and the Experience of Love.* Cambridge: Cambridge University Press.

Knight, G. Wilson. 1947. *The Crown of Life.* London: Methuen.

Knight, Stephen. 1980. *Form and Ideology in Crime Fiction.* Bloomington: Indiana University Press.

Langer, Susanne. 1953. *Feeling and Form: A Theory of Art.* New York: Scribner.

Lanham, Richard A. 1976. *The Motives of Eloquence.* New Haven: Yale University Press.

Larner, Christina. 1984. *Witchcraft and Religion: The Politics of Popular Belief.* Oxford and New York: Basil Blackwell.

Leinwand, Theodore B. 1986. "'I Believe We Must Leave the Killing Out': Deference and Accommodation in *A Midsummer Night's Dream.*" *Renaissance Papers:* 11–30.

Léry, Jean de. 1927. *Le Voyage au Brésil.* Edited by Charly Clerc. Paris: Payot.

Lévinas, Emmanuel. 1987. *Time and the Other [and additional essays].* Translated by Richard A. Cohen. Pittsburgh: Duquesne University Press.

Lyly, John. 1902. *Endimion.* In *The Complete Works,* edited by R. Warwick Bond. 3 vols. Oxford: Clarendon Press.

Macfarlane, Alan. 1971. *Witchcraft in Tudor and Stuart England: A Regional and Comparative Study.* 1970. Reprint. New York and Evanston, Ill.: Harper and Row.

Mandel, Ernest. 1984. *Delightful Murder: A Social History of the Crime Story.* Minneapolis: University of Minnesota Press.

Manning, Roger. 1988. *Village Revolts.* Oxford: Oxford University Press, 1988.

Marcus, Leah. 1988. *Puzzling Shakespeare: Local Reading and Its Discontents.* Berkeley: University of California Press.

Marsh, Ngaio. 1966. *Killer Dolphin.* Boston: Little Brown.

Marston, John. 1965. "To My Equal Reader." In *The Fawn,* edited by Gerald A. Smith. Lincoln: University of Nebraska Press.

Martin, Christopher. 1988. "Sidney's *Defence:* The Art of Slander and the Slander of Art." *Sidney Newsletter* 9: 3–10.

Montrose, Louis. 1980. "The Purpose of Playing: Reflections on a Shakespearean Anthropology." *Helois* n.s. 7: 50–74.

————. 1988. "'Shaping Fantasies': Figuration of Gender and Power in Elizabethan Culture." In *Representing the English Renaissance,* 31–64. See Greenblatt 1988.

Muir, Kenneth. 1965. "Introduction." *Shakespeare: The Comedies.* Englewood Cliffs, N.J.: Prentice-Hall.

———, Kenneth. 1973. Introduction. The Arden edition of *Macbeth.* London: Methuen.

——— and S. Schoenbaum, eds. 1971. *A New Companion to Shakespeare Studies.* London: Cambridge University Press.

Mullaney, Steven. 1988a. *The Place of the Stage.* Chicago: University of Chicago Press.

———. 1988b. "Strange Things, Gross Terms, Curious Customs: The Rehearsal of Cultures in the Late Renaissance." In *Representing the English Renaissance.* See Greenblatt 1988.

Nelson, T. G. A. 1990. *Comedy.* Oxford: Oxford University Press.

Nevo, Ruth. 1987. *Shakespeare's Other Language.* New York: Methuen.

Ong, Walter. 1982. *Orality and Literacy.* London and New York: Methuen.

Orgel, Stephen. 1988. "The Authentic Shakespeare." *Representations* 21: 1–25.

———. 1986. "Prospero's Wife." In *Rewriting the Renaissance,* 50–64. See Ferguson et al. 1986.

Palmer, John. 1961. *Political and Comic Characters of Shakespeare.* London: Macmillan and Co.

Patterson, Annabel. 1989. *Shakespeare and the Popular Voice.* Oxford: Basil Blackwell.

Powlick, Leonard. 1974. "*Cymbeline* and the Comedy of Anticlimax." In *Shakespeare's Late Plays: Essays in Honor of Charles Crow,* edited by Richard C. Tobias and Paul Zolbrod. Athens: Ohio University Press.

Puttenham, George. 1936. *The Arte of English Poesie.* Edited by Gladys Doidge Willcock and Alice Walker. Cambridge: Cambridge University Press.

Rabkin, Norman. ed. 1964. *Approaches to Shakespeare.* New York: McGraw-Hill.

Rappaport, Steve. 1989. *Worlds within Worlds: Structures of Life in Sixteenth Century London.* Cambridge: Cambridge University Press.

Ridley, M. R., ed. 1958. The Arden edition of *Othello.* Cambridge: Harvard University Press.

Robinson, J. W. 1964. "'Palpable Hot Ice': Dramatic Burlesque in *A Midsummer Night's Dream.*" *Studies in Philology* 61: 192–204.

Rosenberg, Marvin. 1978. *The Masks of Macbeth.* Berkeley: University of California Press.

Rudich, Norman. 1976. *Weapons of Criticism: Marxism in America and the Literary Tradition.* Palo Alto, Calif.: Ramparts Press.

Rushdie, Salman. 1990. "In Good Faith." *Newsweek.* 12 Feb.: 52–57.

Sayers, Dorothy. 1978. "Introduction." In E. C. Bentley, *Trent's Last Case.* New York: Perennial Library.

Scarre, Geoffrey. 1987. *Witchcraft and Magic in 16th and 17th Century Europe.* Atlantic Highlands, N.J.: Humanities Press International.

Schwartz, Murray M. 1970. "Between Fantasy and Imagination: A Psychological Exploration of *Cymbeline.*" In *Psychoanalysis and Literary Process,* edited by Frederic Crews. Cambridge, Mass.: Winthrop.

——— and Coppélia Kahn, eds. 1980. *Representing Shakespeare: New Psychoanalytic Essays.* Baltimore and London: Johns Hopkins University Press.

Segal, Erich. 1968. *Roman Laughter.* Studies in Comparative Literature 29. Cambridge, Mass.

Shakespeare, William. 1974. *The Riverside Shakespeare.* Edited by G. Blakemore Evans, et al. Boston: Houghton, Mifflin.

———. 1981. *Shakespeare's Plays in Quarto.* Edited by Michael J. B. Allen and Kenneth Muir. Berkeley: University of California Press.

———. 1973. *Macbeth.* Arden Edition. Edited by Kenneth Muir. London: Methuen.

———. 1979. *A Midsummer Night's Dream.* Arden Edition. Edited by Harold F. Brooks. London: Methuen.

———. 1954. *A Midsummer Night's Dream.* Edited by Helge Kokeritz. New Haven: Yale University Press.

———. 1981. *Much Ado about Nothing.* Arden Edition. Edited by A. R. Humphreys. London: Routledge.

———. 1958. *Othello.* Arden Edition. Edited by M. R. Ridley. Cambridge: Harvard University Press.

———. 1987. *The Tempest.* Oxford Shakespeare. Edited by Stephen Orgel. Oxford: Oxford University Press.

———. 1981. *The Tempest.* Pelican Edition. Edited by Northrop Frye. 1970. Reprint. New York: Penguin Books.

Shaw, George Bernard. 1934. *Prefaces by Bernard Shaw.* London: Constable and Company.

Shepherd, Geoffrey, ed. 1965. *An Apology for Poetry or The Defence of Poesy by Sir Philip Sidney.* London: Thomas Nelson.

Sidney, Philip. 1928. *The Defence of Poesie.* London: Printed for William Ponsonby, 1595. The Facsimile Text Society. London: Noel Douglas.

Skura, Meredith Ann. 1989. "Discourse and the Individual: The Case of Colonialism in *The Tempest.*" *Shakespeare Quarterly* 40: 42–69.

———. 1980. "Interpreting Posthumus's Dream from Above and Below: Families, Psychoanalysts, and Literary Critics." In *Representing Shakespeare.* See Schwartz and Kahn 1980.

Snyder, Susan. 1979. *The Comic Matrix of Shakespeare's Tragedies.* Princeton: Princeton University Press.

Sousa, Gabriel Soares de. 1939. *Notìcia do Brasil.* Edited by Pirajà da Silva. Sao Paulo: Livraria Martins Editora.

Sousa, Geraldo de. 1987. "Closure and the Antimasque of *The Tempest.*" *Journal of Dramatic Theory and Criticism* 2: 41–51.

Speaight, Robert. 1973. *Shakespeare on the Stage.* Boston: Little, Brown.

Spenser, Edmund. 1932–1949. "The Teares of the Muses." In *The Works of Edmund Spenser: A Variorum Edition,* edited by Edwin Greenlaw, et al. 8 vols. Baltimore: Johns Hopkins University Press.

Staden, Hans. 1928. *The True History of His Captivity.* 1928. Translated by Malcolm Letts. London: George Routledge and Sons, 1928.

Stallybrass, Peter and Allon White. 1986. *The Politics and Poetics of Transgression.* Ithaca: Cornell University Press.

Stewart, J. I. M. 1949. *Character and Motive in Shakespeare.* London and New York: Longmans, Green.

————. 1958. *The Long Farewell.* New York: Harper and Row.

Stone, Lawrence. 1979. *Family, Sex, and Marriage in England 1500–1800.* New York: Harper Colophon Books, 1979.

Strong, Roy. 1977. *The Cult of Elizabeth: Elizabethan Portraiture and Pageantry.* Berkeley: University of California Press.

————. 1987. *Gloriana: The Portraits of Queen Elizabeth I.* New York: Thames and Hudson.

Styan, J. L. 1967. *Shakespeare's Stagecraft.* Cambridge: Cambridge University Press.

Summers, Montague. 1956. *The History of Witchcraft and Demonology.* New York: University Books.

Swinburne, Henry. 1985. *A Treatise of Spousals, or Matrimonial Contracts.* 1686. Facimile reprint. New York and London: Garland. 1985.

Thomas, Keith. 1971. *Religion and the Decline of Magic.* London: Weidenfeld and Nicholson.

Todorov, Tzvetan. 1984. *The Conquest of America: The Question of the Other.* Translated by Richard Howard. New York: Harper and Row.

Traub, Valerie. 1989. "Prince Hal's Falstaff: Positioning Psychoanalysis and the Female Reproductive Body." *Shakespeare Quarterly* 40: 456–74.

Traversi, Derek. 1957. *Shakespeare from Richard II to Henry V.* Stanford, Calif.: Stanford University Press.

Trousdale, Marion. 1981. "Shakespeare's Oral Text." *Renaissance Drama* n.s. 12: 95–115.

Turner, Victor. 1977. *The Ritual Process: Structure and Anti-Structure.* 1969. Reprint. Ithaca: Cornell University Press. 1977.

Unamuno, Miguel de. 1985. "Prologue" to *San Manuel Bueno.* In *San Manuel Bueno, Martir, & la Novelo de Don Sandalio.* Edited by C. A. Longhurst. New York: St. Martin's Press.

Velz, John. 1977. "Shakespeare Inferred." In *Teaching Shakespeare.* See Heffner 1977.

Walter, John. 1985. "A 'Rising of the People'? The Oxfordshire Rising of 1596." *Past and Present* 107: 90–143.

Watts, Harold. 1981. "The Sense of Regain: A Theory of Comedy." In *Comedy: Meaning and Form,* by Robert W. Corrigan. 2d ed. New York: Harper and Row.

Webbe, William. 1586. *A Discourse of English Poetrie.* London.

Wells, Robin Headlam. 1983. *Spenser's "Faerie Queene" and the Cult of Elizabeth.* London: Croom Helm.

Wells, Stanley, ed. 1986. *The Cambridge Companion to Shakespeare.* Cambridge: Cambridge University Press.

Whigham, Frank. 1984. *Ambition and Privilege: The Social Tropes of Elizabethan Courtesy Theory.* Berkeley: University of California Press.

White, Hayden. 1978. *Tropics of Discourse: Essays in Cultural Criticism.* Baltimore: Johns Hopkins University Press.

Williams, Ethel Carelton. 1970. *Anne of Denmark.* London: Longman.

Williams, Raymond. 1981. *The Sociology of Culture.* New York: Schocken Books.

Wilson, John Dover. 1964. *The Fortunes of Falstaff.* Cambridge: Cambridge University Press.

Wilson, Thomas. 1553/1562. *The Arte of Rhetorique . . . newlie sette foorthe.* London. 1553, 1562.

Winks, Robin W. ed. 1980. *Detective Fiction: A Collection of Critical Essays.* Englewood Cliffs, N.J.: Prentice-Hall.

Zitner, S. P. 1958. "Gosson, Ovid, and the Elizabethan Audience." *Shakespeare Quarterly* 9: 206–28.

Notes on Contributors

M. AROGYASAMI is completing a doctorate at Brigham Young University on the aesthetic theory of Bharata Muni and its use in Anglo-American culture.

SUSAN BAKER is Professor of English at the University of Nevada. With Dorothea Kehler, she recently published *In Another Country: Feminist Perspectives on Renaissance Drama*. Her articles on Shakespeare and Webster have appeared in *Comparative Drama*, *Shakespeare Quarterly*, and Texas Studies in Language and Literature.

CHRISTY DESMET is Associate Professor of English at the University of Georgia. She recently published *Reading Shakespeare's Characters: Rhetoric, Ethos, and Identity*.

GERALDO U. DE SOUSA is Associate Proessor of English at Xavier University in Cincinnati and the co-author of *Shakespeare: A Study and Research Guide*. His work has appeared in *Shakespeare Quarterly*, *Essays in Theater*, *Research Opportunities in Renaissance Drama*, and *The Journal of Dramatic Theory and Criticism*.

MARY FREE is Associate Professor and Associate Chair of English at Florida International University (North Miami). Her articles on Renaissance and modern drama have appeared in *Renaissance Papers*, *Shakespeare Studies*, and *South Atlantic Review*.

THELMA N. GREENFIELD is Professor Emérita of English at the University of Oregon. Her books include *The Eye of Judgment: Reading the New Arcadia* and *The Induction in Elizabethan Drama*; with Waldo McNeir, she edited the volume *Pacific Coast Studies in Shakespeare*.

EJNER JENSEN is Professor of English at the University of Michigan. His books include *Ben Jonson's Comedies on the Modern Stage* and *Shakespeare and the Ends of Comedy*.

MARCIA MCDONALD is Associate Professor of English at Belmont University in Nashville. She has published on the subject of pedagogy in the *ADE Bulletin;* currently she is studying the figure of Youth in Renaissance drama.

ALAN POWERS is Professor of English at Bristol Community College in Fall River, Massachusetts. He has published his research in *Upstart Crow, Folklore,* and *Spinner,* and his opinions in the *Berkshire Eagle* and the *New York Times Magazine.*

FRANCES TEAGUE is Professor of English at the University of Georgia. She has published *The Curious History of "Bartholomew Fair"* and *Shakespeare's Speaking Properties;* with John Velz, she edited *One Touch of Shakespeare.*